Be Prepared

for the

AP

Computer
Science
Exam in Java

Maria Litvin
Phillips Academy, Andover, Massachusetts

Practice exam contributors:

Sally Bellacqua
Thomas Jefferson High School for Science and Technology, Alexandria, Virginia

Roger Frank
Ponderosa High School, Parker, Colorado

Dave Wittry
Troy High School, Fullerton, California

Skylight Publishing
Andover, Massachusetts

Library of Congress Catalog Card Number: 2002093457

ISBN 0-9654853-5-8

Skylight Publishing
9 Bartlet Street, Suite 70
Andover, MA 01810

web: http://www.skylit.com
e-mail: sales@skylit.com
          support@skylit.com

3 4 5 6 7 8 9 10   08 07 06 05

Printed in the United States of America

Brief Contents

Contents

About the Authors

Maria Litvin has taught computer science and mathematics at Phillips Academy in Andover, Massachusetts, since 1987. She is an Advanced Placement Computer Science exam reader and Question Leader and, as a consultant for The College Board, provides AP training for high school computer science teachers. Maria is a recipient of the 1999 Siemens Award for Advanced Placement for Mathematics, Science, and Technology for New England and of the 2003 RadioShack National Teacher Award. Prior to joining Phillips Academy, Maria taught computer science at Boston University. Maria is the author of the earlier, C++ version of *Be Prepared* and co-author of *C++ for You++: An Introduction to Programming and Computer Science*, which became one of the leading high school textbooks for AP Computer Science courses. More recently, Maria and Gary Litvin co-wrote two textbooks, *Java Methods: an Introduction to Object-Oriented Programming*, and *Java Methods AB: Data Structures*, now used for AP CS courses in hundreds of schools.

Sally Bellacqua teaches at Thomas Jefferson High School for Science and Technology in Fairfax County, Virginia, where she is the lead teacher for the school's AP Computer Science program. She runs teacher training workshops and has developed curriculum for CS, AP CS, and AP Calculus. She co-authored two workbooks of computer science materials, the first in Pascal and the second in C++, used throughout the county's high schools, and contributed practice exam questions to the C++ version of *Be Prepared*. Currently she is helping implement Java into the county's CS curriculum. Sally earned her bachelors degree in mathematics from Immaculate Heart College in Los Angeles and her masters in mathematics from the University of Illinois.

Roger Frank has taught AP Computer Science and mathematics at Ponderosa High School since 1992. Previously, he worked in industry, including positions as Hardware Engineering Manager and later National Technical Director for Sun Microsystems, along with other software and hardware engineering positions at Digital Equipment Corp., International Medical Corporation, the Los Alamos National Laboratory, and others. He holds a bachelors degree in Electronic and Computer Engineering, an MBA, and a masters in mathematics education.

Dave Wittry teaches a variety of computer science classes at Troy High School, a magnet school for science, math, and technology in Fullerton, California. He has been instrumental in developing and teaching the innovative computer science curriculum, which has contributed to Troy's immense success as a California Distinguished School, a National Blue Ribbon School of Excellence, and a New American High School — one of only 17 showcase schools in the nation. For the past four years, he has been a reader for the AP Computer Science Exam. Dave earned a BA in Computer Science/Mathematics from Lake Forest College in Lake Forest, Illinois, and an MS in Computer Science from Southern Illinois University.

Acknowledgments

Gary Litvin helped make this book a reality by working closely with the authors and editing all the sample questions and practice exams. He contributed ideas and wrote solutions for some free-response questions and created the companion web site for this book.

Our most sincere thanks to David Levine of St. Bonaventure University. We are fortunate to have benefited from David's vast experience as an AP Exam Leader and his keen technical insight into computer science, OOP, and Java. David recommended many important improvements, helped us catch technical and stylistic mistakes, and pointed out questions that needed clarification.

We are very grateful to Jacques Hugon of Phillips Academy in Andover, Massachusetts, who took the time to read a draft very thoroughly, suggested many improvements, and corrected a number of mistakes.

Our special thanks to Margaret Litvin for making this book more readable with her thorough and thoughtful editing.

Finally, we thank the Boy Scouts of America for allowing us to allude to their motto in the book's title.

How to Use This Book

Multiple-choice questions in the review chapters are marked by their number in a box:

Their solutions are delimited by ⬆ and ⬇.

Comments that are relevant only to the AB exam are delimited by ⌈ and ⌋. For example:

⌈ The AB exam also includes standard data structures: linked lists, stacks, queues, and trees. ⌋

The companion web site

        http://www.skylit.com/beprepared/

is an integral part of the book. It contains annotated solutions to free-response questions from last year's exams, the latest *Case Study* information, and relevant links. The *MBS Case Study* is likely to stay for the 2005 and 2006 exams, but another case study may eventually replace it. Check this book's web site for the current information and be sure you have the latest edition of *Be Prepared*.

> **Our practice exams may be more difficult than the actual exams, so don't panic if they take more time. We have included three parts in most of our free-response questions while actual exam questions may have only two parts.**

In the past, A and AB exams shared one or two free-response questions. Our A and AB practice exams do not overlap, but all the questions in our A exams are useful practice for the AB exam as well. Similarly, many questions in each of our AB exams require only A-level material.

Introduction

The AP exams in computer science test your understanding of basic concepts in computer science as well as your fluency in Java programming. There are two levels of the exam. The A-level exam covers roughly the material of a one-semester introductory college course in computer science (CS-1). The AB-level exam covers a typical introductory college course plus a second course on data structures (CS-1 + CS-2). Chapter 1 in this book will help you decide which exam you should take.

Exam questions are developed by the AP CS Development Committee of The College Board, and exams are put together by Educational Testing Service, the same organization that administers the SAT and other exams. In 2002, The College Board offered 34 courses in 19 disciplines, and 937,951 students took 1,585,516 exams. The most up-to-date information on the AP exams offered and participation statistics can be found on The College Board's *AP Central* web site, `http://apcentral.collegeboard.com`.

In the spring of 2004, the computer science exams will use Java for the first time. At the same time, the program's emphasis has shifted from implementation of algorithms and coding proficiency to object-oriented software design and development. Planning for the switch from C++ to Java took several years to complete. Developing exams is a very big effort for The College Board; training teachers in a new programming language is another big undertaking. So it is safe to say that Java will be here to stay for a few years.

> **Answers to exam questions written in a programming language other than Java will not receive credit.**

A working knowledge of Java is necessary but not sufficient for a good grade on the exam. First and foremost, you must understand the basic concepts of computer science, object-oriented programming (OOP), and some common algorithms. ⌈ The AB exam also includes standard data structures: lists, stacks, queues, priority queues, hash tables, trees, and big-O analysis of algorithms. ⌋

As for Java: you don't have to know the whole language, just the subset described in The College Board's *Advanced Placement Course Description for Computer Science* (available at `http://apcentral.collegeboard.com`). You must also be familiar with The College Board's materials developed specifically for the AP exams: the *Marine Biology Simulation Case Study* ⌈ and, for the AB exam, *Implementation Classes and Interfaces*. ⌋

This is a lot of material to cover, and it is certainly not the goal of this book to teach you everything you need to know from scratch. For that you need a complete textbook with exercises and programming projects. (We recommend *Java Methods: an Introduction to Object-Oriented Programming*, Skylight Publishing, 2001 ⌈ and for the AB exam, also its sequel, *Java Methods AB: Data Structures*, Skylight Publishing, 2003 ⌋.) Most students who take the exam are enrolled in an AP computer science course at their school. A determined student can prepare for the exam on his or her own; it may take anywhere between three and twelve months, and a good textbook will be even more important.

The goals of this book are:

- to describe the exam format and requirements;

- to describe the AP Java subset;

- to provide an effective review of what you should know with emphasis on the more difficult topics and on common omissions and mistakes;

- to help you identify and fill the gaps in your knowledge;

- to offer sample exam questions with answers, hints, and solutions for you to practice on to and analyze your mistakes.

The AP exams in computer science are paper-and-pencil affairs. While you need a computer with a Java compiler to learn how to program and how to implement common algorithms in Java, this book does not require the use of a computer. In fact it is a good idea not to use one when you work on practice questions, so that you can get used to the exam's format and environment. One-hundred-percent correct Java syntax is not the emphasis here. Small mistakes (a missed semicolon or a brace) that a compiler would normally help you catch will probably not even affect your exam score. You'll need a computer only to access *AP Central* and our web site for the latest updates and past exam free-response solutions.

Chapter 1 of this book explains the format, required materials, and the Java subset for the exams and provides information about exam grading and exam-taking hints. Chapter 2 covers the elements of Java required for the exam. Chapter 3 deals with OOP topics. Chapter 4 deals with common algorithms for searching and sorting. Chapter 5 reviews additional AB exam topics: lists, stacks, queues, trees, and so on. Chapter 6 reviews the *Marine Biology Simulation* (*MBS*) *Case Study*. Chapter 7 is actually on the web at this book's companion web site, `http://www.skylit.com/beprepared/`. It offers annotated solutions to free-response questions from past exams. Review chapters contain sample multiple-choice questions with detailed explanations of all the right and wrong answers. At the end of the book are four complete practice exams — two A and two AB, with no overlap — followed by answers and solutions.

Good luck!

Chapter 1. Exam Format, Grading, and Hints

1.1. Exam Format and Materials

Both the A and AB exams consist of two sections. The first section presents 40 multiple-choice questions for one hour and fifteen minutes (1.5 to 2 minutes per question on average). The second section presents four free-response questions for one hour and forty-five minutes (20-30 minutes per question). The free-response questions usually consist of two or three parts each. The total duration of the exam is three hours. No computers, calculators, or any other devices, books, or materials are allowed.

The multiple-choice questions are a mixture of questions related to general computer science terms, program design decisions, specific elements of Java syntax, properties of classes, logical analysis of fragments of Java code, OOP concepts, and about five questions related to the *Case Study*. ⌈ The AB exam also includes questions about data structures: linked lists, stacks, queues, trees, priority queues, hash tables, heaps, etc., and "big-O" analysis of algorithms. ⌋

The free-response questions usually aim to cover a wide range of material: arrays, strings, classes and interfaces, sorting and searching, Java library classes (within the AP subset), and so on. ⌈ The AB exam may include questions on two-dimensional arrays, linked lists, trees, and other data structures. ⌋ In past exams, students have not been asked to write complete programs. Usually, they were asked to write a method that performs a specified task under a given header for the method. The second part of the question often refers to the method implemented in the first part, but each part is graded separately and your implementation of Part (a) does not have to be correct in order for you to get full credit for Part (b). Part (c) may ask questions about your implementation or ask you to write an additional method that uses Parts (a) and/or (b). In that case you are to assume that the methods in the previous parts work as intended, regardless of what you wrote for them.

Free-response questions may also include a "design" question, in which you are asked to design a small class in one part, then use it in other parts. Your design will be graded based on the appropriateness of the features of your class, appropriate names for methods and variables, and other criteria. In the design part, you do not need to implement your design.

One free-response question is based on the *Case Study*. It may ask you to extend a *Case Study* class and to write a new method or rewrite an existing method.

Exam materials given to you at the exam will include a booklet containing the needed case study code and *Quick Reference* — a list of the library classes and their methods included in the AP subset⌈ and, for the AB exam, *Implementation Classes and Interfaces* ⌋. These materials are provided for reference — it is expected that you will already be very familiar and comfortable with the case study and required library classes before the exam. `http://www.skylit.com/beprepared/` has current links to these materials.

1.2.   The Java Subset

The Development Committee has defined a restricted subset of Java that will be tested on the exams. The purpose of the subset is to focus the AP CS program more on general concepts than on the specifics of Java and to limit the scope of material, especially material related to the peculiarities of Java. The subset is described in The College Board's *Advanced Placement Course Description for Computer Science*; we have a link to it from this book's web site `http://www.skylit.com/beprepared/`. ⌈ The AB "superset" also defines the `ListNode` and `TreeNode` classes and the `Stack`, `Queue`, and `PriorityQueue` interfaces (see Chapter 5). ⌋

What is in the subset? Actually, quite a bit.

A exam:

- `boolean`, `int`, and `double` primitive data types. `(int)` and `(double)` casts. **Other primitive data types, including** `char`, **are not in the subset and should be avoided on exams.**

- Assignment (`=`), arithmetic (`+`, `-`, `*`, `/`, `%`), increment (`++`, `--`), compound assignment (`+=`, `-=`, `*=`, `/=`, `%=`), relational (`<`, `>`, `<=`, `>=`, `==`, `!=`), and logical (`&&`, `||`, `!`) operators. **Use only the postfix form of ++ and -- (x++ or x--), and do not use them in expressions**.

- `+` and `+=` operators for concatenating strings. `String`'s `compareTo`, `equals`, `length`, `substring`, and `indexOf(String s)` methods. `\n`, `\\`, and `\"` escape sequences in literal strings.

- `System.out.print` and `System.out.println`.

- One-dimensional arrays, `array.length`, arrays of objects, initialized arrays such as `int x[] = {1,2,3};`

- `if-else`, `for`, `while`, `return`. **But `do-while` and `switch` are not included.**

- Classes, interfaces, and abstract classes, `extends`. Class cast (as in `String s = (String)myList.get(i);`). Calling superclass's constructor (as in `super(...)`). Passing `this` object to a method (as in `otherObject.someMethod(this)`).

- Constructors, the `new` operator, `public` and `private` methods, `static` methods, `static final` variables (constants), overloaded methods, `null`. **All instance variables are `private`.** Default initialization rules are not in the subset and are unlikely to come up on the exam.

- `NullPointerException`, `ArrayIndexOutOfBoundsException`, `ArithmeticException`.

- `throw new NoSuchElementException();`
  `throw new IllegalStateException();`

- Library classes and methods:
  String: `length(), substring(...), indexOf(String s)`
  Integer: `Integer(int x), intValue()`
  Double: `Double(double x), doubleValue()`
  Math: `abs(double x), pow(double base, double exp), sqrt(double x)`
  Random: `nextInt(int n), nextDouble()`

  Also understand `toString` methods for all objects, the `Comparable` interface and `compareTo`, `equals` and `compareTo` for `String`, `Integer`, and `Double`.

- `ArrayList` (see Section 2.6).

⌈ AB exam:

All of the above, plus you should be able to:

- Design and implement interfaces, abstract classes, subclasses. Call a superclass's method from a subclass (as in `super.someMethod(...)`).

- Use small subsets of methods for collection interfaces and classes `List`, `ArrayList`, `LinkedList`, `Iterator`, `ListIterator`, `Set`, `TreeSet`, `HashSet`, `Map`, `TreeMap`, `HashMap` (see Chapter 5).
⌋

If you feel you must stray from the subset in your free-response solution, you might have misunderstood the problem and making it harder than it is.

The things that are <u>not</u> in the AP subset and should be avoided include the following:

- Java syntax abominations, such as the `?_:_` operator and the "comma" operator

- `++` and `--` in expressions (as in `a[i++]`)

- Primitive data types other than `boolean`, `int`, and `double` (`char` is <u>not</u> in the subset)

- All bit-wise logical operators

Also not in the subset and will not be tested:

- The `switch` statement, the `do-while` loop, `continue` in loops

- The prefix form of `++` and `--` operators (`++k`, `--k`)

- Library classes (such as `StringBuffer`, `Arrays`, `DecimalFormat`, etc.), unless specifically listed in the subset

- `System.in`; any input and output other than `System.out.print` and `System.out.println`

1.3. Grading

The exams are graded on a scale from 1 to 5. Grades of 5 and 4 are called "extremely well qualified" and "well-qualified," respectively, and usually will be honored by colleges that give credit or placement for AP exams in computer science. A grade of 3, "qualified," especially on the A exam, may be denied credit or placement at some colleges. Grades of 2, "possibly qualified," and 1, "no recommendation," are basically useless.

Table 1-1 presents published statistics and grade distributions on the 2002 A and AB exams, which were in C++. In 2002, 15,660 candidates nationwide took the A exam and 7,799 candidates took the AB exam.

The multiple-choice and free-response sections weigh equally in the final grade.

	Computer Science A		Computer Science AB	
	Number	%	Number	%
Students	15,660	100.0	7,799	100.0
Grade:				
5	3,060	19.5	2,676	34.3
4	3,955	25.3	979	12.6
3	2,881	18.4	2,079	26.7
2	1,370	8.7	827	10.6
1	4,394	28.1	1,238	15.9
3 or Higher	9,896	63.2	5,734	73.6

Table 1-1. 2002 grade distributions for A and AB exams

The College Board uses a weighted combination of the multiple-choice and free-response scores to determine the final total score:

```
totalScore = MC_coeff * (countCorrect - 0.25*countWrong) +
             FR_coeff * FR_score;
```

For multiple-choice questions, one point is given for each correct answer and 1/4 point is subtracted for each wrong answer. Free-response questions are graded by a group of high school teachers and college professors. Scores are based on a *rubric* established by the Chief Reader, Question Leader, and a small group of exam readers. Each free-response question is graded out of 9 points, with partial credit given according to the rubric. The final score is obtained by adding the MC and FR weighted scores. The MC and FR coefficients are chosen in such a way that they give equal weights to the multiple-choice and free-response sections of the exam. For example, if the exam has 40 multiple-choice questions and 4 free-response questions, weights of 1.25 for multiple-choice and 1.3889 for free-response will give each section a maximum total of 50, for a maximum possible total score of 100.

Four cut-off points determine the grade. Table 1-2 shows the maximum composite scores and cut-off points used for the 1999 exams. In that year, 75% or more correct answers on the A exam and 70% or more correct answers on the AB exam would get you a 5. The cut-off points are determined by the Chief Reader and may vary slightly from year to year based on the score distributions and close examination of a sample of individual exams.

A Max composite score 80 (1.00 * MC + 1.1111 * FR)		AB Max composite score 100 (1.25 * MC + 1.3889 * FR)	
Composite score	AP Grade	Composite score	AP Grade
60 - 80	5	70 - 100	5
45 - 59	4	60 - 69	4
33 - 44	3	41 - 59	3
25 - 32	2	31 - 40	2
0 - 24	1	0 - 30	1

Table 1-2. 1999 score-to-grade conversion

1.4.   A or AB?

Table 1-1 shows that a larger percentage of AB exam takers got a 5. That's how it should be — if you don't feel that you can get a 4 or 5 on the AB exam, you don't need to take it. If you haven't covered all the AB material, or are not comfortable with it, take the A exam. It makes little sense to get a 2 or 1 on the AB exam if you could get a 5 or 4 on the A exam. The practice exams in this book will help you make up your mind.

> **Statistical analysis of published results from the 1999 exam shows that over 90% of students who got at least 27 out of 40 on the multiple-choice section received a 4 or a 5 for the whole exam. This may or may not be true for our practice exams. You will know only after the exam!**

Most colleges will take your AP courses and exam grades into account in admissions decisions if you take your exams early enough. But acceptance of AP exam results for credit and/or placement varies widely among colleges. In general, the A exam corresponds to a CS-1 course (Introductory Computer Science or Computer Programming I), a one-semester course for computer science majors. The AB exam corresponds to CS-1 + CS-2; that is, the first programming course plus a course on data structures, usually a one-year sequence for computer science majors. Some colleges give one-semester credit for the A exam and two-semester credit for the AB exam, as intended. But other colleges may only give one semester credit, regardless of the exam. They may also base their decision on your grade. For example, you may get a full year credit only if you got a 5 on the AB exam. Some colleges may not give any credit at all.

The AP program in computer science is a rigorous and demanding program that is comparable to or exceeds the level of the respective first-year computer science courses at most colleges.

> **If you plan to major in computer science and your college of choice does not recognize a good grade on the AP exam for credit and/or placement, you should examine the reasons carefully. Decide for yourself whether these reasons are valid or just stem from the bias of that college or its computer science department.**

But if the college that you definitely want to attend does not give any admissions preference or additional credit for the AB exam, it may be better to swallow your pride and focus on getting a 5 on the A exam.

To do well on the AB exam, you have to be comfortable enough with Java classes to write constructors and methods, and to call superclass methods. You must also know linked lists, binary trees, stacks and queues, priority queues, hashing, and big-O analysis of algorithms.

> **If you know this material, you shouldn't be afraid of the AB exam. Don't assume that it is "just harder." The AB exams simply include more topics. It is not assumed that for the AB exam you must write code better or faster.**

The exams share many questions, and, once you learn the data structures part, the AB exam questions are not necessarily harder than the questions on the A exam. The AB exam questions have to be more diverse in order to cover all the material in the same number of questions; this may actually make the exam easier for you if you have studied all the AB material. For example, you may just *love* recursive handling of binary trees, but be prone to mistakes in programs that involve iterations and arrays. The AB exam usually has at least one free-response question on linked lists or stacks/queues and one on trees, while the A exam may have a seemingly infinite number of questions on simple classes, arrays, and strings.

1.5.   Exam Taking Hints

Some things are obvious:

- If you took the time to read a multiple-choice question and all the answer choices but decided to skip it, take an extra ten seconds and guess. Most likely you have eliminated one or two wrong answers even without noticing.

- If a common paragraph refers to a group of questions and you took the time to read it, try each question in the group.

- Do read the question before jumping to the code included in the question.

But there are a few important things to know about answering free-response questions.

> **Remember that all free-response questions have equal weight. Don't assume that the first question is the easiest and the last is the hardest.**

> **In a nutshell: be neat, straightforward, and professional; keep your exam reader in mind; don't show off.**

More specifically:

1. Stay within the AP Java subset.

2. Remember that the elegance and superior efficiency of your code <u>do not</u> count. More often than not, a brute-force approach is the best. You may waste a lot of time writing tricky, non-standard code and trick yourself in the process or mislead your exam readers who, after all, are only human. No one will test your code on a computer, of course.

3. Remember that Part (b) and Part (c) of the question are graded independently from the previous parts, and may actually be easier: Part (a) may ask you to implement a method and Part (b) may simply ask you to use it.

    Call method(s) specified in Part (a) in subsequent parts, even if your Part (a) is incorrect or left blank — do not re-implement code from Part (a) unnecessarily in Part (b) or Part (c).

4. Bits of "good thinking" count. You may not know the whole solution, but if you have read and understood the question, write bits of code that may earn you partial credit points. But don't spend too much time improvising incorrect code.

5. Do not erase or cross out a solution if you have no time to redo it, even if you think it is wrong. You <u>won't</u> be penalized for incorrect code and may get partial credit for it. Exam readers are instructed not to read any code that you crossed out. But if you wrote two solutions, make sure to cross one out: otherwise only the first one on the page will be graded.

6. Glance at method preconditions and postconditions quickly — they usually restate the task in a more formal way and sometimes give hints. Assume that preconditions are satisfied — don't add unnecessary checks to your code.

7. One common mistake is to forget a `return` statement in a non-`void` method. Make sure the returned value matches the specified type.

8. If an algorithm is suggested for a method, don't fight it, just do it!

9. Remember that the exam readers grade a vast number of exams in quick succession during a marathon grading session every June. Write as neatly as possible. Space out your code (don't save paper).

10. Always indent your code properly. This helps you and your exam reader. If you miss a brace but your code is properly indented, the reader (as opposed to a Java compiler) may accept it as correct. Similarly, if you put each statement on a separate line, a forgotten semicolon may not be held against you.

11. Follow the Java naming style: names of all methods, variables, and parameters start with a lowercase letter. Use meaningful, but not too verbose, names for variables. `count` may be better than `a`; `sum` may be better than `temp`; `row`, `col` may be better than `i`, `j`. But `k` is better than `loopControlVariable`. If the question contains examples of code with names, use the same names when appropriate.

12. Don't bother with comments, they do not count and you will lose valuable time. Occasionally you can put a very brief comment that indicates your intentions for the fragment of code that follows. For example:

```
// Draw left border:
...
...
```

13. Don't worry about `imports` — assume that all the necessary library classes are imported.

14. Code strictly according to pre- and postconditions. Avoid extraneous "bells and whistles" — you will lose points. Never add `System.out.print/println` in solutions unless specifically asked to do so.

15. Use recursion when appropriate: almost always in methods that deal with binary trees; otherwise if recursion is specifically requested or especially tempting.

16. Don't try to catch the exam authors on ambiguities: there will be no one to hear your case, and you'll waste your time. Instead try to grasp quickly what was *meant* and write your answer.

Chapter 2. Exam Topics: Language Properties

2.1. Variables; Arithmetic, Relational, and Logical Operators

Primitive data types included in the subset are `boolean`, `int`, and `double`. In Java, an `int` always takes four bytes, regardless of a particular computer or Java compiler, and its range is from -2^{31} to $2^{31} - 1$. A double takes 8 bytes and has a huge range, but its precision is about 15 significant digits.

> **Remember to declare local variables. It is safer to declare all variables at the top of the method body. If you declare a variable inside a nested block, make sure it is used only in that block. If you declare a variable in a `for` loop, it will be undefined outside that loop.**

For example:

```
public int find(int[] a, int target)
{
  if (a.length > 0)
  {
    int iMin = 0;
    for (int i = 1; i < a.length; i++)
      if (a[i] < a[iMin])
        iMin = i;

    int count = 0;

    for (i = 0; i < a.length; i++)
      if (a[i] == a[iMin])
        count++;
  }
  return count;
}
```

Error: i is undefined here

Error: count is undefined here

A safer version:

```
public int countMins(int[] a)
{
  int i, iMin = 0;
  int count = 0;

  if (a.length > 0)
  {
    iMin = 0;
    for (i = 1; i < a.length; i++)
      if (a[i] < a[iMin])
        iMin = i;

    count = 0;
    for (i = 0; i < a.length; i++)
      if (a[i] == a[iMin])
        count++;
  }
  return count;
}
```

Do not declare count *here:*
int count = 0;
would be a mistake

You won't be penalized for declarations inside the code, but if you declare all variables above the code, it makes it easier to read and may help you avoid mistakes.

1

Which of the following statements is true?

(A)   In Java, data types in declarations of symbolic constants are needed only for documentation purposes.

(B)   When a Java interpreter is running, variables of the `double` data type are represented in memory as strings of decimal digits with a decimal point and an optional sign.

(C)   A variable's data type determines where it is stored in computer memory when the program is running.

(D)   A variable's data type determines whether that variable may be passed as an argument to a particular method.

(E)   A variable of the `int` type cannot serve as an operand for the / operator.

  This question gives us a chance to review what we know about data types.

A is false: symbolic constants are not all that different from variables. The difference is that a constant declaration includes a keyword `final`. Class constants are often declared as final `static` variables. For example:

```
public static double final PI = 3.14;
```

B is false, too. While real numbers may be written in programs in decimal notation, a Java compiler converts them into a special floating-point format that takes eight bytes and is convenient for computations.

C is false. The data type by itself does not determine where the variable is stored. Its location in memory is determined by where the variable is used and its allocation: whether it is a local variable in a method or an instance variable.

E is false, too. In Java, you can write a/b, where both a and b are integers. The result is truncated to an integer.

D is true. Sometimes an argument of a different type may be promoted to the type expected by the method (e.g., an `int` can be promoted into `double` when you call, say, `Math.sqrt(x)` for an `int x`). But this is not always the case (e.g., a `double` won't work in place of a `String`). The answer is D.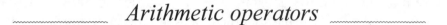

Arithmetic operators

> **The most important thing to remember about Java's arithmetic operators is that the data type of the result, even each intermediate result, is the same as the data type of the operands. In particular, the result of division of one integer by another integer is truncated to an integer.**

For example:

```
int n = 3;
double result;

result = (n + 1) * n / 2;        // result is 6.0
result = (n / 2) * (n + 1);      // result is 4.0
result = (1 / 2) * n * (n + 1);  // result is 0.0
```

To avoid truncation you have to watch the data types and sometimes use the cast operator. For example:

```
int a, b;
double ratio;
...
ratio = (double)a / b;       // Or a / (double) b;
// But not ratio = (double)(a/b) -- this is a cast applied too late!
```

If at least one of the operands is a `double`, there is no need to cast the other one — it is promoted to a `double` automatically. For example:

```
double x;
int factor = 3;
x = 2.0 / factor;   // Correct result: x = .6666...
```

2

Which of the following expressions does not evaluate to 0.4?

(A)   `(int)4.5 / (double)10;`
(B)   `(double)(4 / 10);`
(C)   `4.0 / 10;`
(D)   `4 / 10.0;`
(E)   `(double)4 / (double)10;`

☞ In B the cast to `double` is applied too late — after the ratio is truncated to 0 — so it evaluates to 0. The answer is B. ✍

In the real world we have to worry about the range of values for different data types. For example, a method that calculates the factorial of *n* as an `int` may overflow the result, even for relatively small *n*.

> **For the AP exam, you have to be aware of what overflow is but you don't have to worry about the specific limits.**

Modulo division

> **The % (modulo division) operator applies to two integers: it calculates the remainder when the first operand is divided by the second.**

For example:

```
int r;
r = 17 % 3;   // r is set to 2
r = 8 % 2;    // r is set to 0
r = 4 % 5;    // r is set to 4
```

Compound assignments, ++ and --

Compound assignment operators are +=, -=, *= , /=, and %=. x ✳= y is the same as x = x ✳ y.

There are two forms of the ++ and -- operators in Java. The prefix form increments (or decrements) the variable before its value is used in the rest of the expression; the postfix form increments (or decrements) it afterwards.

> The AP Development Committee discourages the use of ++ or - - in expressions. Use ++ and - - only in separate statements.

For example:

```
while (i <= n)           while (i <= n)
{                        {
                            sum += i;
    sum += i++;             i++;
}                        }
```

You won't lose points over ++ or - - in expressions if you use them correctly, but they won't earn you any credit either!

> It is bad style <u>not</u> to use increment or compound assignment operators where appropriate:

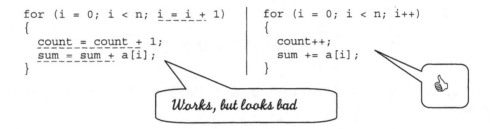

```
for (i = 0; i < n; i = i + 1)    for (i = 0; i < n; i++)
{                                {
    count = count + 1;               count++;
    sum = sum + a[i];                sum += a[i];
}                                }
```

Again, this incurs no penalty but looks ugly.

Arithmetic expressions are too easy to be tested alone. You may encounter them in questions that combine them with logic, iterations, recursion, and so on.

Relational operators

In the subset, the relational operators ==, !=, <, >, <=, >= will apply to `ints` and `doubles`. Remember that "is equal to" is represented by == (not to be confused with the assignment operator, =). Write it clearly. `a != b` is equivalent to `!(a == b)`, but `!=` is stylistically better.

> The == and != operators can be also applied to any objects, but their meanings are different from what you expect: they compare the <u>addresses</u> of two objects. The result of == is true if and only if the two variables refer to exactly the same object. You rarely care about that: most likely you want to compare the <u>contents</u> of two objects, for instance two strings. Then you need to use the `equals` or `compareTo` method.

For example:

```
if (str.equals("Stop")) ...
```

On the other hand, == or != are used when you need to compare an object to null. null is a Java reserved word that stands for a reference with a value of zero. It is used to indicate that a variable currently does not refer to any valid object. For example:

```
if (str != null && str.equals("Stop")) ...
// str != null avoids NullPointerException -- can't call a null's method
```

You can also write

```
if ("Stop".equals(str)) ...
```

— this works because "Stop" is not null; it works even if str is null.

Logical operators

The logical operators &&, ||, and ! normally apply to Boolean values and expressions. For example:

```
boolean found = false;              boolean found = false;
...                                 ...
while (i >= 0 && !found)            while (i >= 0 && found == false)
{                                   {
  ...                                 ...
}                                   }
```

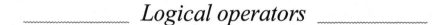

Works, but is more verbose

Do not write

```
while (... && !found == true)
```

— this works, but is redundant.

3

Assuming that x, y, and z are integer variables, which of the following three logical expressions are equivalent to each other, that is, have the same values for any values of x, y, and z?

     I.   `(x == y && x != z) || (x != y && x == z)`

    II.   `(x == y || x == z) && (x != y || x != z)`

   III.   `(x == y) != (x == z)`

(A)   I and II only
(B)   II and III only
(C)   I and III only
(D)   I, II, and III
(E)   None of the three

Expression III is the key to the answer: all three expressions state the fact that exactly one out of the two equalities, `x == y` or `x == z`, is true. Expression I states that either the first and not the second or the second and not the first is true. Expression II states that one of the two is true and one of the two is false. Expression III simply states that they have different values. All three boil down to the same thing. The answer is D.

De Morgan's laws

The exam may include questions on De Morgan's Laws:

    `!(a && b)` is the same as `!a || !b`
    `!(a || b)` is the same as `!a && !b`

4

The expression `!((x <= y) && (y > 5))` is equivalent to which of the following?

(A)   `(x <= y) && (y > 5)`
(B)   `(x <= y) || (y > 5)`
(C)   `(x >= y) || (y < 5)`
(D)   `(x > y) || (y <= 5)`
(E)   `(x > y) && (y <= 5)`

☞ The given expression is pretty long, so if you try to plug in specific numbers you may lose a lot of time. Use De Morgan's Laws instead:

$$! ((x <= y) \quad \&\& \quad (y > 5))$$

$$! (x <= y) \quad || \quad ! (y > 5)$$

$$(x > y) \quad || \quad (y <= 5)$$

The answer is D. ☜

> When ! is distributed, && changes into || and vice-versa

Short-circuit evaluation

> **An important thing to remember about the Java logical operators, && and ||, is *short-circuit evaluation*. If the value of the first operand unambiguously defines the result, then the second operand is <u>not</u> evaluated.**

5

Consider the following code segment:

```
int x = 0, y = 3;
String op = "/";

if (op.equals("/") && (x != 0) && (y/x > 2))
{
  System.out.println("OK");
}
else
{
  System.out.println("Failed");
}
```

Which of the following statements about this code is true?

(A)   There will be a compile error because String and int variables are intermixed in the same condition.
(B)   There will be a run-time divide-by-zero error.
(C)   The code will compile and execute without error; the output will be OK.
(D)   The code will compile and execute without error; the output will be Failed.
(E)   The code will compile and execute without error; there will be no output.

☞ A and E are just filler answers. Since x is equal to 0, the condition cannot be true, so C should be rejected, too. The question remains whether it bombs or executes. In Java, once x != 0 fails, the rest of the condition, y/x > 2, won't be evaluated and y/x won't be computed. The answer is D. ☜

The relational expressions in the above question are parenthesized. This is not necessary because relational operators always take precedence over logical operators. If you are used to lots of parentheses, use them, but you can skip them as well. For example, the Boolean expression from Question 5 can be written with fewer parentheses:

```
if (op.equals("/") && x != 0 && y/x > 2)
```

&& also takes precedence over ||, but it's clearer to use parentheses when && and || appear in the same expression. For example:

```
if ((0 < a && a < top) || (0 < b && b < top)) ...
```

2.2. Conditional Statements and Loops

You can use simplified indentation for `if-else-if` statements.

For example:

```
if (score >= 70)
  grade = 5;
else if (score >= 60)
  grade = 4;
...
else
  grade = 1;
```

But don't forget braces and proper indentation for nested ifs. For example:

```
if (exam.equals("A"))
{
  if (score >= 60)
    grade = 5;
  else if ...
    ...
}
else if (exam.equals("AB"))
{
  if (score >= 70)
    grade = 5;
  else if ...
    ...
}
```

Consider the following code segment, where x is a variable of the type double:

```
if (x > 0.001)
{
   if ((int)(1.0 / x) % 2 == 0)
     System.out.println("even");
   else
     System.out.println("odd");
}
else
   System.out.println("small");
```

Which of the following code segments are equivalent to the one above (that is, produce the same output as the one above regardless of the value of x)?

I.
```
if (x <= 0.001)
   System.out.println("small");
else if ((int)(1.0 / x) % 2 == 0)
   System.out.println("even");
else
   System.out.println("odd");
```

II.
```
if (x > 0.001 && (int)(1.0 / x) % 2 == 0)
   System.out.println("even");
else if (x <= 0.001)
   System.out.println("small");
else
   System.out.println("odd");
```

III.
```
if ((int)(1.0 / x) % 2 == 0)
{
   if (x <= 0.001)
     System.out.println("small");
   else
     System.out.println("even");
}
else
{
   if (x <= 0.001)
     System.out.println("small");
   else
     System.out.println("odd");
}
```

(A)   I only
(B)   II only
(C)   I and II
(D)   II and III
(E)   I, II, and III

Segment I can actually be reformatted as:

```
if (x <= 0.001)
  System.out.println("small");
else
{
  if ((int)(1.0 / x) % 2 == 0)
    System.out.println("even");
  else
    System.out.println("odd");
}
```

So it's the same as the given segment with the condition negated and `if` and `else` swapped. Segment II restructures the sequence, but gives the same result. To see this we can try different combinations of true/false for `x <= 0.001` and
`(int)(1.0 / x) % 2 == 0`. Segment III would work, too, but it has a catch: it bombs when `x` is equal to 0. The answer is C.

───── *for and* while *loops* ─────

The `for` loop,

```
for (initialize; condition; increment)
{
    ...    // Do something
}
```

is equivalent to the `while` loop:

```
initialize;
while (condition)
{
    ...    // Do something
    increment;
}
```

increment can mean any change in the values of the variables that control the loop; actually it can be a *decrement*.

`for` loops are shorter and more idiomatic in some instances. They shouldn't be discriminated against. For example:

```
i = 0;
while (i < a.length)
{
    sum += a[i];
    i++;
}
```

```
for (i = 0; i < a.length; i++)
    sum += a[i];
```

O.K.

Better, more idiomatic

In a `for` or `while` loop, the condition is evaluated at the beginning of the loop and the program does not go inside the loop if the condition is false. Thus, the body of the loop may be skipped entirely if the condition is false at the very beginning.

7

Consider the following methods:

```
public int fun1(int n)              public int fun2(int n)
{                                   {
    int product = 1;                    int product = 1;
    int k;                              int k = 2;
    for (k = 2; k <= n; k++)            while (k <= n)
    {                                   {
        product *= k;                       product *= k;
    }                                       k++;
    return product;                     }
}                                       return product;
                                    }
```

For which integer values of n do `fun1(n)` and `fun2(n)` return the same result?

(A)   Only n > 1
(B)   Only n < 1
(C)   Only n == 1
(D)   Only n >= 1
(E)   Any integer n

☞ The best approach here is purely formal: since the initialization, condition, and increment in the `for` loop in `fun1` are the same as the ones used with the `while` loop in `fun2`, the two methods are equivalent. The answer is E.

8

Consider the following code segment:

```
while (x > y)
{
  x--;
  y++;
}
System.out.print(x - y);
```

Assume that x and y are int variables and their values satisfy the conditions $0 \le x \le 2$ and $0 \le y \le 2$. Which of the following describes the set of all possible outputs?

(A)   0
(B)   -1, 1
(C)   -1, -2
(D)   0, -1, -2
(E)   0, -1, 1, -2, 2

☞ If $x \le y$, then the while loop is never entered and the possible outputs are 0, -1, and -2 (for the pairs (0,0), (0,1), (0,2), (1,1), (1,2), (2,2)). If $x > y$, then the loop is entered and after the loop we must have $x \le y$, so x - y cannot be positive. The answer is D. ↵

_____ *OBOBs* _____

When coding loops, beware of the so-called "off-by-one bugs" ("OBOBs"). These are mistakes of running through the iterations one time too many or one time too few.

9

Suppose the `isPrime` method is defined:

```
// precondition:  p >= 2
// postcondition: Returns true if p is a prime number, false otherwise.
public static boolean isPrime(int p) { < code not shown > }
```

Given

```
int n = 101;
int sum = 0;
```

Which of the following code segments correctly computes the sum of all prime numbers from 2 to 101?

(A)
```
while (n != 2)
{
  n--;
  if (isPrime(n)) sum += n;
}
```

(B)
```
while (n >= 2)
{
  n--;
  if (isPrime(n)) sum += n;
}
```

(C)
```
while (n != 2)
{
  if (isPrime(n)) sum += n;
  n--;
}
```

(D)
```
while (n >= 2)
{
  if (isPrime(n)) sum += n;
  n--;
}
```

(E)
```
while (n >= 2 && isPrime(n))
{
  sum += n;
  n--;
}
```

☞ It is bad style to start the body of a loop with a decrement, so choices A and B are most likely wrong. Indeed, both A and B miss 101 (which happens to be a prime) because n is decremented too early. In addition, B eventually calls `isPrime(1)`, violating `isPrime`'s precondition. C misses 2 — an OBOB on the other end. E might look plausible for a moment, but it actually quits as soon at it encounters the first non-prime number. The answer is D. ☜

break and return *in loops*

In Java it is okay to use break and return inside loops. return immediately quits the method from any place inside or outside a loop. This may be a convenient shortcut, especially when you have to write nested loops and you are pressed for time. For example:

```java
// postcondition: Returns true if all values in list
//                are different, false otherwise
public boolean allDifferent(int[] list)
{
  int i, j;

  for (i = 0; i < list.length; i++)
    for (j = i + 1; j < list.length; j++)
      if (list[i] == list[j])
        return false;
  return true;
}
```

You can also use break, but remember that in a nested loop break takes you out of the inner loop but not out of the outer loop. break may be dangerous and is not in the AP subset. Avoid redundant, verbose, and incorrect code like this:

```java
// postcondition: Returns true if all values in list
//                are different, false otherwise
public boolean allDifferent(int[] list)
{
  int i, j;
  boolean foundDuplicates;

  for (i = 0; i < list.length; i++)
  {
    for (j = i + 1; j < list.length; j++)
    {
      if (list[i] == list[j])
      {
        foundDuplicates = true;
        break;
      }
      else
      {
        foundDuplicates = false;
      }
    }
  }
  if (foundDuplicates == true)
    return false;
  else
    return true;
}
```

Out of the inner for *but still in the outer* for.

If you insist on using Boolean flags, you need to be extra careful:

```
// postcondition: Returns true if all values in list
//                are different, false otherwise
public boolean allDifferent(int[] list)
{
  int i, j;
  boolean foundDuplicates = false;

  for (i = 0; i < list.length; i++)
  {
    for (j = i + 1; j < list.length; j++)
    {
      if (list[i] == list[j])
      {
        foundDuplicates = true;
        break;
      }
    }
  }
  return !foundDuplicates;
}
```

The `continue` statement is not in the AP subset and should be avoided.

2.3.   Strings

In Java, a string is an object of the type `String`, and, as for other types of objects, a `String` variable holds a reference to (address of) the string. Strings are immutable: none of string's methods can change the string. An assignment statement

```
str1 = str2;
```

copies the reference from `str2` into `str1`, so they both refer to the same memory location.

A *literal string* is a string of characters within double quotes. A literal string may include "escape sequences" \n (newline), \" (a double quote), and \\ (one backslash). For example,

```
System.out.print("Hello\n");
```

has the same effect as

```
System.out.println("Hello");
```

The `String` class supports the `+` and `+=` operators for concatenating strings. `String` is the only class in Java that supports special syntax for using operators on its objects.

The operator

```
s1 += s2;
```

appends `s2` to `s1`. In reality it creates a new string by concatenating `s1` and `s2` and then sets `s1` to refer to it. It is equivalent to

```
s1 = s1 + s2;
```

What is the output of the following code segment?

```
String str1 = "Happy ";
String str2 = str1;
str2 += "New Year! ";
str2.substring(6);
System.out.println(str1 + str2);
```

(A) Happy New Year!
(B) Happy Happy New Year!
(C) Happy New Year! New Year!
(D) Happy New Year! Happy New Year!
(E) Happy New Year! Happy

☞ After `str2 = str1`, `str1` and `str2` point to the same memory location that contains `"Happy "`. But after `str2 += "New Year! "`, these variables point to different things: `str1` remains `"Happy "` (strings are immutable) while `str2` becomes `"Happy New Year! "`. `str2.substring(6)` does not change `str2` — it calls its `substring` but does not use its returned value (a common beginner's mistake: again, strings are immutable). The answer is B. ☜

_____ *String methods* _____

The `String` methods included in the subset are:

```
int length()
boolean equals(String other)
int compareTo(String other)
String substring(int from)
String substring(int from, int to)
int indexOf(String s)
```

> **Use the `equals` method to compare a string to another string. The `==` and `!=` operators, applied to two strings, compare their <u>addresses</u>, not their values.**

`str1.equals(str2)` returns `true` if and only if `str1` and `str2` have the same values (i.e., consist of the same characters).

`str1.compareTo(str2)` returns a positive number if `str1` is greater than `str2` (lexicographically), zero if they are equal, and a negative number if `str1` is less than `str2`.

`str.substring(from)` returns a substring of `str` starting at the `from` position to the end, and `str.substring(from, to)` returns `str`'s substring starting at the `from` position and up to but <u>not including</u> `to` position (so the length of the returned substring is `to - from`). Positions are counted from 0. For example, `"Happy".substring(1,4)` would return `"app"`.

`str.indexOf(s)` returns the starting position of the first occurrence of `s` in `str`, or `-1` if not found.

Consider the following method:

```java
public String process(String msg, String delim)
{
    int pos = msg.indexOf(delim);
    while (pos >= 0)
    {
        msg = msg.substring(0, pos) + " "
                        + msg.substring(pos + delim.length());
        pos = msg.indexOf(delim);
    }
    return msg;
}
```

What is the output of the following code segment?

```java
String rhyme = "Twinkle\ntwinkle\nlittle star";
String rhyme2 = process(rhyme, "\n")
System.out.println(rhyme + "\n" + rhyme2);
```

(A) `little star`
     `Twinkle twinkle little star`

(B) `little star`
     `Twinkle`
     `twinkle`
     `little star`

(C) `Twinkle`
     `twinkle`
     `little star`
     `Twinkle winkle ittle tar`

(D) `Twinkle`
     `twinkle`
     `little star`
     `Twinkle twinkle`
     `little star`

(E) `Twinkle`
     `twinkle`
     `little star`
     `Twinkle twinkle little star`

`process` receives and works with a <u>copy</u> of a reference to the original string (see Section 2.8). The method can reassign the copy, as it does here, but the original reference still refers to the same string. This consideration, combined with immutability of strings, assures us that `rhyme` remains unchanged after the call `process(rhyme)`.

The `rhyme` string includes two newline characters, and, when printed, it produces

    `Twinkle`
    `twinkle`
    `little Star`

So the only possible answers can be C, D or E. Note that we can come to this conclusion before we even look at the `process` method! This method repeatedly finds the first occurrence of `delim` in `msg`, cuts it out, and replaces it with a space. No other characters can be replaced or lost. The resulting message prints on one line. The answer is E.

2.4.   `Integer` and `Double` Classes

In Java, variables of primitive data types (`int`, `double`, etc.) are not objects. In some situations it is convenient represent numbers as objects. For example, you might want to store numeric values in an `ArrayList` (see Section 2.6), but elements of an `ArrayList` must be objects. The `java.lang` package provides several "wrapper" classes that represent primitive data types as objects. Two of these classes, `Integer` and `Double`, are in the AP subset.

The `Integer` class has a constructor that takes an `int` value and creates an `Integer` object representing that value. The `intValue` method of an `Integer` object returns the value represented by that object as an `int`. For example:

```
Integer obj = new Integer(123);
...
int num = obj.intValue();  // num gets the value of 123
```

Likewise, `Double`'s constructor creates a `Double` object that represents a given `double` value. The method `doubleValue` returns the `double` represented by a `Double` object:

```
Double obj = new Double(123.45);
...
double x = obj.doubleValue();  // x gets the value of 123.45
```

> **Use the `equals` method of the `Integer` or of the `Double` class if you want to compare two `Integer` or two `Double` variables, respectively.**

For example:

```
Integer a = new Integer(...);
Integer b = new Integer(...);
...
if (a.equals(b))
  ...
```

If you apply a relational operator `==` or `!=` to two `Integer` or two `Double` variables, you will compare their <u>addresses</u>, not values.

Both the `Integer` and `Double` classes implement the `Comparable` interface (see Section 3.6), so each of these classes has a `compareTo` method. As usual, `obj1.compareTo(obj2)` returns a positive integer if `obj1` is greater than `obj2` (i.e., `obj1`'s numeric value is greater than `obj2`'s numeric value), a negative integer if `obj1` is less than `obj2`, and zero if their numeric values are equal.

2.5.   Arrays

There are two ways to declare and create a one-dimensional array:

```
someType[] a = new someType[ size ];
someType[] b = {value₀, value₁, ..., value_{N-1}};
```

For example:

```
double[] samples = new double[100];
int[] numbers = {1, 2, 3};
String[] cities = {"Atlanta", "Boston", "Cincinnati", "Dallas"};
```

The first declaration declares an array of `doubles` of size 100. Its elements get default values (zeroes), but this fact is not in the AP subset. The second declaration creates an array of `ints` of size 3 with its elements initialized to the values 1, 2, and 3. The third declaration declares and initializes an array of four given strings.

We can refer to `a`'s elements as `a[i]`, where `a` is the name of the array and `i` is an index (subscript), which can be an integer constant, variable, or expression.

▌ Indices start from 0.

`a.length` (<u>with no parentheses</u>) refers to the size of the array. `a[a.length - 1]` refers to the last element.

Once an array is created, its size cannot be changed. The only way to expand an array is to create a bigger array and copy the contents of the original array into the new one. The old array is discarded (or, more precisely, recycled by a process called "garbage collection"). For example:

```
int[] a = new int[100];
...
int[] temp = new int[a.length * 2];
for (int i = 0; i < a.length; i++)
  temp[i] = a[i];
a = temp;   // reassign a to the new array; the old array is discarded
```

▌ If a and b are arrays, a = b does not copy elements from b into a: it just reassigns the reference a to b, so that both a and b refer to the same array.

The following method reverses the order of elements in an array of strings:

```
public void reverse(String[] words)
{
  int i = 0, j = words.length - 1;
  String temp;
  while (i < j)
  {
    temp = words[i]; words[i] = words[j]; words[j] = temp;
    i++;
    j--;
  }
}
```

The Java Virtual Machine (the run-time interpreter) checks that an array index is within the valid range, from 0 to `array.length - 1`. If an index value is invalid, the interpreter "throws" an `ArrayIndexOutOfBoundsException` — reports a run-time error, the line number for the offending program statement, and a trace of the method calls that led to it.

An exception is a run-time error, not a compile-time error.

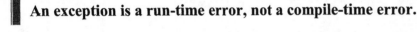

Consider the following method:

```
// precondition:  counts contains n values, n > 1
// postcondition: returns true if there are no two elements in
//                counts whose values are the same or are consecutive
//                integers; false otherwise
public boolean isSparse(int[] counts, int n)
{
  int j, k, diff;

  < code >
}
```

Which of the following code segments can be used to replace < *code* > so that the method `isSparse` satisfies its postcondition?

I.
```
for (j = 0; j < n; j++)
{
  for (k = j + 1; k < n; k++)
  {
    diff = counts[j] - counts[k];
    if (diff >= -1 && diff <= 1)
      return false;
  }
}
return true;
```

II.
```
for (j = 1; j < n; j++)
{
  for (k = 0; k < j; k++)
  {
    diff = counts[j] - counts[k];
    if (diff >= -1 && diff <= 1)
      return false;
  }
}
return true;
```

III.
```
for (j = 0; j < n; j++)
{
  for (k = 1; k < n; k++)
  {
    diff = counts[j] - counts[k];
    if (Math.abs(diff) <= 1)
      return false;
  }
}
return true;
```

(A) I only
(B) II only
(C) I and II only
(D) I and III only
(E) I, II, and III

☞ Note that in this question not all `counts.length` elements of `counts` are used, just the first n. Their subscripts range from 0 to $n-1$. The precondition states that $n > 1$, so there is no need to worry about an empty array or an array of just one element. Looking at the inner loop in each segment you can quickly see that they work the same way. So the difference is in how the loops are set up; more precisely, in the limits in which the indices vary. In Segment I the outer loop starts with the first item in the list; the inner loop compares it with each of the subsequent items. In Segment II the outer loop starts with the second item in the list; the inner loop compares it with each of the previous items. Both of these are correct and quite standard in similar algorithms. This eliminates A, B, and D. Segment III at first seems harmless, too, but it has a catch: the inner loop doesn't set a limit for `k` that depends on `j`, so when `j` is greater than 0, `k` may eventually take the same value as `j`, (e.g. `j` = 1, `k` = 1). The method will erroneously detect the same value in `counts` when it is actually comparing an item to itself.
The answer is C. ▨

13

Suppose the method `int sign(int x)` returns 1 if x is positive, -1 if x is negative, and 0 if x is 0. Given

```
int[] nums = {-2, -1, 0, 1, 2};
```

what are the values of the elements of `nums` after the following code is executed?

```
int k;
for (k = 0; k < nums.length; k++)
{
  nums[k]  -= sign(nums[k]);
  nums[k]  += sign(nums[k]);
}
```

(A)   -2, -1, 0, 1, 2
(B)   -1, 0, 0, 0, 1
(C)   0, 0, 0, 0, 0
(D)   -2, 0, 0, 2, 3
(E)   -2, 0, 0, 0, 2

☞ Remember that the first statement within the loop changes `nums[k]`, which may change the sign of `nums[k]`, too. Jot down a little table:

Before		After -=		After +=
a[k]	sign of a[k]	a[k]	sign of a[k]	a[k]
-2	-1	-1	-1	-2
-1	-1	0	0	0
0	0	0	0	0
1	1	0	0	0
2	1	1	1	2

The answer is E. ☟

Array return type

Occasionally you may need to return an array from a method. Suppose you want to restructure the `reverse` method above so that it <u>returns</u> a new array containing the values from a given array in reverse order. The original array remains unchanged. It can be coded as follows:

```
public String[] reverse(String[] words)
{
  String[] result = new String[words.length];

  int i;
  for (i = 0; i < words.length; i++)
    result[i] = words[words.length - 1 - i];

  return result;
}
```

⌈ *Two-dimensional arrays* ⌋

⌈ <u>The AB exam</u> includes rectangular two-dimensional arrays. These are similar to one-dimensional arrays but use two indices, one for the row and one for the column. For example:

```
double[][] matrix = new double[3][5]; // 3 rows by 5 cols
int r, c;
...
matrix[r][c] = 1.23;
```

If m is a two-dimensional array, m.length represents the number of rows and m[0].length (i.e., the length of the first row) represents the number of columns.

Only rectangular 2-D arrays are considered in the AP subset; therefore, the lengths of all the rows are the same and `m[0].length` represents the length of any row.

The following method calculates and returns the sums of the values in each column of a 2-D array:

```
// precondition:  table is a 2-D array
// postcondition: returns a 1-D array containing sums of all the values
//                in each column of table
public double[] totalsByColumn(double[][] table)
{
  int nRows = table.length;
  int nCols = table[0].length;
  double[] totals = new double[nCols];
  int r, c;

  for (c = 0; c < nCols; c++)
  {
    totals[c] = 0.0;
    for (r = 0; r < nRows; r++)
      totals[c] += table[r][c];
  }
  return totals;
}
```

14

Consider the following code segment:

```
String[][] m = new String[6][3];
int k;

for (k = 0; k < m.length; k++)
{
  m[k][m[0].length - 1] = "*";
}
```

Which of the following best describes the result when this code segment is executed?

(A)   All elements in the first row of m are set to `"*"`
(B)   All elements in the last row of m are set to `"*"`
(C)   All elements in the last column of m are set to `"*"`
(D)   The code has no effect
(E)   `ArrayIndexOutOfBoundsException` is reported

The first index is row, and the `for` loop is set up for all rows. The answer is C.

⌐

2.6.   The `ArrayList` class

`java.util.ArrayList` is a Java library class that implements a list of items using an array of objects.

> **An `ArrayList` holds objects (e.g., strings). If you want to hold elements of primitive data types, use a standard array or convert numbers into objects using the corresponding "wrapper" class — `Integer` for `ints`, `Double` for `doubles`.**

`ArrayList` provides methods for getting and setting the value of a particular element, adding a value at the end of the list, removing a value, and inserting a value at a given position. As in standard arrays, indices start from 0.

An `ArrayList` is automatically resized when it runs out of space. `ArrayList`'s "no-args" constructor (i.e., the constructor that takes no arguments) allocates an array of some default initial capacity and size 0 (no values stored in it). As values are added, their number may exceed the current capacity. Then the capacity is doubled, a new array is allocated, the old values are copied into the new array, and the old array is discarded. All this happens behind the scenes — you don't have to worry about any of it.

The AP subset includes the following methods of `ArrayList`:

`int size()`	Returns the number of values currently stored in the list
`boolean add(Object x)`	Adds x at the end of the list; returns `true`
`Object get(int index)`	Returns the value stored at `index`
`Object set(int index, Object x)`	Sets the value of the element at `index` to x; returns the old value
`Object remove(int index)`	Removes the value at `index` and shifts the subsequent values towards the beginning of the list; returns the old value stored at `index`
`void add(int index, Object x)`	Inserts x at `index`, shifting the current value stored at `index` and all the subsequent values towards the end of the list

The `add` and `remove` methods adjust the size of the array appropriately. The methods that take an `index` parameter check that the index is in the valid range, from 0 to `size() - 1` and "throw" `IndexOutOfBoundsException` if the index is not in that range.

15

What is the output of the following code segment?

```
ArrayList list = new ArrayList();
list.add("A");
list.add("B");
list.add("C");
list.add("D");
list.add("E");
int k;
for (k = 1; k <= 3; k++)
{
    list.remove(1);
}
for (k = 1; k <= 3; k++)
{
    list.add(1, new Integer(k));
}
for (k = 0; k < list.size(); k++)
{
    System.out.print(list.get(k) + " ");
}
```

(A) A C D E 1 2 3
(B) 1 2 3 B C D E
(C) A 3 2 1 E
(D) A E 1 2 3
(E) IndexOutOfBoundsException

☞ This question is not as tricky as it might seem. First we create an empty list and add five values to it: A, B, C, D, E. Then we remove the value at index 1 three times. This is the second element and each time we remove it, the subsequent values shift to the left. A, E remain. Then we insert three Integer values. Note that we always insert at index 1. After the first insertion we get A, 1, E. After the second we get A, 2, 1, E. The third insertion produces A, 3, 2, 1, E. The third for loop traverses the whole list and prints out the values. Note that when an object is passed to System.out.print or System.out.println, its toString method is called to convert that object into a string, so both String and Integer objects will be printed correctly. (This is a case of polymorphism.) The answer is C. ☜

2.7.   Classes

A Java program consists of classes. The term *class* refers to a class of objects.

You should know the following concepts and terms:

class	*private* and *public* members
object	*encapsulation* and *information hiding*
instance of a class	*client* of a class
constructor	*accessor*
new operator	*modifier*
garbage collection	*static* methods
instance variable or *field*	*public static final* fields (constants)

An object that belongs to a particular class is also called an *instance* of that class, and the process of creating an object is called *instantiation*.

A class definition includes *constructors*, *methods*, and data members. The constructors describe how objects of the class can be created; the methods describe what an object of this class can do; the data members (a.k.a. *instance variables* or *fields*) describe the object's attributes — the current state of an object.

―――――――― *Constructors* ――――――――

Constructors describe ways to create an object of a class and initialize the object's instance variables.

> **All constructors have the same name as the class. Constructors do not have any return data type, not even `void`.**

A constructor may take arguments (parameters) that help define a new object. A constructor that takes no arguments is called a "no-args" constructor.

A new object is created using the `new` operator. For example, suppose you have defined a class `School`:

```
public class School
{
  // Constructor:
  public School(String name, int numStudents) { < code not shown > }
  ...
}
```

Then you can create a `School` object elsewhere in the code:

```
School sgt = new School("School for Gifted and Talented", 1200);
```

If a class has instance variables `myName` and `myNumStudents` —

```
public class School
{
  ...
  private String myName;
  private int myNumStudents;
}
```

— the constructor can set them to values of the arguments passed to it:

```
public School(String name, int numStudents)
{
  myName = name;
  myNumStudents = numStudents;
}
```

> **The prefix "my" is often used in AP CS examples to make the names of instance variables different from the names of parameters passed to constructors and methods. Other names can be used, as long as they don't clash with each other.**

In Java, objects that are no longer used in the program are automatically destroyed and the memory they occupy is recycled. This mechanism is called *garbage collection*.

`public` *and* `private`

Class members, both data and methods, may be *public* or *private*.

> **Public members are accessible anywhere in the code; private members are accessible only within the class's constructors and member methods.**

In the AP subset, constructors are always public.

> **It is a common practice in OOP (and a requirement on the AP exam) to make all instance variables <u>private</u>.**

Private members hide the implementation details of a class from other classes, its clients. This concept is known as *encapsulation*. A *client* class uses your class through constructors and public methods. In general, it is a good idea to supply as little information to client classes as possible. This concept is known as *information hiding*. For example, if a method is used only internally within that class, it should be made <u>private</u>.

Accessors and modifiers

Since all instance variables are private, they are not directly accessible in client classes. It is common to provide special public methods, called *accessors*, that return the values of instance variables. For example:

```
public class School
{
  ...
  public String getName()
  {
    return myName;
  }
  ...
}
```

Accessors' names often start with a "get." Accessors do not change the state of the object.

A public method that sets a new value of an instance variable is called a *modifier*. Modifiers' names often start with a "set." For example:

```
public class School
{
  ...
  public void setName(String name)
  {
    myName = name;
  }
  ...
}
```

The "accessor" and "modifier" designations are somewhat informal — a class may have a method that sets an instance variable to a new value and at the same time returns, say, the old value.

16

Consider the following class:

```
public class Clock
{
  private int hours;
  private int mins;

  public Clock(int h, int m)
  {
    hours = h;
    mins = m;
  }

  // postcondition: moves this clock one minute forward
  public void move()
  {
    < missing code >
  }

  public void set(int h, int m)
  {
    hours = h;
    mins = m;
    normalize();
  }

  private void normalize()
  {
    while (mins >= 60)
    {
      mins -= 60;
      hours++;
    }
    hours %= 12;
  }
}
```

Which of the following could replace < *missing code* > in the move method?

I.   this = new Clock(hours, mins + 1);

II. mins++;
     normalize();

III. set(hours, mins + 1);

(A) I only
(B) II only
(C) I and II only
(D) II and III only
(E) I, II, and III

☞ Option I is wrong: it attempts to replace `this` with a new object instead of changing this one, which results in a syntax error. The other two options are acceptable: it is okay to access private instance variables and call private and public methods inside the same class. The answer is D.

(Note that it would be better to add a call to `normalize` in `Clock`'s constructor, too, just to make sure the clock is set correctly, even if `mins` ≥ 60. Alternatively, the constructor could throw an `InvalidStateException` if its parameters didn't make sense.) ↵

Static (class) variables and methods

Sometimes an attribute belongs to a class as a whole, not to individual objects. Such variables are called *class variables* and are designated with the keyword `static`. In the AP subset, static variables are always `public final` variables (constants). For example:

```
public class School
{
  public static final int highestGrade = 12;
  ...
}
```

A class may also have static methods — methods that do not involve any particular instances of a class and do not access any instance variables. For example, the Java library class `Math` has static methods `abs`, `sqrt`, `pow`. (For your convenience, it also includes the `public static final` "variables" `PI` that represents π, the ratio of a circle's circumference to its diameter, and `E` that represents e, the base of the natural logarithm.) Static methods are called and static constants are accessed using the dot notation, with the class's name as the prefix. For example:

```
double volume = 4.0 / 3.0 * Math.PI * Math.pow(r, 3);
```

2.8.   Methods

In Java, all methods belong to classes. It is universal Java style that all method names start with a lowercase letter.

An *instance* method is called for a particular object; then the object's name and a dot are used as a prefix in a call, as in `obj.someMethod(...)`. If a method is called from another method of <u>the same</u> object, the prefix is not needed and you write simply `someMethod(...)`. Class (`static`) methods belong to the class as a whole and are called using the class's name with a dot as a prefix. For example: `Math.sqrt(...)`.

A method takes a specific number of arguments of specific data types. Some methods take no arguments. A method call may include a whole expression as an argument; then the expression is evaluated first and the result is passed to the method. An expression may include calls to other methods. For example:

```
double x, y;
...
x = Math.sqrt(Math.abs(2*y - 1));
```

A method usually returns a value of the specified data type, but a `void` method does not return any value. The return value is specified in the `return` statement.

> **It is considered a "major error" (-1 point) to read the new values for a method's arguments from `System.in` from inside the method.**
>
> **It is a minor error (-1/2 point) to print the return value to `System.out` from inside the method (when it is not requested) and an additional error if a required `return` statement is missing in a non-`void` method.**

For example:

```
// precondition:  n >= 1
// postcondition: Returns the sum of all integers from 1 to n.
public int addNumbers (int n)
{
   int k;
   int sum = 0;                        Mistake  👎

   n = System.in.read();       // n is passed to this method from main or
                                //    from another calling method

   for (k = 1; k <= n; k++)         Mistake  👎
   {
      sum += k;
   }

   System.out.println(sum);    // Not intended and not described
                                //    in the postcondition

   return sum;
}
```

Recall that `Math`'s static method `min` returns the value of the smaller of two integers. If a, b, c, and m are integer variables, which of the following best describes the behavior of a program with the following statement?

```
m = Math.min(Math.min(a, c), Math.min(b, c));
```

(A)   The statement has a syntax error and will not compile.
(B)   The program will run but go into an infinite loop.
(C)   a will get the smaller value of a and c; b will get the smaller value of b and c; m will get the smallest value of a, b, and c.
(D)   m will be assigned the smallest of the values a, b, and c.
(E)   None of the above

☞ Any expression of the appropriate data type, including a method call that returns a value of the appropriate data type, may be used in a larger expression or as an argument to a method. The code above is basically equivalent to:

```
int temp1 = Math.min(a, c);
int temp2 = Math.min(b, c);
m = Math.min(temp1, temp2);
```

So m gets the smallest of the three values. The answer is D. ↵

_____ *Arguments of primitive data types* _____

In Java, all arguments of primitive data types are passed to methods "by value."

When an argument is passed by value, the method works with a copy of the variable passed to it, so it has no way of changing the value of the original.

18

Consider the following method:

```
public void fun(int a, int b)
{
    a += b;
    b += a;
}
```

What is the output from the following code?

```
int x = 3, y = 5;
fun(x, y);
System.out.println(x + " " + y);
```

(A)   3 5
(B)   3 8
(C)   3 13
(D)   8 8
(E)   8 13

☞ x and y are ints, so they are passed to fun by value. fun works with copies of x and y, named a and b. What is happening inside fun is irrelevant here because x and y do not change after the method call. The answer is A. ☜

_____ *Objects passed to methods* _____

> **All objects are passed to methods as references. A method receives a <u>copy</u> of a reference to (address of) the object.**

When a variable gets an "object" as a value, what it actually holds is a reference to (address of) that object. Likewise, when an object is passed to a method, the method receives a copy of the object's address, and therefore it potentially <u>can</u> change the original object. Usually all instance variables of an object are private, so to change the object, the method would have to call one of the object's *modifier* methods.

But note that the `String`, `Integer`, and `Double` classes represent *immutable* objects, that is, objects that have no modifier methods. Even though these objects are passed to methods as references, no method can change them. For example, there is no way in Java to write a method

```
// postcondition:  Converts s to upper case
public void toUpperCase(String s)
{
  ...
}
```

because the method has no way to change the string passed to it. For immutable objects, you have to create and return from the method a new object with the desired properties:

```
// postcondition:  Returns s converted to upper case
public String toUpperCase(String s)
{
  ...
}
```

Aliasing

A more complicated concept is *aliasing*. In general, it is good to understand, but it is unlikely to come up on the exams. The following explanation is for a more inquisitive reader.

Consider a method:

```
// postcondition: point2 receives coordinates of point1 rotated
//                 90 degrees counterclockwise around the origin
public void rotate90 (Point point1, Point point2)
{
  point2.setY(point1.getX());
  point2.setX(-point1.getY());
}
```

In this example, `rotate90` takes two `Point` objects as arguments. Like all objects, these are passed to the method as references. Note that a `Point` object here is not immutable because it has the `setX` and `setY` methods. The code looks pretty harmless: it sets `point2` coordinates to the new values obtained from `point1` coordinates. However, suppose you call `rotate90(point, point)` hoping to change the coordinates of `point` appropriately. The compiler will not prevent you from doing that, but the result will not be what you expected. Inside the method, `point1` and `point2` actually both refer to `point`. The first statement will set `point`'s y equal to x, and the original value of y will be lost. If `point` coordinates are, say, x = 3, y = 5, instead of getting x = -5, y = 3, as intended, you will get x = -3, y = 3. This type of error is called an aliasing error.

In Java, aliasing may happen only when arguments are objects and they are not immutable (or when arguments are arrays and the method moves values from one array to another). In the above example, it would be safer to make `rotate90` return a new value, as in

```
public Point rotate90 (Point point)
{
  return new Point(point.getX(), -point.getY());
}
```

return

A method that is not `void` must return a value of the designated type using the `return` statement. `return` works with any expression, not just variables. For example:

```
return (-b + Math.sqrt(b*b - 4*a*c)) / (2*a);
```

An often overlooked fact is that a `boolean` method can return the value of a Boolean expression. For example, you can write simply

```
return x >= a && x <= b;
```

as opposed to the redundant and verbose

```
if (x >= a && x <= b)
    return true;
else
    return false;
```

A `void` method can use a `return` (within `if` or `else`) to quit early, but there is no need for a `return` at the end of the method.

Returning objects

A method's return type can be a class, and a method can return an object of that class. Often a new object is created in the method and then returned from it. For example:

```
public String getFullName(String firstName, String lastName)
{
  return firstName + " " + lastName;
}
```

A method whose return type is a class can also return a `null` (a reference with a zero value that indicates that it does not refer to any valid object). For example:

```
public String getAddress(String name)
{
  for (int i = 0; i < myListOfNames.length; i++)
  {
    if (myListOfNames[i].equals(name))
      return myListOfAddresses(i);
  }
  return null; // not found
}
```

Overloaded methods

Methods of the same class with the same name but different numbers or types of parameters are called *overloaded* methods. (The order of different types of parameters is important, too.)

> **The compiler treats overloaded methods as different methods. It figures out which one to call depending on the number and types of the arguments.**

The `String` class, for example, has two forms of the `substring` method:

```
String substring(int from)
String substring(int from, int to)
```

If you call `"Happy".substring(2)` then the first overloaded method will be called, but if you call `"Happy".substring(1, 3)` then the second overloaded method will be called. Another example of overloading is `Math.abs(x)`, which has different versions of the static method abs, including `abs(int)` and `abs(double)`. `System.out.print(x)` has overloaded versions for all primitive data types as well as for `String` and `Object`.

The `ArrayList` class has two overloaded add methods: `add(x)`, which adds x at the end of the list, and `add(index, x)`, which inserts x at a given index.

Overloading is basically a stylistic device. You could instead give different names to different forms of a method, but it would be hard to remember them. Overloaded methods do not have to have the same return type, but usually they do because they perform similar tasks. The return type alone cannot distinguish between overloaded methods.

> **All constructors of a class have the same name, so they are overloaded by definition and must differ from each other in the number and/or types of their parameters.**

19

Consider the following class declaration:

```
public class Date
{
  public Date() { < code not shown > }
  public Date(String monthName, int day, int year)
            { < code not shown > }
  public void setDate(int month, int day, int year)
            { < code not shown > }

    < other class members not shown >
}
```

Consider modifying the Date class to make it possible to initialize variables of the type Date with month (given as a month name or number), day, and year information when they are declared, as well as to set their values later using the member method setDate. For example, the following code should define and initialize three Date variables:

```
Date d1 = new Date();
d1.setDate("May", 11, 2004);
Date d2 = new Date("June", 30, 2010);
Date d3 = new Date(6, 30, 2010);
```

Which of the following best describes the additional features that should be present?

(A) An overloaded version of setDate with three int arguments
(B) An overloaded version of setDate with one String and two int arguments
(C) A constructor with three int arguments
(D) Both an overloaded version of setDate with three int arguments and a constructor with three int arguments
(E) Both an overloaded version of setDate with one String and two int arguments and a constructor with three int arguments

 This is a verbose but simple question. Just match the declarations against the provided class features:

```
Date d1 = new Date();              ────────────  ✓ Date()

Date d2 = new Date("June", 30, 2010);  ───  ✓ Date(String, int, int)

Date d3 = new Date(6, 30, 2010);      ─────── Date(int, int, int)

d1.setDate("May", 11, 2004);       ───────── void setDate(String, int, int)

           not used                ───────  ✓ void setDate(int, int, int)
```

As we can see, what's missing is a constructor with three `int` arguments and a version of `setDate` with one `String` and two `int` arguments. The answer is E. ⮐

Questions 20-22 refer to the following partial class definition:

```
public class TicketSales
{
    public  TicketSales(String movieName) { < code not shown > }

    // precondition:  1 <= week <= 52
    // postcondition: sets box office receipts for a given week
    public void setWeekSales(int week, double dollars)
    { < code not shown > }

    // Finds and returns the week with best sales
    private int findBestWeek() { < code not shown > }

    < Other methods not shown >

    private String myName;
    private double[] mySales;
            // mySales[0], ..., mySales[51] hold sales totals for 52 weeks
}
```

20

The method `findBestWeek` is declared `private` because

(A) `findBestWeek` is not intended to be used by clients of the class.
(B) `findBestWeek` is intended to be used only by clients of the class.
(C) Methods that work with private instance variables of the `array` type cannot be public.
(D) Methods that have a loop in their code cannot be public.
(E) Methods that return a value cannot be public.

☞ In this question only the first two choices deserve any consideration — the other three are fillers. You might get confused for a moment about what a "client" means, but common sense helps: a client is anyone who is not yourself, so if a client needs to use something of yours, you have to make it public. Private things are for yourself, not for clients. The answer is A. ⮐

21

The constructor for the `TicketSales` class initializes the `mySales` array to hold 52 values. Which of the following statements will do that?

(A) `double mySales[52];`
(B) `double mySales = new double[52];`
(C) `double [] mySales = new double[52];`
(D) `mySales = new double[52];`
(E) `mySales.setSize(52);`

☞ This is a syntax question. Choice A has invalid syntax. E is absurd: an array does not have a `setSize` method (or any other methods). B assigns an array to a `double` variable — a syntax error. Both C and D appear syntactically plausible and in fact either one will compile with no errors. But C, instead of initializing an instance variable `mySales`, will declare and initialize a <u>local</u> variable with the same name. This is a very common nasty bug in Java programs. The answer is D. ⏎

22

Given the declaration

```
TicketSales movie = new TicketSales("Monsters, Inc.");
```

which of the following statements sets the third week sales for that movie to 245,000?

(A) `movie = TicketSales(3, 245000.00);`
(B) `setWeekSales(movie, 3, 245000.00);`
(C) `movie.setWeekSales(3, 245000.00);`
(D) `movie(setWeekSales, 3, 245000.00);`
(E) `setWeekSales(3, 245000.00);`

☞ This is another syntax question. The variable `movie` of the type `TicketSales` is defined outside the class, in a client of the class. The key word in this question is "sets." It indicates that a member method, a modifier, is called, and the way to call a member method from a client is with dot notation. (Besides, A assumes that there is a constructor with two arguments; B and D look like calls to non-existing methods; E forgets to mention `movie` altogether.) The answer is C. ⏎

2.9.   Random Numbers

Random numbers simulate chance in computer programs. For example, if you want to simulate a roll of a die, you need to obtain a random number from 1 to 6 (with any one of these values appearing with the same probability). "Random" numbers are not truly random — their sequence is generated using a certain formula — but they are good enough for many applications. Java provides a library class `Random` in its `java.util` package, which has methods for generating the "next" random integer or the "next" random `double`. These methods are <u>not static</u> — you need to create a `Random` object first and then call its `nextInt` and `nextDouble` methods. `nextInt(n)` returns a random integer from 0 to $n-1$; `nextDouble()` returns a `double` x from 0 (inclusive) to 1 (exclusive). For example:

```
Random generator = new Random();
int numPoints = generator.nextInt(6) + 1;
      // sets numPoints to a random number from 1 to 6
int xCoord = generator.nextDouble();   // sets xCoord and yCoord
int yCoord = generator.nextDouble();   //  to random numbers
      // 0 <= xCoord < 1; 0 <= yCoord < 1
```

> **`nextInt` and `nextDouble` are not static in `Random` but rather depend on a particular instance of `Random`.**

If you create a `Random` object using `Random`'s no-args constructor, it starts a unique sequence of random numbers. (The random number generator uses an initial value, called a "seed," as a starting point. The no-args constructor seeds the generator with a value derived from the current system time. `Random` has another constructor that takes the seed as a parameter, but this constructor is not in the AP subset.)

23

Which of the following is a list of all possible outputs of the following code segment?

```
Random g = new Random();
String memo = "MEMO";
System.out.print("[" + memo.substring(g.nextInt(3), g.nextInt(3) + 2)
                  + "]");
```

(A)   `[ME], [EM]`

(B)   `[ME], [EM], [MO]`

(C)   `[EM], [MO], [O], []`

(D)   `[], [M], [ME], [EM], [MO]`

(E)   `[], [M], [E], [ME], [EM], [MO], [MEM], [EMO], [MEMO]`

☞ The two calls to g.nextInt(3) look the same, but they return different values — two successive values in the random number sequence. The "from" argument of memo.substring can be 0, 1, or 2, and the "to" argument can be 2, 3, or 4. Any combination of these from/to values results in a valid substring (including substring(2,2), which returns an empty string). The answer is E. ☜

2.10. Input and Output

The AP subset does not include any classes or methods for data input. If a question involves user input it may be stated as follows:

```
double x = < call to a method that reads a floating-point number >
```

or

```
int x = IO.readInt();   // Reads user input
```

Output is limited to System.out.print and System.out.println calls.

You do not have to worry about formatting numbers. Java converts an int or a double value passed to System.out.print or System.out.println into a string using default formatting.

You can pass any object to System.out.print or System.out.println. These methods handle an object by calling its toString method. Integer and Double classes have reasonable toString methods defined. If you are designing a class, it is a good idea to supply a reasonable toString method for it. For example:

```
public class Fraction
{
  ...
  public string toString()
  {
    return myNum + "/" + myDenom;
  }
}
```

Otherwise, your class inherits a generic toString method from Object.

> The System.out.print and System.out.println methods take only <u>one</u> argument.

If you need to print several things, use the + operator for concatenating strings. You can also concatenate a string and an `int` or a `double`: the latter will be converted into a string. For example:

```
System.out.println(3 + " hours " + 15 + " minutes.");
```

The displayed result will be

```
3 hours 15 minutes.
```

You can also concatenate a string and an object: the object's `toString` method will be called to convert it into a string. For example:

```
int n = 3, d = 4;
Fraction f = new Fraction(n, d);
System.out.println(f + " = " + (double)n / (double)d);
```

The displayed result will be

```
3/4 = 0.75
```

Just be careful not to apply a + operator to two numbers or two objects other than strings: in the former case the numbers will be added rather than concatenated; the latter will cause a syntax error.

2.11. Exceptions

An exception is a <u>run-time</u> event that signals an abnormal condition in the program. Some run-time errors, such as invalid user input or an attempt to read past the end of a file, are considered fixable. The `try-catch-finally` syntax allows the programmer to catch and process the exception and have the program recover. This type of exception is called a *checked exception*.

 Checked exceptions and the `try-catch` statements are not in the AP subset.

Other errors, such as an array index out of bounds or an attempt to call a method of a non-existing object (null reference) are considered fatal: the program displays an error message with information about where the error occurred, then quits. This type of exception is called an *unchecked exception*.

In Java, an exception is an object. The Java library implements many types of exceptions, and if necessary you can derive your own exception class from one of the library classes. We say that a program "throws" an exception.

For AP CS exams, you are expected to understand `ArithmeticException`, `ArrayIndexOutOfBoundsException`, `NullPointerException`, and `ClassCastException`. These types of exceptions are represented by library classes and thrown by the Java Virtual Machine (or by library methods); all you need to do is understand what they mean.

An `ArithmeticException` is thrown in case of an arithmetic error, such as integer division by zero. (You would expect `Math.sqrt(x)` to throw an `ArithmeticException` for a negative x, but it doesn't. Java exception handling is inconsistent at times.)

`ArrayIndexOutOfBoundsException` is self-explanatory: it is thrown when an array index is negative or is greater than `array.length - 1`. `ArrayList` methods throw a similar `IndexOutOfBoundsException`.

`NullPointerException` is thrown when you forget to initialize an object-type instance variable or an element of an array and then try to call its method. For example:

```
public class MyClass
{
  private String myName;   // myName is set to null
  ...
    int n = myName.length(); // if myName has not been initialized
                             // by MyClass's constructor, this statement will
                             // throw a NullPointerException
  ...
}
```

Another example:

```
public class Dice
{
  private Random gen;   // gen is set to null
  ...
    int n = gen.nextInt(6);  // gen has to be initialized here or
                             // by Dice's constructor --
                             //    gen = new Random();
                             // if not, this will throw a
                             // NullPointerException
```

A third example:

```
        Integer[] a = new Integer[10];
        int x = a[0].intValue();      // a[0] is null --
                                      // throws a NullPointerException
```

A `ClassCastException` is thrown when you are trying to cast an object into a class type to which it does not belong. For example:

```
ArrayList list = new ArrayList();
list.add("123.456");
Double x = (Double)list.get(0);  // ClassCastException: trying to cast
                                 //   a string "123.456" into a Double
```

Throwing your own exceptions

Occasionally you need to "throw" your own exception. For example, you are implementing the `dequeue` method for a queue data structure. What is your method to do when the queue is empty? Throw a `NoSuchElementException`.

`throw` is a Java reserved word. The syntax for using it is

```
throw < exception >;
```

For example:

```
if (items.size() == 0)
   throw new NoSuchElementException();
```

Throw an `IllegalStateException` if an object is not ready for a particular method call. For example:

```
public void stop()
{
  if (!isMoving())
    throw new IllegalStateException();  // displays a message and quits
  speed = 0;
  ... etc.
}
```

> **Your code does not need to explicitly throw an `ArithmeticException`, `NullPointerException`, `ClassCastException`, or `ArrayIndexOutOfBoundsException` — Java does it for you automatically when the triggering condition occurs.**

24

Consider the following class:

```
public class TestSample
{
  public TestSample(n)
  {
    int k;
    for (k = 0; k < n; k++)
    {
      myList.add(new Integer(k));
    }
  }

  public double getBestRatio()
  {
    int k;
    double maxRatio = ((Integer)myList.get(1)).intValue() /
                      ((Integer)myList.get(0)).intValue();

    for (k = 1; k < myList.size() - 1; k++)
    {
      double ratio = ((Integer)myList.get(k+1)).intValue() /
                     ((Integer)myList.get(k)).intValue();
      if (ratio > maxRatio)
      {
        maxRatio = ratio;
      }
    }
    return maxRatio;
  }

  private ArrayList myList;
}
```

What is the result of the following code segment?

```
TestSample t = new TestSample(1);
System.out.println(t.getBestRatio());
```

(A) NullPointerException
(B) ArithmeticException
(C) IndexOutOfBoundsException
(D) ClassCastException
(E) Infinity

☞ Luckily we don't have to look at the getBestRatio method. The programmer has forgotten to initialize myList and calls its add method in the constructor. The answer is A.

Now suppose we added

```
myList = new ArrayList();
```

at the top of the constructor. What would happen then? getBestRatio would call myList.get(1), but we would have added only one value to myList. The answer would be C, IndexOutOfBoundsException.

Now suppose we changed

```
TestSample t = new TestSample(1);
```

to

```
TestSample t = new TestSample(2);
```

What would happen then? The answer would be B, ArithmeticException, because we have an integer division by 0.

Actually, the programmer probably meant to write

```
double maxRatio = (double)((Integer)myList.get(1)).intValue() /
                          ((Integer)myList.get(0)).intValue();
```

What would happen if we added this cast to a double? We would still expect an ArithmeticException for floating-point division by 0, but Java actually prints "Infinity." The answer would be E (but you do not have to know that).

Note that the objects *are* cast correctly: we put Integers into myList, and we cast objects we get from myList back into Integers. So ClassCastException does not occur. ☜

Chapter 3. Program Design and OOP Concepts

3.1. Computer Systems

You are probably aware by now that a typical computer system <u>hardware</u> has at least one *processor*, (a.k.a. CPU), some *RAM* (*random-access memory*), secondary storage devices (such as magnetic disks, CD-ROM drives, floppy disk drives, etc.) and *peripherals* (modems, printers, sound cards and speakers, mice or other pointing devices, etc.).

Chances are you also have worked with an *operating system*, a piece of <u>software</u> that controls the computer system and interacts with a user. Linux, Windows XP, and OS X, are examples of operating systems. A *compiler* is also a piece of software. It checks syntax in programs written in a high-level programming language and translates them into machine code. In Java, a compiler translates the *source code* (program text) into machine-independent *bytecodes* — instructions for the *Java Virtual Machine*. The virtual machine acts as a run-time *interpreter* that reads bytecodes and executes the appropriate instructions on a particular computer. A *debugger* is a program that helps you run and test your program in a controlled way and find errors ("bugs") in it. The editor, compiler, interpreter, debugger, and other *software development tools* may be combined in one package called an *IDE* (Integrated Development Environment), which has a *GUI* (graphical user interface).

Issues of system reliability and security and the legal and ethical issues related to computer use are not precisely defined in the AP exam guidelines. Questions about these things would have to be rather general.

3.2. Program Design and Development Methodology

Computer science courses try to emphasize *problem solving*, as opposed to just programming in a particular language or using specific hardware platforms. The exam topics related to general software design and development methodology emphasize *procedural* and *data abstraction*, *functional decomposition*, and the *reusability* of code. These topics are discussed in the context of *object-oriented* software design and development. Here is a very brief glossary of the relevant terms:

Specifications — a detailed description of what a piece of software should accomplish and how it should behave and interact with the user. Specifications may be given for a whole system, one module, even one class or method.

Object-oriented programming — a programming methodology based on designing the program as a world of interacting objects arranged in hierarchies of classes and using encapsulation and polymorphism.

Top-down design — a design methodology in which you first define the general structure of the program, laying out high-level classes and their interaction, and then refine the design of each class, identifying subtasks and smaller classes or methods. Then you refine the design of subtasks, individual methods, and so on.

Top-down development — similar to top-down design: you first lay out your code at a high level, defining general classes and methods. These methods may call lower-level methods, which are not yet implemented. You can compile and sometimes even test high-level pieces of your code by substituting "stubs" — empty or greatly simplified placeholders — for still uncoded low-level methods.

Data structure — a way of organizing data combined with methods of accessing and manipulating the data. For example, a two-dimensional array with methods or operators for retrieving and changing the values of its elements is a data structure that may be useful for representing tables.

Encapsulation and information hiding — making all instance variables and helper methods that are used only inside the class private. The clients of a class can then use that class only through its public constructors and methods.

Procedural abstraction — a description of a procedure that is not tied to a specific hardware platform, particular data types, or other details. A high-level programming language, such as Java, already assures a degree of procedural abstraction by isolating a programmer from the particular hardware platform. An algorithm is even more abstract. It can be described using pseudocode, flowcharts, and other tools independent of any particular programming language.

Reusable code — debugged and tested libraries, classes, or fragments of code that are somewhat general in nature and can be reused in other projects. Reusing code shortens software development projects, no matter what methodology is being employed.

Team development — OO languages, such as Java, allow you to split a project into separate pieces and assign their development to different team members. Encapsulation and information hiding facilitate team development by limiting the amount of interaction needed between developers.

User interface — the behavior of a program as it interacts with a user: screens, menus, commands, messages, graphics, sounds, and so on.

These are very general concepts, and it is not easy to come up with multiple-choice or free-response questions that test in-depth understanding of these concepts. In past exams, design and implementation questions were limited to specific data structures and algorithms, but sometimes used these terms in their descriptions. The new exams may include a free-response "design" question that asks you to design a small class, then use some of its features (see Section 3.7).

3.3. Inheritance

Inheritance allows a programmer to state that one class *extends* another class, inheriting its features. In Java terminology, a *subclass* extends a *superclass*. `extends` is a Java reserved word. For example:

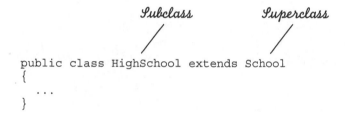

```
public class HighSchool extends School
{
  ...
}
```

Inheritance implements the IS-A relationship between objects: an object of a subclass type IS-A (is also an object of the) superclass. A high school is a kind of school. A `HighSchool` object IS-A (kind of) `School` object. Technically this means that in your program you can use an object of a subclass whenever an object of its superclass is expected. For example:

```
School sch = new HighSchool(...);
```

If you have a constructor or a method (elsewhere, in a client class), which expects a `School` type of parameter passed to it, you can call it with a `HighSchool` type of argument. Objects of a subclass inherit the data type of the superclass.

In Java, a class can directly extend only one superclass — there is no *multiple inheritance* for classes. But you can derive different subclasses from the same superclass:

```
public class HighSchool extends School ...
public class ElementarySchool extends School ...
public class DrivingSchool extends School ...
```

The IS-A relationship of inheritance is not to be confused with the HAS-A relationship between objects. That *X* "has a" *Y* simply means that *Y* is a data member (an instance variable) in *X*. For example, you might say that a `HighSchool` HAS-A `MarchingBand`, but not a `HighSchool` IS-A `MarchingBand`.

Subclass methods

A subclass inherits all the public methods of its superclass and you can call them in the subclass without any "dot prefix." For example, if `School` has a method

```
public String getName() { ... }
```

`HighSchool`'s `apRegister` can call it directly:

```
public class HighSchool extends School
{
  ...
  public void makeApForm()
  {
    String registrationForm = getName() + ...;
    ...
  }
  ...
}
```

`HighSchool`'s clients can call `getName`, too, for any `HighSchool` object:

```
HighSchool hs = new HighSchool(...);
String name = hs.getName();
```

A subclass can add its own methods. It can also *override* (redefine) a method of the superclass by providing its own version with exactly the same signature (the same name, return type, and number and types of parameters). For example, `School` may have a `toString` method, and `HighSchool`'s `toString` may override it.

⌐ In the AB subset only: occasionally it may be necessary to make an explicit call to a superclass's public (or protected) method from a subclass. This is accomplished using the `super.` prefix. For example:

```
public class HighSchool extends School
{
  ...
  public String toString()
  {
    return super.toString() + collegeAcceptance() + ...;
  }
  ...
}
```
⌐

The superclass's <u>private</u> methods are not callable in the subclass.

Subclass constructors

Constructors are not inherited: a subclass has to provide its own.

A subclass's constructors can explicitly call the superclass's constructors using the keyword `super`. For example:

```
public class School
{
  public School(String name, int numStudents)
  {
    myName = name;
    myNumStudents = numStudents;
  }
  ...
}

public class ElementarySchool extends School
{
  public ElementarySchool(String name, int numStudents, int highestGrade)
  {
    super(name, numStudents); // Calls School's constructor
    myHighestGrade = highestGrade;
    ...
  }
  ...
  private int myHighestGrade;
}
```

If `super` is used, it must be the first statement in the subclass's constructor.

Subclass variables

A subclass inherits all the class (static) and instance variables of its superclass. However, the instance variables are usually private (always private in the AP subset).

The superclass's private variables are not directly accessible in its subclass. So you might as well forget that they are inherited — instead, use public accessors and modifiers to get and set values of the superclass's instance variables.

Superclass public constants (`public static final` variables) are directly accessible everywhere.

A subclass can add its own static or instance variables.

25

Consider the following partial definitions:

```
public class MailingList
{
  public MailingList() { people = new ArrayList(); }
  public void add(String name) { people.add(name); }
  public ArrayList getPeople() { return people; }

  private ArrayList people;
}

public class Subscribers extends MailingList
{
  public Subscribers() { super(); }

  // postcondition: returns the number of names in people
  private int size()
  {
    return < expression >;
  }

  < Other methods not shown >
}
```

Which of the following should replace < *expression* > in the `size` method of the
`Subscribers` class so that the method works as specified?

(A) `super.size();`
(B) `people.size();`
(C) `super.people.size();`
(D) `getPeople().size();`
(E) None of the above

The `MailingList` class HAS-A(n) `ArrayList people` as an instance variable, but
`MailingList` Is-Not-A(n) `ArrayList`: it does not extend `ArrayList`. The
programmer has not provided a `size` method for the `MailingList` class (a design
mistake), so choice A is wrong. B or C might look plausible at first, but `people` is
private in `MailingList`, so it is not directly accessible in `Subscribers`. But
`MailingList` has a public method `getPeople`, and this method is inherited and
accessible in the `Subscribers` class. `getPeople` returns an `ArrayList`, which has a
method `size` that returns the size of the list. The answer is D. Also note that

```
    return getPeople().size();
```

is equivalent to

```
    ArrayList temp = getPeople();
    return temp.size();
```

3.4.   Class Hierarchies

If you have a class, you can derive one or several subclasses from it. Each of these classes can in turn serve as a superclass for other subclasses. You can build a whole tree-like hierarchy of classes, in which each class has one superclass. For example:

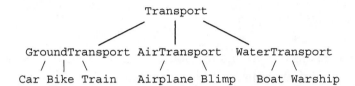

In fact, in Java all classes do belong to one big hierarchy; it starts at a class `Object`. If you do not specify that your class extends any particular class, then it extends `Object` by default. Therefore, every object IS-A(n) `Object`. The `Object` class provides a few common methods, including `equals` and `toString`, but these methods are not very useful and usually get redefined in classes lower in the hierarchy.

Class hierarchies exist to allow reuse of code from higher classes in the lower classes without duplication and to promote a more logical design. A class lower in the hierarchy inherits the data types of all classes above it. For example, if we have classes

```
public class Animal { ... }
public class Dog extends Animal { ... }
public class Spaniel extends Dog { ... }
```

all of the following declarations are legal:

```
Spaniel s = new Spaniel(...);
Dog d = new Spaniel(...);
Animal a = new Spaniel(...);
```

But if you also define

```
public class Horse extends Animal { ... }
```

then

```
Horse x = new Spaniel(...);
```

is an error, of course: `Spaniel` does not extend `Horse`.

Abstract classes

Classes closer to the top of the hierarchy are more abstract — the properties and methods of their objects are more general. As you proceed down the hierarchy, the classes become more specific and the properties of their objects are more concretely spelled out. Java syntax allows you to define a class that is officially designated `abstract`. For example:

```
public abstract class Solid { ... }
```

An abstract class can have constructors and methods; however, some of its methods may be declared `abstract` and left without code. For example:

```
public abstract class Solid
{
  ...
  public abstract double getVolume();
  ...
}
```

This indicates that every `Solid` object has a method that returns its volume; but the actual code may depend on the specific type of solid. For example, the `Sphere` and `Cube` subclasses of `Solid` will define `getVolume` differently.

A class in which all the methods are defined is called *concrete*. Naturally, abstract classes appear near the top of the hierarchy and concrete classes sit below. You cannot instantiate an abstract class, but you can declare variables or arrays of its type. For example:

```
        Solid s1 = new Sphere(radius);
        Solid s2 = new Cube(side);
        Solid[] solids = { new Sphere(100), new Cube(100) };
```

Questions 26-27 refer to the following partial class definitions:

```
public abstract class Account
{
  public Account() { ... }
}

public class BankAccount extends Account
{
  public BankAccount(double amount)
  {
    super();
    balance = amount;
  }

  private double balance;
}

public class CheckingAccount extends BankAccount
{
  public CheckingAccount(String name, double amount)
  {
    < Missing statements >
  }
  ...

  private String customerName;
}
```

26

Which of the following is an acceptable replacement for < *Missing statements* > in `CheckingAccount`'s constructor?

I. ```
    balance = amount;
    customerName = name;
    ```

II. ```
    super(amount);
    customerName = name;
    ```

III. ```
     super(name, amount);
     ```

(A)  I only
(B)  II only
(C)  I and II
(D)  II and III
(E)  I, II and III

☞ `balance` is private in `BankAccount`, so it is not accessible in `CheckingAccount`. Option I cannot be right. `BankAccount` does not have a constructor with two arguments, so III cannot be right either. Option II is the way to go. The answer is B. ☜
     ```

[27]

Which of the following declarations are valid?

I. `Account acct = new BankAccount(10.00);`

II. `CheckingAccount acct = new BankAccount(10.00);`

III. `BankAccount acct = new CheckingAccount("Amy", 10.00);`

(A) I and II
(B) II and III only
(C) I and III
(D) I, II, and III
(E) None of the three

It may appear that Option I is wrong because an abstract class `Account` cannot be instantiated. But in fact we are not instantiating `Account` — we are instantiating `BankAccount` and assigning the newly created `BankAccount` object to an `Account` variable. Since a `BankAccount` IS-A(n) `Account`, we are okay. We only have to make sure that `BankAccount` has a constructor that takes one `double` parameter (which it does). Options II and III are clearly problematic as a pair: either a `BankAccount` IS-A `CheckingAccount` or a `CheckingAccount` IS-A `BankAccount`, but not both. Here `CheckingAccount` extends `BankAccount`, so Option III is okay (again, provided `CheckingAccount` has a constructor that takes a `String` and `double` parameters). The answer is C.

3.5. Polymorphism

Polymorphism is a mechanism that assures that the correct method is called for an object disguised as a more generic type. In the above example, if we call

```
double volume = solids[0].getVolume();
```

the compiler does not know whether `solids[0]` is a `Sphere` or a `Cube`. The decision of which `getVolume` method to call is postponed until run-time. In Java implementation, each object holds a pointer to a table of entry points to its methods; thus any object itself "knows" what type of object it is. This technique is called *dynamic method binding* — which method is called is decided at run time, not compile time.

> **Polymorphism is implemented in the language; all you have to do is understand it and use it correctly.**

One common situation when polymorphism comes into play occurs when different types of objects are mixed together in an array or list, as shown in the above example. This code

```
for (int i = 0; i < solids.length; i++)
  totalVolume += solids[i].getVolume();
```

works no matter what `Solid`s are stored in the `solids` array because the appropriate `getVolume` method is called for each element of the array. This is true even if several different `Solid`s were in the `solids` array.

Another situation for polymorphism occurs when a method takes a more generic type of parameter and a client class passes a more specific type of argument to the method. For example, one of the overloaded versions of `System.out`'s `print` method takes an `Object` type as a parameter. This method may be implemented as follows:

```
public void print(Object x)
{
  if (x != null)
    print(x.toString());
  else
    print("<null>");
}
```

This method works for any type of object x with a reasonable `toString` method defined (including `Integer`, `Double`, etc.). Polymorphism assures that the correct `toString` is called for each type of x.

28

Given

```
public class Person
{
  Person(String name) { myName = name; }
  public String getName() { return myName; }
  public String toString { return getName(); }

  private String myName;
}

public class OldLady extends Person
{
  public OldLady(String name, int age) { super(name); myAge = age; }
  public String getName() { return "Mrs. " + super.getName(); }
  public int getAge() { return myAge; }

  private int myAge;
}
```

what is the output of the following statements?

```
Person p = new OldLady("Robinson", 92);
System.out.println(p + ", " + ((OldLady)p).getAge());
```

(A)   `Mrs. Robinson, 92`
(B)   `Robinson, 92`
(C)   `Robinson`
(D)   `ClassCastException`
(E)   No output due to infinite recursion

⌐ Strictly speaking this is an AB question, but it won't hurt A-exam takers to study it. ⌐

In this question we have to restore a somewhat convoluted sequence of events:

1.   The variable `p` is disguised as a `Person` type, but it is actually an `OldLady`.

2.   `p + ", "` calls `p`'s `toString` method. `OldLady` inherits `toString` from `Person`, so `Person`'s `toString` is called.

3.   `toString` in turn calls `getName`. Which one? This is the trickiest point. Both `Person` and `OldLady` have a `getName` method, but, <u>due to polymorphism,</u> `OldLady`'s `getName` will be called (notwithstanding the fact that we call it from `Person`'s `toString` method).

4.   `OldLady`'s `getName` takes `"Mrs. "` and appends to it the result of `super.getName()`. The latter explicitly calls `Person`'s `getName`, which simply returns the name.

5.   Finally we cast p back to the `OldLady` type — we need this to call its `getAge` method. A `Person` does not have `getAge`, and the compiler does not keep track of what type we assigned to p. `getAge`'s result is appended to the output string.

Choice B tries to make you forget about polymorphism or suggests that polymorphism does not apply here. It does. C is an awkward attempt to confuse you about p's data type. Deep inside, p is not just a `Person` but an `OldLady`, so it does have a `getAge` method once we cast it to `OldLady`. If p were only a `Person`, the cast to `OldLady` would cause a `ClassCastException`, as suggested in D. E hints that `getName` infinitely calls itself. This does not happen here: `OldLady`'s `getName` explicitly calls `Person`'s `getName` as indicated by the `super.` prefix (this is the AB-only part). We would have infinite recursion only if we forgot `super.`. The answer is A.

3.6.   Interfaces

In Java, an interface is even more "abstract" than an abstract class. An interface has no constructors or instance variables and no code at all — just headings for methods. All its methods are public and abstract. For example:

```
public interface Fillable
{
  void fill(int x);
  int getCurrentAmount();
  int getMaximumCapacity();
}
```

(No need to repeat public abstract for each method in interfaces — it is understood.)

A class "implements" an interface by supplying code for all the interface methods. `implements` is a reserved word. For example:

```
public class Car implements Fillable
{
  ...
  public void fill(int gallons) { fuelAmount += gallons; }
  public int getCurrentAmount() { return fuelAmount; }
  public int getMaximumCapacity() { return fuelTankCapacity; }
}

public class VendingMachine implements Fillable
{
  ...
  public void fill(int qty) { currentStock += qty; }
  public int getCurrentAmount() { return currentStock; }
  public int getMaximumCapacity() { return 20; }
}
```

> **For a concrete class to implement an interface, it must define <u>all</u> the methods required by the interface. It must also explicitly state that it implements the interface. A class that claims it implements an interface but does not define some of the interface methods must be declared abstract.**

A class can extend only one class, but it can implement several interfaces:

```
public class C extends B implements I1, I2, I3 { ... }
```

Each interface adds a secondary data type to the objects of the class that implements it. If a class *C* implements interface *I*, objects of C can be disguised as type *I* objects and polymorphism applies (the same way as for subclasses). For example, we can have a method:

```
// postcondition: All objects in a are filled to capacity
public void fillUp(Fillable[] a)
{
  for (int k = 0; k < a.length; k++)
    a[k].fill (a[k].getMaximumCapacity() - a[k].getCurrentAmount());
}
```

The formula works polymorphically for any types of different Fillable objects that might be stored in the array a.

> **If class *C* implements interface *I*, all subclasses of *C* automatically implement *I*.**

Interfaces help us write more general methods, facilitating code reuse.

The Comparable interface

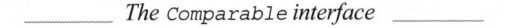

The library (built-in) interface java.lang.Comparable is widely used for designating objects that can be compared in some way. We need to compare objects in order to arrange them in order (sorting), perform a Binary Search, or implement certain data structures ⌈ such as Binary Search Trees ⌋.

The Comparable interface specifies only one method:

```
int compareTo(Object other);
```

The method returns a positive integer if this object is "greater than" the other, zero if they are "equal," and a negative integer if this object is "less than" the other. (Sort of like this - other.) It is up to the programmer to decide what "smaller" and "greater" might mean for a particular type of objects.

`compareTo` takes one parameter of the `Object` type — for type independence, but it is usually assumed that the parameter belongs to the same class, and the parameter is cast back into its actual type in the code. For example:

```
public class Flight implements Comparable
{
   ...
   public int compareTo(Object other)
   {
     return getDepartureTime() - ((Flight)other).getDepartureTime();
   }
}
```

`String`, `Integer`, and `Double` all implement `Comparable`, but naturally they do so in different ways. Strings are compared lexicographically. The comparison is case-sensitive, and all uppercase letters precede all lowercase letters. `Integer` and `Double` objects are compared as usual, based on their numeric values.

The `Comparable` interface does not require an `equals` method to compile, but it is better to override the `equals` method inherited from `Object` and make it consistent with `compareTo`, to avoid possible errors later. For example:

```
public boolean equals(Object other)
{
   return other != null && compareTo(other) == 0;
}
```

29

Consider the following class:

```
public class Fraction implements Comparable
{
  public int getNum() { return num; }
  public int getDenom() { return denom; }
  public double doubleValue() { return (double)num / denom; }

  < Other constructors and methods not shown >

  private int num, denom;
}
```

Which of the following would appropriately implement a `compareTo` method, required by the `Comparable` interface?

I.
```
public int compareTo(Fraction other)
{
  return getNum() * other.getDenom() -
         getDenom() * other.getNum();
}
```

II.
```
public int compareTo(Object other)
{
  double x = doubleValue();
  double y = ((Fraction)other).doubleValue();
  if (x < y) return -1;
  else if (x > y) return 1;
  else return 0;
}
```

III.
```
public int compareTo(Object other)
{
  return (int)(doubleValue() - ((Fraction)other).doubleValue());
}
```

(A) I only
(B) II only
(C) I and II
(D) II and III
(E) I, II, and III

☞ Option I would be problematic on an actual exam. First, it assumes that students know how to subtract fractions, which is not in the course description. Second, it is ambiguous with regard to possible arithmetic overflow: can we assume that the numerators and denominators of the fractions are small enough so that their products do not overflow the int range? Luckily we can eliminate this answer because the compareTo method is defined incorrectly: the parameter must be an Object, not a Fraction. If we put Fraction there, the compiler will report a cryptic error message "Fraction must be declared abstract" (because compareTo(Object) is not defined). Option II works, even though it provides a rather truncated result of the comparison: compareTo can return only 0, 1, or -1. Recall that only the sign of a comparison result really matters. Option III fulfills the formal requirements, but fractions that differ "by a small fraction" will be deemed equal. This is not in the spirit of compareTo for arithmetic objects. If a question like this happened to slip past exam editors, we'd say the answer was B. ☜

30

What is the output from the following code segment?

```
Comparable x = new Integer(123);              // Line 1
System.out.println(x.compareTo("123"));       // Line 2
```

(A) 0
(B) A positive integer
(D) A syntax error on Line 1
(D) A syntax error on Line 2
(E) A ClassCastException

☞ There are three separate issues here. First, on Line 1, we are assigning an Integer object to a variable of the Comparable type. Is this okay? Yes, because the Integer class implements Comparable. Second, on Line 2 we are passing a string to x's compareTo method. Is this okay? Yes, because compareTo's parameter has the Object type, so we can pass to compareTo any object, including a String. Third, how do we compare an Integer to a String? Well, we can't. Integer's compareTo assumes that the object passed to it is another Integer, and the code will try to cast it into Integer. But the argument actually happens to be a String. The program will be aborted with a run-time error, ClassCastException. The answer is E. ☜

3.7. "Design" Question

The free-response section of the exam may include a "design" question. This type of question asks you to design (<u>but not implement</u>) a simple class that represents a given situation or model. This is the "design" part. Other parts may ask you to write some code of a client class that uses some constructors or methods from the class you designed. A design question first appeared on the 2003 AB exam (still in C++).

> **Note that you are not asked to implement your class in the design part, only to design it. It would be a huge waste of time to write code for your class.**

Designing a class means specifying its constructors and their parameters, public (and possibly private) methods, and fields — public constants and private instance variables.

In writing the design part, pay special attention to the following:

- Use reasonable and consistent style with proper indentation and generous spacing between statements.

- DO NOT include comments, preconditions, or postconditions — they are not required.

- Choose meaningful names for your class, its methods and their parameters, and for variables. Follow the same naming style as shown in the other parts of the exam: a class name starts with an uppercase letter; the names of all methods, their parameters, and instance variables start with a lowercase letter. Make sure that all constructors have the same name as the class. Names of instance variables may have the prefix "my" (e.g., `myBalance`, `myInterestRate`).

- Put all constructors and public methods first. Make all methods public, unless there is a specific hint in the question that some of them are "helper" methods used only inside this class — then make them private.

- In addition to specified constructors, it may be a good idea to provide a no-args constructor that takes no arguments.

- Make all instance variables private and group them together.

- Specify appropriate return types for all methods. Recall that constructors do not have a return type, not even `void`.

- Provide public "accessor" methods as specified in the question. An accessor returns the value of the respective data member. Accessor names may start with "get." For example:

```
public void getBalance() { ... }
```

- Provide "modifier" methods as specified in the question. Modifiers set the values of one or several data members. Modifier names may start with "set" or "make." For example:

```
public void makeDeposit(double amount) { ... }
```

- Group all accessors together in a group and all modifiers in another group to make your class definition more readable.

Again, do not write any code in the design part of the question.

Part (b) may ask you to write a fragment of code from a client class that uses your class designed in Part (a) . In writing code in Part (b) pay special attention to the following:

- Use constructors and call public methods of your Part (a) class with appropriate numbers and types of arguments, consistent with what you wrote in Part (a). Use this opportunity to double-check your definitions in Part (a).

- Never refer directly to private instance variables of your Part (a) class in the client class; rather, call accessors and modifiers.

- It is allowed (and often desirable) to reuse in the client class the same names for variables as you used for similar formal parameters in methods in Part (a). For example, if in Part (a) you wrote

```
public void makeDeposit(double amount) { ... }
```

then in Part (b) you may write

```
double amount = ...;
...
account.makeDeposit(amount);
```

_____ *A sample question* _____

The World Population Institute keeps track of demographic trends in different countries or "population zones." Each population zone is described by its name, population growth rate, and a table of population counts by age. The age ranges from 0 (under one year old) to some maximum age.

When a new population zone is created in the program, it receives a name and a table of population counts by age. It may also receive a growth rate parameter. If not supplied, the growth rate is set to 1.0 (no growth).

Operations on a population zone include the following:

- retrieve zone's name

- retrieve zone's growth rate

- set a new growth rate

- retrieve the total population

- retrieve the total population below a given age

- adjust the distribution to simulate aging of the population by one year (filling the "zero" slot with a new value calculated from a formula that includes the growth rate factor).

(This simplified model does not take deaths into account.)

A population zone will be represented in a program by a class called `PopulationZone`. A separate class, `Demographics`, will store a list of population zones, such as all countries in the world.

(a) Write a class definition for `PopulationZone`, putting only "..." in the bodies of constructors and methods. In writing this definition you must:

- choose appropriate names for methods, data members, and parameters;

- use overloaded methods where appropriate;

- provide the functionality specified above;

- make data representation consistent with the above specifications;

- make design decisions that are consistent with information-hiding principles.

Comments are not required but may be used if desired.

DO NOT write the implementations of the constructors or the member methods of the `PopulationZone` class.

(b)   Consider the class `Demographics` partially specified below.

```
public class Demographics
{
  public double teenRatio(PopulationZone z)
  {
    < Code not shown >
  }

  public String findMostTeens()
  {
    < Code not shown >
  }

  private ArrayList countries;
}
```

Write a member method `teenRatio` that computes and returns the ratio of all teenagers (ages 13 through 19) to the total population in a given population zone. In writing `teenRatio`, you may use any of the methods of the `PopulationZone` class that you specified in Part (a). Assume that these methods work as specified, regardless of what you wrote in Part (a).

Complete the method `teenRatio` below.

```
// postcondition:  returns the ratio of all teenagers
//                 (ages 13 through 19) to the total
//                 population in z
public double teenRatio(PopulationZone z)
```

(c)   Write the method `findMostTeens` of the `Demographics` class. This method returns the name of the country from the `countries` list with the highest ratio of teenagers to the total population. (In the unlikely event that two or several population zones have exactly the same highest teen ratio, the method returns any one of them.) In writing this method you can use the class from Part (a) and the method from Part (b) and assume that they work as specified regardless of what you wrote in those parts.

Complete the method `findMostTeens` below.

```
// postcondition:  returns the name of the country
//                 from the list countries with the
//                 highest ratio of teenagers to the
//                 total population; if several countries
//                 have the same highest ratio, returns any
//                 one of their names
public String findMostTeens()
```

(a)

```
class PopulationZone
{
  public PopulationZone() { ... }

  public PopulationZone(String name, int[] countsByAge) { ... }

  public PopulationZone(String name, int[] countsByAge,
                                      double growthRate) { ... }
  public String getName() { ... }
  public double getGrowthRate() { ... }
  public int getPopulation() { ... }
  public int getPopulation(int ageLimit) { ... }
  public void setGrowthRate(double growthRate) { ... }
  public void ageByOneYear() { ... }

  private String myName;
  private double myGrowthRate;
  private int[] myCountsByAge;
}
```

(b)

```
public double teenRatio(PopulationZone z)
{
  return (double)(z.getPopulation(20) - z.getPopulation(13))
         / z.getPopulation();
}
```

(c)

```
public String findMostTeens()
{
  int k, kMax = 0;
  double ratio;
  double maxRatio = teenRatio(countries.get(0));

  for (k = 1; k < countries.size(); k++)
  {
    ratio = teenRatio(countries.get(k));
    if (ratio > maxRatio)
    {
      maxRatio = ratio;
      kMax = k;
    }
  }
  return ((PopulationZone)countries.get(kMax)).getName();
}
```

Pay attention to OBOBs in Part (b), and note the correct syntax for dealing with ArrayList in Part (c).

Chapter 4. Algorithms

4.1. Iterations

Most programming languages provide iteration control structures, such as the `while` and `for` loops in Java. Simple loops are good for iterating (repeating the same operation) over a range of numbers or over the elements of a one-dimensional array ⌈ or a linked list ⌋.

A `for` loop is a convenient and idiomatic way to *traverse* a one-dimensional array:

```
int k, len = a.length;

for (k = 0; k < len; k++)
{
    System.out.println(a[k]);     // ... or do whatever you need to do
                                  //        with each element
}
```

⌈ For working with two-dimensional arrays you usually need *nested* loops. The following code, for example, traverses a two-dimensional array m:

```
int r, c, nRows = m.length, nCols = m[0].length;

for (r = 0; r < nRows; r++)
{
    for (c = 0; c < nCols; c++)
    {
        System.out.println(m[r][c]);   // ... or do whatever...
    }
}
```
⌋

Note that braces are optional if the body of the loop has only one statement:

```
for (i = 1; i < n; i++)
    for (j = 0; j < i; j++)
        if (a[i] == a[j])
            count++;
```

In a "triangular" nested loops, the outer loop may run, say, for i from 1 to $n-1$ and the inner loop may run for j from 0 to $i-1$. In the above example the inner loop runs i times for $i = 1, ..., n-1$, so the total number of comparisons is

$$1 + 2 + ... + (n-1) = \frac{n(n-1)}{2}$$

85

⌈ The <u>AB exam</u> material includes linked list traversal. A `for` loop can be used for this, too:

```
ListNode head;
...
ListNode p;
for (p = head; p != null; p = p.getNext())
{
   System.out.println(p.getValue());
}
```

The library classes `ArrayList` and `LinkedList` support *iterators* (see Section 5.2). A list has a method `iterator` that returns an `Iterator` object. A `while` loop is convenient for traversing a list using an iterator:

```
LinkedList list = new LinkedList();
...
Iterator iter = list.iterator();
while (iter.hasNext())
{
   Object x = iter.next();
   ...
}
```
⌋

Max and min

A common example of using loops is to find a maximum or a minimum value (or its position) in an array:

```
// precondition:  Array a holds values a[0], ..., a[n-1]; n >= 1
// postcondition: Returns maxValue such that maxValue >= a[k]
//                for any 0 <= k <= n-1 and maxValue = a[k] for some k.
public double max(double[] a, int n)
{
   double maxValue = a[0];
   int k;

   for (k = 1; k < n; k++)
   {
      if (a[k] > maxValue)
         maxValue = a[k];
   }
   return maxValue;
}
```

[31]

Consider the following method:

```
public int mysteryMax(int[] a)
{
  int sum, m = 0;
  int i, k;

  for (i = 0; i < a.length; i++)
  {
    sum = 0;
    for (k = i; k < a.length; k++)
    {
      sum += a[k];
      if (sum > m)
        m = sum;
    }
  }
  return m;
}
```

If a contains -1, -3, 2, -3, 2, 1, what value will be returned by mysteryMax(a)?

(A)   -2
(B)   -1
(C)   1
(D)   2
(E)   3

☞ The method returns the largest sum of several consecutive elements in a (or 0 if all the values are negative). The answer is E. ☚

32

Consider the following method:

```
// precondition:  n >= 2; a[0] ... a[n-1] are filled with values.
// postcondition: Returns the largest sum of any two different elements.
public double maxSum(double[] a, int n)
{
  < code >
}
```

Which of the following code segments can replace < *code* > so that the method works as specified?

I.
```
double max = a[0] + a[1];
int i, j;

for (i = 1; i < n; i++)
  for (j = 0; j < i; j++)
    if (a[i] + a[j] > max)
      max = a[i] + a[j];
return max;
```

II.
```
double max1 = a[0], max2 = a[0];
int i;

for (i = 1; i < n; i++)
  if (a[i] > max1)
    max1 = a[i];

for (i = 1; i < n; i++)
  if (a[i] != max1 && a[i] > max2)
    max2 = a[i];

return max1 + max2;
```

III.
```
double max1 = a[0], max2 = a[1];
int i;

if (a[1] > a[0])
{
  max1 = a[1];
  max2 = a[0];
}

for (i = 2; i < n; i++)
{
  if (a[i] > max1)
  {
    max2 = max1;
    max1 = a[i];
  }
  else if (a[i] > max2)
    max2 = a[i];
}

return max1 + max2;
```

(A)   I only
(B)   II only
(C)   I and II
(D)   I and III
(E)   I, II, and III

☞ This is a lot of code for one question, so we need to focus on the key points. Segment I is inefficient but most straightforward: using triangular nested loops we generate sums for all the different pairs of elements and choose the largest of them. Segment II is based on a different idea: to find the largest value, then the second largest value in two separate traversals of the array. But it has two problems. First, if the largest value happens to be a[0], then the second for loop will never update max2. Second, it will fail if the largest value appears in the array more than once. The postcondition states that the method is looking for the largest sum of two different elements, but these could have the same value.

To work, this approach would need a couple of minor fixes:

```
int iMax1 = 0, iMax2 = 0;
int i;

for (i = 1; i < n; i++)
  if (a[i] > a[iMax1])
    iMax1 = i;

if (iMax1 == 0)
  iMax2 = 1;

for (i = 1; i < n; i++)
  if (i != iMax1 && a[i] > a[iMax2])
    iMax2 = i;

return a[iMax1] + a[iMax2];
```

In Segment III we find both the largest and the second largest elements in one sweep. Note how the largest element becomes the second largest when we find another one with a greater value. It works fine. The answer is D. ☟

Insert in order

Many applications, including Insertion Sort, require you to insert a value into a sorted array while preserving the order:

```
// precondition:  a[0] <= a[1] <= ... <= a[n-1].  n < a.length
// postcondition: Values a[k], ..., a[n-1] are shifted
//                appropriately into a[k+1], ..., a[n] and newValue
//                is inserted into a[k] so that the ascending order
//                is preserved.
void insertInOrder(int[] a, int n, int newValue)
{
  if (n >= a.length)
    return;

  // Shift values to the right by one until you find the
  //     place to insert:

  int k = n;              // Start at the end
  while (k > 0 && a[k-1] > newValue)
  {
    a[k] = a[k-1];
    k--;
  }
  a[k] = newValue;
}
```

In the above code, we shift the values in the array to the right by one to create a vacant slot and then insert the new value into the vacancy thus created. Note that the shifting has to proceed from the end, so that each shifted value is placed into a vacant slot and does not overwrite any data (Figure 4-1).

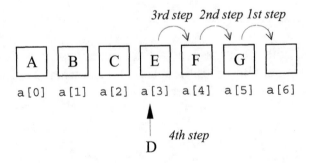

Figure 4-1. Inserting a new value in the middle of an array

33

Consider an array a that contains n integer values sorted in ascending order
(n < a.length). Which of the following code segments correctly inserts newValue
into a, preserving the ascending order?

I.
```
int k;
for (k = n; k > 0; k--)
{
  if (a[k-1] <= newValue)
  {
    a[k] = newValue;
    k = 0;
  }
  else
    a[k] = a[k-1];
}
```

II.
```
int k = n;
while (k > 0 && a[k-1] > newValue)
{
  a[k] = a[k-1];
  k--;
}
a[k] = newValue;
```

III.
```
int j, k = 0;

while (k < n && a[k] < newValue)
  k++;

for (j = n-1; j >= k; j--)
{
  a[j+1] = a[j];
}
a[k] = newValue;
```

(A)   I only
(B)   II only
(C)   III only
(D)   I and II
(E)   II and III

☞ When you have to decide whether such code is correct, check the boundary conditions
first: does it work if we have to insert the value at the very beginning or at the very end of
the array? Segment I, for example, looks good at first — similar to the insertInOrder
method described above. But if newValue is smaller than all the values in the array,
nothing is inserted. Segment II is equivalent to the insertInOrder code above.
Segment III uses a more step-wise approach: first find the place to insert, then shift the
values above that place, then insert. In Segment III, it is sufficient to check that this code
works for newValue being the smallest and the largest — that means there are no tricks.
The answer is E. ⏎

⌐ *Loop invariants* ⌐

⌐ AB exam takers should be familiar with the concept of *loop invariant*. A loop invariant is an assertion about the loop that is relevant to the purpose of the loop and that holds true before and after each iteration through the loop. This assertion is usually expressed as a relation between the variables involved in the loop. Loop invariants are used to reason about programs formally and to prove their correctness without tracing all the iterations through a loop. If you can establish that an assertion is true before the first iteration, and also prove that for any iteration if the assertion is true before that iteration it will remain true after that iteration, then your assertion is a loop invariant. If you are familiar with mathematical induction, you can see how it works here. If not, you can still answer questions about loop invariants without too much trouble.

34

Consider the following code segment:

```
int count = 0;
int n = 41;
int k = 2;

while (k <= n)
{
  if (isPrime(k))
    count++;
  k++;
}
```

Which of the following statements are loop invariants for the above code?

    I. k is a prime.
   II. 41 is a prime.
  III. count is equal to the number of primes from 2 to $k-1$.

(A)   I only
(B)   II only
(C)   III only
(D)   I and II
(E)   None of the three

☞ Statement I is not an invariant because it varies: k may or may not be a prime as we iterate through the loop. More precisely, k is a prime before the first iteration (k = 2) and before the second iteration (k = 3), but not after it (k = 4). This eliminates A and D. Statement II is not an invariant for a different reason. Certainly 41 is a prime — so are 37, 43, 47, and an infinite number of other integers. Also, Washington, DC, is the capital of the United States. These facts, while true, do not help us reason about the purpose or correctness of the above code. But Statement III is a typical invariant: it links the values of the variables count and k and reflects the purpose of the loop, namely counting all the primes from 2 to n. The answer is C. ↵   ⌋

4.2.   Sequential Search and Binary Search

A typical application of a simple loop is *Sequential Search*:

```
// precondition:  Array a holds values a[0], ..., a[n-1].
// postcondition: Returns pos such that 0 <= pos < n and a[pos] == target,
//                or -1 if target is not among a[0], ..., a[n-1].
public int sequentialSearch(int[] a, int n, int target)
{
  int k;

  for (k = 0; k < n; k++)
  {
    if (a[k] == target)
      return k;
  }
  return -1;
}
```

Sequential Search works for any array: the values in the array may be in random order. If an array is sorted (that is, if its elements are arranged in ascending or descending order), then Binary Search is a much more efficient method.

Binary Search is a "divide and conquer" method for quickly finding a target value in a sorted array. Suppose the array is sorted in ascending order. We take an element in the middle (or approximately in the middle) of the array and compare it to the target. If they are equal, we're done. If the target is greater, we continue the search in the right half of the array; if it's smaller, we continue in the left half. For example:

```
// precondition:  Array a contains n values sorted in ascending order.
// postcondition: Returns the position of the element equal to target
//                 or -1 if target is not in the array.
public int binarySearch(int[] a, int n, int target)
{
  int left = 0;
  int right = n - 1;
  int middle;

  while (left <= right)
  {
    middle = (left + right) / 2;
    if (target == a[middle])
      return middle;
    else if (target < a[middle])
      right = middle - 1;      // Continue search in the left half
    else
      left = middle + 1;       // Continue search in the right half
  }
  return -1;
}
```

Binary Search in an array of 2^k - 1 elements requires at most k iterations. In other words, Binary Search in an array of n elements requires $\log_2 n$ iterations. Thus in an array of 1,000,000 elements it would need at most 20 iterations. By comparison, Sequential Search in an array of n elements takes, on average, $n/2$ iterations; in the worst case it may take n iterations.

35

Suppose that two programs, one using Binary Search and the other using Sequential Search, take (on average) the same amount of time to find a random target value in a sorted array of 30 elements. Roughly how much faster than the Sequential Search program will the Binary Search program run on an array of 1000 elements?

(A)   2 times faster
(B)   10 times faster
(C)   16 times faster
(D)   33 times faster
(E)   50 times faster

☞ Binary Search takes 5 iterations for 30 elements ($32 = 2^5$) and 10 iterations for 1000 elements ($1024 = 2^{10}$). So Binary Search will run roughly two times longer on a 1000-element array than on a 30-element array. Sequential search will run roughly 33 times longer ($1000 \approx 30 \cdot 33$). On 1000 elements, Binary Search will be $33/2 = 16.5$ faster. The answer is C. ☂

36

An e-mail address is a string made of alphanumeric characters, one or several "dots," and one "@." The short substring after the last dot is called the domain name suffix. For example, in `jane.lee@math.bestacad.org`, "org" is the suffix. Which of the following methods can be used to find the beginning position of the suffix?

    I.   A modified Sequential Search in which we scan through the whole array keeping track of the last occurrence of a given character

    II.   A modified Sequential Search which proceeds backwards, starting at the end of the array

    III.   A modified Binary Search in which each alphanumeric character is treated as '0' and a dot and @ are treated as '1'

(A)   I only
(B)   II only
(C)   III only
(D)   I and II
(E)   II and III

☞ The task is basically to find the last dot in a string. Method I is not the most efficient, but it works:

```
for (k = 0; k < email.length(); k++)
  if (email.charAt(k) == '.')
    dotPos = k;

// Characters, charAt, and char constants are not in the AP subset

return dotPos;
```

Method II works a bit faster:

```
for (k = email.length() - 1; k >= 0; k--)
  if (email.charAt(k) == '.')
    return k;
```

The description of Method III tries to confuse you with a binary system which has no relation to Binary Search. The latter won't work here because the string is not sorted and dots are scattered among alphanumeric characters. The answer is D. ⏎

4.3.   Selection and Insertion Sorts

Sorting means arranging a list of items in ascending or descending order, according to the values of the items or some key that is part of an item. Sorting algorithms are usually discussed for lists represented as arrays. ⌈ On the <u>AB exam</u>, sorting questions may involve linked lists, queues, or priority queues. ⌋

Selection Sort and **Insertion Sort** are called *quadratic sorts* because they use two straightforward nested loops and the number of required comparisons is approximately proportional to n^2.

Selection Sort

In *Selection Sort* we iterate for k from n down to 2: we find the largest among the first k elements and swap it with the k-th element.

```
// precondition:  Array a contains a[0], ..., a[n-1] (n >= 1)
// postcondition: Elements are sorted in ascending order.
public void selectionSort(int[] a, int n)
{
  int i, k, maxPos;
  int temp;

  for (k = n; k >= 2; k--)
  {
    maxPos = 0;
    for (i = 1; i < k; i++)
    {
      if (a[i] > a[maxPos])
        maxPos = i;
    }
    // Swap a[maxPos], a[k-1]
    temp = a[maxPos]; a[maxPos] = a[k-1]; a[k-1] = temp;
  }
}
```

In the above method, the inner loop runs $k-1$ times, for $k = n, n-1, ..., 2$.

The total number of comparisons in Selection Sort is always the same:

$$(n-1)+(n-2)+...+1 = \frac{n(n-1)}{2}$$

In another variation of *Selection Sort* we find the smallest among the elements a[k], ..., a[n-1] and swap it with a[k] (for $k = 0, ..., n-2$).

Insertion Sort

In *Insertion Sort*, we iterate for *k* from 2 up to *n*. We keep the first ($k-1$) elements sorted and insert the *k*-th element among them where it belongs:

```
// precondition:  Array a contains a[0], ..., a[n-1] (n >= 1)
// postcondition: Elements are sorted in ascending order.
public void insertionSort(int[] a, int n)
{
  int i, k;
  int temp;

  for (k = 2; k <= n; k++)
  {
    temp = a[k-1];
    for (i = k-1; i > 0; i--)
    {
      if (a[i-1] <= temp)
        break;
      else
        a[i] = a[i-1];
    }
    a[i] = temp;
  }
}
```

In this version of Insertion Sort, if the array is already sorted, then the inner loop runs just one comparison and we immediately break out of it. Then the method needs a total of $n-1$ comparisons. This is the best case: instead of *quadratic* time, the method executes in *linear* time.

The worst case for this implementation of Insertion Sort is when the array is sorted in reverse order. Then the inner loop runs $k-1$ times and the whole method will need as many comparisons as Selection Sort:

$$1 + 2 + ... + (n-1) = \frac{n(n-1)}{2}$$

The average case is about half that number, still approximately proportional to n^2.

The methods above are just examples of how Selection and Insertion Sorts can be implemented. Other variations are possible.

|37|

Consider the task of sorting the elements of an array in ascending order. Which of the following statements are true?

    I.   Selection Sort always requires more comparisons than Insertion Sort.
   II.   Insertion Sort always requires more moves than Selection Sort.
  III.   Insertion Sort, on average, requires more moves than Selection Sort.

(A)   I only
(B)   II only
(C)   III only
(D)   I and II
(E)   II and III

This question gives us a chance to review the properties of the two quadratic sorts. As we have seen, Statement I is false: although, on average, Selection Sort requires more comparisons, Insertion Sort in the worst case (an array sorted in reverse order) will take as many comparisons as Selection Sort. Statement II is false, too: in the best case, when the array is already sorted, Insertion Sort does not require any moves. (Selection Sort, too, with a slight modification, can avoid any moves when the array is already sorted.) Statement III is the vague part: what do we mean, "on average"? First of all, our array must be large enough to support some conclusions. Sorting an array of three elements will not be representative. Let's assume that we set up an experiment where we generate a fairly large array of random numbers, sort it using each of the two algorithms, and count the number of moves. Intuition tells us that Insertion Sort, on average, needs more moves. Indeed, the k-th iteration through the outer loop may require anywhere from 0 to k moves, $k/2$ moves on average. In Selection Sort each iteration through the outer loop requires one swap, which can be counted as three moves. The answer is C.

⌈ Insertion Sort works better with a linked list than with an array because inserting an element in the middle of a linked list is easier — you just have to rearrange a few links. With a linked list, you can scan the first $k-1$ elements, starting at the head of the list, and insert the k-th element among them. ⌋

4.4.   Recursion

You may find recursion pleasant or difficult, depending on your taste. If you happen to hate it and you are taking the A exam, you can still take a stab at the multiple-choice questions on recursion.

38

Consider the following method:

```
public void mystery(int n)
{
  int i;
  if ( n <= 0)
    return;

  for (i = 0; i < n; i++)
  {
    System.out.print("-");
  }

  for (i = 0; i < n; i++)
  {
    System.out.print("+");
  }

  System.out.println();

  mystery(n-1);              // Recursive call
}
```

What is the output when mystery(4) is called?

(A)
```
----++++
```

(B)
```
----++++
----++++
----++++
----++++
```

(C)
```
----+
----++
----+++
----++++
```

(D)
```
-+
--++
---+++
----++++
```

(E)
```
----++++
---+++
--++
-+
```

This method calls itself — that's what recursion is. Note two things about it. First, if n <= 0, the method doesn't do anything. An exit from a recursive method, perhaps after some work but without recursive calls, is called the *base case* (or the *stopping case*). In this method the base case does nothing. Second, when the method calls itself, it calls itself with an argument that is less by one than the original. The argument has to change, usually decrease in some way in the direction of the base case, if the recursion is to terminate at some point.

Instead of trying to unwrap and trace all the recursive calls in this method, first try to reason more formally about its properties. The method prints some minuses followed by the same number of pluses. When called with $n = 4$, the method right away prints one line with 4 minuses and 4 pluses. But that is not all: after printing the first line, the method calls mystery(3), which must do the same thing as mystery(4) but on a smaller scale. The answer is E.

Now suppose we change the mystery method in the previous question, placing the recursive call <u>above</u> the for loops:

39

Consider the following method:

```
public void mystery(int n)
{
  int i;

  if (n <= 0)
    return;
  mystery(n-1);                // Recursive call
  for (i = 0; i < n; i++)
  {
    System.out.print("-");
  }
  for (i = 0; i < n; i++)
  {
    System.out.print("+");
  }
  System.out.print();
}
```

What is the output when mystery(4) is called?

< *Same answer choices as in Question 38* >

☞ This question is a bit trickier, but D and E are still the only plausible answers:

```
(D)                     (E)
-+                      ----++++
--++                    ---+++
---+++                  --++
----++++                -+
```

We have to choose D because the last thing mystery(4) does is print ----++++.

(If you are more mathematically inclined, you can reason as follows. mystery(4) prints a triangle pointing either up or down. Let's take a guess at this method's general behavior: say, "mystery(n) prints a triangle with *n* rows that points up." Suppose it's true for *n* = 3. Then mystery(4) first prints a triangle with 3 rows in the recursive call, then adds the longest fourth row. Our guess fits, so the answer should be D.) ↵

40

Consider the following method:

```
public void mysteryMix(String str)
{
  int len = str.length();
  if (len >= 3)
  {
    mysteryMix (str.substring(0, len/3));
    System.out.print (str.substring(len/3, 2*len/3));
    mysteryMix (str.substring(2*len/3));
  }
}
```

What is the output when mysteryMix("la-la-la!") is called?

(A) la-la-la!
(B) ala-a
(C) ala-la-la-l
(D) lla-l
(E) a-la-a!

☞ Many AP questions mix unrelated subjects. This question tests both recursion and strings, and it is a tough question. We start with a string of nine characters, but immediately call mysteryMix recursively for a string of three characters. So it makes sense to see first what happens when we call, say, mysteryMix("xyz"). This call just prints the middle character, "y", and does nothing else: when len is 3 the two recursive calls do nothing. Now back to the original string of nine characters. The two recursive calls print one character each and System.out.print prints three characters, so the output must have five characters. This eliminates A, C, and E. The first character printed is the middle character in the first one-third of the string, which is "a". The answer is B. ↵

Recursive implementation of Binary Search

The description of the Binary Search algorithm is recursive in nature, and it can be implemented recursively with ease.

[41]

Consider the following incomplete recursive implementation of Binary Search:

```
// precondition:  Array a contains values stored from a[left]
//                to a[right], sorted in ascending order.
// postcondition: Returns the position of the element equal to target
//                or -1, if target is not among the values
//                a[left], ..., a[right].
public int binarySearch(int[] a, int left, int right, int target)
{
  int targetPos = -1;
  int middle;

  < statement 1 >
  {
    middle = (left + right) / 2;
    if (target == a[middle])
      < statement 2 >
    else if (target < a[middle])
      targetPos = binarySearch(a, left, middle - 1, target);
    else
      targetPos = binarySearch(a, middle + 1, right, target);
  }
  return targetPos;
}
```

Which of the following could be used to replace *< statement 1 >* and *< statement 2 >* so that the `binarySearch` method works as intended?

< statement 1 >	*< statement 2 >*
(A) `while (left <= right)`	`return targetPos;`
(B) `while (left <= right)`	`return middle;`
(C) `while (left < right)`	`targetPos = middle;`
(D) `if (left <= right)`	`targetPos = middle;`
(E) `if (left < right)`	`return middle;`

☞ In the choice between `while` and `if`, `if` wins, because this is a <u>recursive</u> solution and recursion <u>replaces</u> iterations. This eliminates A, B, and C. In D and E either choice works for Statement 2, but Statement 1 in E misses the case when `left == right`. The answer is D. ☜

⎡ **AB exams** very often include a free-response question on binary trees, so you have to be comfortable with recursive methods that deal with binary trees. Dealing with them in any other way is usually not practical under the time constraints of the exam. Binary Trees are reviewed in Chapter 5. ⎦

4.5.   Mergesort ⎡ and Quicksort ⎦

Mergesort and *Quicksort* are two recursive sorting algorithms based on the "divide and conquer" principle. Both algorithms take, on average, $n \log n$ comparisons, as opposed to n^2 comparisons in quadratic sorts. This difference can be very significant for large arrays. For example, for 1024 elements, Mergesort and Quicksort may run 100 times faster than Selection Sort and Insertion Sort.

The idea of *Mergesort* is simple: divide the array into two approximately equal halves; sort (recursively) each half, then merge them together into one sorted array (Figure 4-2). Mergesort usually requires a temporary array for holding the two sorted halves before they are merged back into the original space.

Split the array into two halves:

```
A:    1   7   4   9 ┊ 3   5   8   6   2
```

Sort each half (recursively) and copy into *temp*:

```
temp:  1   4   7   9 ┊ 2   3   5   6   8
```

Merge elements in ascending order from the two sorted halves back into the array:

Figure 4-2.   Mergesort

42

Consider the following implementation of Mergesort:

```
// precondition:   0 <= n1 <= n2 < a.length
// postcondition: a[n1], ..., a[n2] are sorted in ascending order.
public void sort(int[] a, int n1, int n2)
{
  int m;

  if (n1 == n2)
    return;

  m = (n1 + n2) / 2;
  sort(a, n1, m);
  sort(a, m+1, n2);
  if (a[m] > a[m+1])           // Optional line
    merge(a, n1, m, n2);
}
```

Compare it with a more conventional version with the `if` statement on the "optional line" removed. Suppose a has 8 elements and `sort(a, 0, 7)` is called. For which of the following values in a will the version with `if` work faster than the version without?

  I.   1 2 3 4 5 6 7 8
 II.   5 6 7 8 2 1 4 3
III.   2 1 4 3 6 5 8 7

(A)   I only
(B)   I and II
(C)   I and III
(D)   I, II, and III
(E)   None of the three

A typical implementation of Mergesort doesn't skip the work even when the array is already sorted. The slight change proposed in this question allows Mergesort to skip all the merging and quickly establish that an array is already sorted, as in Array I. This version also avoids merging when the array is partially sorted, namely when all the values in the left half of the array are smaller than any value in the right half, as in Array III. In that case, after the two recursive calls to `sort` the array becomes sorted and the call to `merge` is skipped.

Since the algorithm is recursive, it will also save time when some portions of the array have these properties — are either sorted or partially sorted — even when the whole array isn't. In Array II, for example, the left half is sorted and the right half is partially sorted. The answer is D.

Quicksort is a little less obvious and <u>it is not required for the A exam</u>.

⌈ It works as follows. Choose a "pivot" element. Rearrange all the elements of the array so that the pivot divides the array into two parts. All the elements to the left of the pivot should be less than or equal to the pivot. All the elements to the right of the pivot should be greater than or equal to the pivot. Sort (recursively) each part.

Quicksort does not require temporary storage. On average, it runs a bit faster than Mergesort, but it is less predictable. You have to be lucky when you choose a pivot; hopefully its value will be close to the median value for the array, so that the pivot divides the array into two roughly equal halves.

43

Suppose the method

```
public void quickSort(int[] a, int k, int m) { ... }
```

implements the recursive Quicksort algorithm that sorts the elements `a[k]`, `...` `a[m]` in ascending order. It is implemented in such a way that `a[k]` serves as the pivot element. Which of the following ordering properties of the array `a` with 1000 elements results in the best running time for `quickSort(a, 0, 999)`?

(A)   When `a[0]`, `...`, `a[999]` are already sorted in ascending order
(B)   When `a[0]`, `...`, `a[999]` are sorted in descending order
(C)   When `a[0]` is the median of `a[0]`, `...`, `a[999]` and the rest of the 999 elements are sorted in ascending order
(D)   When `a[999]` is the median of `a[0]`, `...`, `a[999]` and the rest of the 999 elements are sorted in ascending order
(E)   When `a[0]`, `...`, `a[999]` are arranged in random order

 Quicksort is a recursive algorithm, which means that the method will be called many times for different segments of the array. For it to run efficiently, the pivot element in these calls must pretty often be close to the median value of the segment. When the array is already sorted, as in A and B, the first element, which is chosen as pivot, is always as far from the median as possible. In such situations the pivot does not split the array into two more or less equal halves; instead it just splits away one element. So these two are the worst cases for Quicksort. In C and D the first element is the median, but this applies only at the top level of recursion. As we proceed deeper with recursive calls, the smaller segments become sorted and we face the same problem as in A and B. The random arrangement ensures that the first element will be somewhat close to the median with some frequency and `quickSort` will work as intended. The answer is E. ⌐

<u>The AB exam</u> also covers Heapsort, which is discussed in Section 5.7.

⌡

4.6. Data Organization Questions

AP CS exams may contain multiple-choice questions on appropriate ways of representing data for specific tasks. Below are a few examples of such questions at the A level. ⌈ AB exam takers have a much larger toolbox of standard data structures — lists, two-dimensional arrays, trees, hash tables, etc. These are discussed in Chapter 5. ⌋

44

Consider designing a data structure that represents information about subscribers in an e-mail server system. Among other attributes, a subscriber has an ID and a number of unread new messages. Information about all subscribers who have unread mail will be stored in an array of `Subscriber` objects. Two possible implementations are being considered:

Method A: Store the array entries in arbitrary order.
Method B: Store the array entries in sorted order by subscriber ID.

Consider the following operations:

Operation 1:   Increment the number of messages for a subscriber with a specified ID.
Operation 2:   Add a new subscriber with a given number of messages to the list of subscribers.

Which of the following is true?

(A)   Both Operation 1 and Operation 2 can be implemented more efficiently using Method A than Method B.
(B)   Both Operation 1 and Operation 2 can be implemented more efficiently using Method B than Method A.
(C)   Operation 1 can be implemented more efficiently using Method A; Operation 2 can be implemented more efficiently using Method B.
(D)   Operation 1 can be implemented more efficiently using Method B; Operation 2 can be implemented more efficiently using Method A.
(E)   Operation 1 and Operation 2 can be implemented equally efficiently using either method.

☞ These types of questions may test your reading comprehension skills, but in terms of real technical difficulty they don't go too far beyond common sense. It certainly helps if you have a good understanding of various data structures and their uses in different algorithms. Here, for example, we have to deal with finding an element with a given key (subscriber ID) in an array and inserting a new value into an array. The relevant ideas that come to mind are Sequential and Binary Search, inserting a value in order, and inserting at the end.

You may want to jot down a little table quickly in order not to get confused in the Methods and Operations; then check the appropriate boxes (what works faster):

	A: random order	B: sorted
1. Increment # msgs — "find"		✓
2. Add a subscr — "insert".	✓	

Clearly, if you need to worry about the order, adding a subscriber to a sorted array will take more work than just slapping him on at the end of a random one. This alone eliminates choices B, C, and E. (Don't try to be too smart, thinking that you may need to reallocate and copy the array if it is not large enough. That is not what this question is about.)

Is it easier to find a value in a sorted array? Of course. If you remember that you can use Binary Search on a sorted array, that's great. But even if you don't, this would be a good guess. The fact that the array is sorted probably can't hurt the search operation. This eliminates A. The answer is D. ☜

Questions 45-46 refer to the following information:

The College Board administers AP exams in N subjects ($N \geq 34$) over K days ($K \geq 14$). Each subject is offered only on one day. The subjects are represented by integers from 1 to N. Two different designs are being considered for an application that keeps track of the exam calendar:

Design 1:

The exam schedule information is held in a one-dimensional array of integers. For each of the K days there is one entry that represents the number of exams on that day, followed by a list of the subjects offered on that day. For example, if the first day has two exams in subjects 29 and 31, and the second day has no exams, the array will start with 2, 29, 31, 0, ...

Design 2:

The schedule is represented as an array of Boolean values consisting of N groups of K values in each group. The `true` value in the k-th element of the n-th group indicates that the n-th subject is offered on the k-th day.

45

Which of the following statements about the space requirements of the implementation of the two designs in Java is true?

(A) Design 1 will require less space.
(B) Design 2 will require less space.
(C) Which design will require more space depends on the value of N.
(D) Which design will require more space depends on the value of K.
(E) Which design will require more space depends on the number of bytes it takes to represent Boolean and integer values on a particular platform.

☞ See the solution for Question 46. ☜

46

Suppose that Design 2 is chosen and that the following method is implemented as efficiently as possible:

Given a subject number between 1 and N and a day number between 1 and K, the method returns `true` if the given subject is offered on the given day and `false` otherwise.

Which of the following statements is true?

(A)   The average time spent in the method is proportional to N.
(B)   The average time spent in the method is proportional to K.
(C)   The average time spent in the method is proportional to the total number of values in the array (N times K).
(D)   The average time spent in the method is proportional to the average number of exams per day.
(E)   The time spent in the method does not depend on N or K, nor on the distribution of exams by day.

☞☞ The above two questions compare space and time requirements for the same data represented as a list (Design 1) and as a *lookup table* (Design 2). You can answer these questions right away if you are familiar with lookup tables. In a lookup table, a data item (here a valid subject/day pair) is represented as a <u>location</u> in an array. Lookup tables usually take more space but provide instantaneous (constant time) access to data regardless of the size of the table.

If you've never heard the term *lookup table*, you can still figure it out.

In Question 45 the space requirement for Design 1 is $K + N$ integers: one for each day (representing the number of exams for that day) and one for each exam (each exam has to be listed under one of the days). The space requirement for Design 2 is $N \cdot K$ Boolean values. Recall that in Java, an integer always takes four bytes, regardless of the particular platform. A Boolean may vary, but even if it takes only one byte, still $4 \cdot (K + N) < N \cdot K$ for large enough N and K (recall that $N \geq 34$, $K \geq 14$). The answer is A. ⏎

In Question 46, you must know that you can go directly to any element of an array, `table[i]`. This property is called *random access* and it's what arrays are all about. The n-th subject is offered on the k-th day if `table[(n-1)*K + (k-1)]` is `true`. (Here, `table` should be really a two-dimensional array, but these are not in the A subset.) The answer is E. ⏎

Chapter 5. AB Topics: Linked Lists, Stacks, Queues, Trees, etc.

⌈ All the material in this chapter is needed only for the <u>AB exam</u>. ⌋

5.1.   Overview

A *collection* refers to a particular way of storing and using data. In Java it is convenient to describe a collection as an interface; different classes that implement that interface provide different implementations of the collection. Table 5-1 lists six types of collections you should be familiar with. These include the `List`, `Set`, and `Map` interfaces from the `java.util` package — only the AP subset of their methods is required — and the `Stack`, `Queue`, and `PriorityQueue` interfaces provided by the AP Development Committee.

> **All of the above collections hold <u>objects</u> (as opposed to `ints` or `doubles` or other primitive data types).**

For the exam you should know the `java.util` classes that implement the `List`, `Set`, and `Map` interfaces as well as the concepts behind these implementations (arrays and linked lists, binary search trees, and hash tables). You should understand the differences between different implementations and their appropriate uses.

The Development Committee does <u>not</u> provide standard implementation classes for the `Stack`, `Queue`, and `PriorityQueue` interfaces, but it is helpful to know at least one simple class that implements each of them because you might be asked to implement some similar methods on the exam.

You should be able to work with linked lists and binary trees in a do-it-yourself way, using the `ListNode` and `TreeNode` classes provided by the AP Development Committee, and have a general understanding of heaps — a particular type of binary trees used for implementing priority queues.

Section 5.8 reviews big-O analysis of algorithms, which is also a required topic.

Interface	Purpose	Implementations
`java.util.List`	A list of items $x_0, ..., x_{n-1}$ that can be accessed through indices; may contain duplicate values	As an array: `java.util.ArrayList` As a linked list: `java.util.LinkedList`
`Stack`	Used for temporary storage in handling nested structures or branching processes; items are accessed in the LIFO (last-in-first-out) manner (`push` and `pop` methods).	No standard implementation is provided; easy to implement using an array or a linked list.
`Queue`	Used for temporary storage in handling items or events in order of arrival; items are accessed in the FIFO (first-in-first-out) manner (`enqueue` and `dequeue` methods).	No standard implementation is provided; easy to implement using a linked list. (Can also be implemented easily, but inefficiently, with an `ArrayList`.)
`java.util.Set`	A set of items; no duplicate values are allowed; there is a way to tell whether a given value is in the set (`contains` method).	As a binary search tree: `java.util.TreeSet` As a hash table: `java.util.HashSet`
`java.util.Map`	A set of pairs: each pair has a key and a value associated with that key; keys form a set (no duplicate keys are allowed); there are ways to add a new pair and to get the value associated with a key (`put` and `get` methods).	As a binary search tree: `java.util.TreeMap` As a hash table: `java.util.HashMap`
`PriorityQueue`	Used for retrieving items in order of their "priority" or rank (`add` and `removeMin` methods).	No standard implementation is provided; can be implemented using a list, but an efficient implementation uses a heap.

Table 5-1   Collections and their implementations on the AP CS AB exam

5.2.   Lists

A *list* is a collection in which items can be accessed through indices. The indices start from 0. We only consider lists that hold objects (not `ints` or `doubles`). If you want to hold integers or doubles, use objects of a wrapper class (`Integer` or `Double`). A list may contain duplicate values (the same object, `obj1 == obj2` or "equal" objects, `obj1.equals(obj2)`).

`java.util.List` is a library interface that describes list methods. The AP subset includes the following methods of `List`:

```
int size();                        // Returns the number of items
                                   //    in the list
boolean add (Object x);            // Adds x at the end of the list
void add (int index, Object x);    // Inserts x at index
Object get (int index);            // Returns the value at index
Object set (int index, Object x);  // Sets the element at index to x;
                                   //    returns the old value
Object remove (int index);         // Removes the item at index;
                                   //    and returns its value
Iterator iterator();               // Returns an Iterator
ListIterator listIterator();       // Returns a ListIterator
                                   //    (iterators are discussed below)
```

Note the following properties of Java lists:

- A list holds references to (i.e., addresses of) objects.

- The same object can be inserted several times into a list and can belong to several lists.

- In general, an object can be modified after it is inserted into a list; however, `Strings`, `Integers`, or `Doubles` are immutable objects, which cannot be modified.

- Indices are checked for the valid range, from `0` to `list.size() - 1`; in an appropriate implementation, methods would throw an `IndexOutOfBoundsException` if called with an invalid index argument.

- `add(index, x)` and `remove(index)` appropriately adjust the indices of all the items that follow the added or removed item and adjust the size of the list.

47

What is the output of the following code segment?

```
List items = ... < creates an empty list >
items.add("One");
items.add("Two");
items.add("Three");
items.add("Four");
int i;
for (i = 0; i < items.size(); i++)
{
   System.out.print(items.remove(i) + " ");
}
System.out.println();
```

(A)   An empty line
(B)   One Two Three Four
(C)   One Two Three
(D)   One Three
(E)   IndexOutOfBoundsException

☞ IndexOutOfBoundsException can't happen because i is never negative and
i < items.size() at each iteration. There must be some output, as "One" is printed
for i = 0. The trick is that after the first iteration, the indices are adjusted: "Two"
becomes the item at 0, "Three" at 1, and "Four" at 2, while i becomes 1. So the
second output value is "Three". After the second iteration, the size of the list becomes
2 and i becomes 2, so the loop is exited. The answer is D. ☜

_____ *java.util.ArrayList* _____

We already reviewed ArrayList in Section 2.6. Here we briefly look at it again in the
context of the Java collections framework.

ArrayList implements the List interface using an array. This provides direct access
to the list's elements, so the get and set methods are efficient.

ArrayList's no-args constructor allocates an array of some default initial capacity and
sets the size to 0 (no values stored in the list). As values are added, their number may
exceed the current capacity. Then the capacity is doubled, a new array is allocated, the
old values are copied into the new array, and the old array is discarded. All of this
happens behind the scenes — you don't have to worry about any of it. Most of the time,
the add() method, which adds an item at the end, works efficiently, but once in a while,
when the list runs out of space, it may take more time for moving the values into a new
array.

The `add(index, x)` and `remove(index)` methods are less efficient because they require shifting all the values that follow the value at index towards the end or towards the beginning of the array, respectively.

java.util.LinkedList

The nodes of a linked list are scattered in memory, but each node contains a reference to the next node. In the last node of the list, the reference is set to `null`.

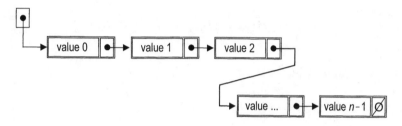

Figure 5-1. A linked list

A linked list with a tail maintains an additional reference to the last node. A doubly-linked list has a reference to the tail and a reverse link from each node to the previous one (Figure 5-2).

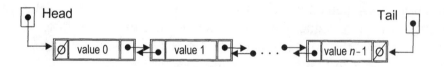

Figure 5-2. A doubly-linked list

`java.util.LinkedList` implements a list as a doubly-linked list.

A linked list <u>does not</u> provide direct access to the list's elements; to get to the *i*-th element you need to start from the beginning (or end) and follow the links until you get to the *i*-th node. The `get(index)` and `set(index, x)` methods are still provided in `LinkedList` to fulfill the requirements of the `List` interface, but these methods are inefficient. On the other hand, you don't need to move items when you insert or remove a new item: a new node can be inserted or removed simply by rearranging a few links.

`java.util.LinkedList` has a few additional methods that are especially efficient for doubly-linked lists:

```
void addFirst(Object x);        // Inserts x at the beginning
void addLast(Object x);         // Inserts x at the end
Object getFirst();              // Returns the first item
Object getLast();               // Returns the last item
Object removeFirst();           // Removes the first item
                                //    and returns its value
Object removeLast();            // Removes the last item
                                //    and returns its value
```

These methods are included in the AP subset.

List traversals and iterators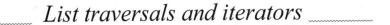

A traversal of a list using indices —

```
for (i = 0; i < list.size(); i++)
{
  Object obj = list.get(i);
  ...
}
```

— works for both `ArrayLists` and `LinkedLists`, but it is inefficient for `LinkedLists`. A better way is to use an *iterator*.

An iterator is an object associated with a list. An iterator maintains the current position in the list and provides a method that checks whether more values are available and a method that returns the next value. The AP subset includes two types of iterators: `java.util.Iterator` and `java.util.ListIterator`. The `List` interface specifies the `iterator` and `listIterator` methods that return an `Iterator` object and a `ListIterator` object for a list, respectively. The `ListIterator` is more involved: in addition to all the `Iterator` methods it has methods for traversing the list in reverse (not in the AP subset) and methods for adding a value and setting an element's value.

`Iterator` and `ListIterator` are actually library interfaces; the `iterator` and `listIterator` methods create and return an iterator object appropriate for the particular type of list. You can think of an iterator as a "caret" or "cursor" positioned between two elements of the list. When an iterator is created, it is positioned before the first element. (A `ListIterator` can be created at a given position, but this constructor is not in the AP subset.)

Only three of `Iterator`'s methods are in the AP subset:

```
boolean hasNext();             // Returns true if there are more
                               //   items to access with this iterator
Object next();                 // Returns the next item
void remove();                 // Removes from the list the item that
                               //   was last returned by the "next" call
```

The additional `ListIterator` methods in the AP subset are:

```
void add (Object x);           // Inserts x at the current position
                               //    (but before the "cursor")
void set (Object x);           // Sets to x the element returned
                               //    by the last call to next
```

A convenient idiom for traversing a list using an iterator uses a `while` loop:

```
Iterator it = list.iterator();
while (it.hasNext())
{
  Object obj = it.next();
  ...
}
```

Iterators are equally efficient for lists implemented as an `ArrayList` and a `LinkedList`, so they are a preferred way of traversing a list when the exact type of the list is not known. For example:

```
public void display(List list)
{
  Iterator it = list.iterator();
  while (it.hasNext())
  {
    System.out.println(it.next());
  }
}
```

48

Consider the following method:

```
// precondition:  list contains strings arranged alphabetically
// postcondition: duplicate values are removed from the list
public void removeDuplicates(List list)
{
  ListIterator it = list.listIterator();
  Object prev = null, current;
  while (it.hasNext())
  {
    < statement1 >;
    if (current.equals(prev))
    {
      < statement2 >;
    }
    prev = current;
  }
}
```

Which of the following are appropriate replacements for < *statement1* > and
< *statement2* > that make the method work as specified?

	< *statement1* >	< *statement2* >
(A)	current = it.next()	it.remove()
(B)	int i = it.next()	list.remove(i)
(C)	int i = it.next().intValue()	list.remove(i)
(D)	current = it.next()	list.remove(it)
(E)	it = it.next()	list.remove(it)

☞ This is a syntax question. `it.next()` returns the next object from the list; it is not an
index into the list. In general, once you start working with an iterator, it is a mistake to
use the <u>list's</u> `add` or `remove` methods because the iterator may get out of sync — you
should stick to calling the <u>iterator's</u> methods. The answer is A. ☜

Note that in the above example we could have used an `Iterator`, not a `ListIterator`,
because we are not calling the iterator's `add` or `set` methods.

Linked lists: do it yourself

Before you can begin building a linked list, you need a way to represent a node of your list. The AP Development Committee has provided a class ListNode to make sure that exam questions can be stated and answered in a consistent way.

```
public class ListNode
{

  // Constructor:
  public ListNode(Object initValue, ListNode initNext)
                        { value = initValue; next = initNext; }

  public Object getValue() { return value; }
  public ListNode getNext() { return next; }
  public void setValue(Object theNewValue) { value = theNewValue; }
  public void setNext(ListNode theNewNext) { next = theNewNext; }

  private Object value;
  private ListNode next;
}
```

The getNext method returns the link to the next node of the list. Suppose head points to the first node in the list. Then the following code will traverse the list and print out all the values in it:

```
ListNode node;
for (node = head; node != null; node = node.getNext())
  System.out.println(node.getValue());
```

Questions 49-50 use the class:

```
public class Student
{
  public Student (String name, double gpa)  { < code not shown > }
   < methods and data members not shown >
}
```

49

Assuming that `ListNode studentList` refers to a linked list of `Student` objects, which of the following code segments correctly allocates a new node for a student with the name "Lobatschewsky" and a GPA of 3.7, and appends it at the beginning of the list?

(A)   `studentList = new Student("Lobatschewsky", 3.7, studentList);`

(B)   `studentList = new ListNode("Lobatschewsky", 3.7, studentList);`

(C)   `studentList = new ListNode(new Student("Lobatschewsky", 3.7),`
                                                    `studentList);`

(D)   `Student x = new Student("Lobatschewsky", 3.7);`
        `studentList.setValue(x);`

(E)   `Student x = new Student("Lobatschewsky", 3.7);`
        `ListNode node = new ListNode(x, null);`
        `studentList.setNext(x);`

☞ Choice A confuses two kinds of objects: `Student`s and `ListNode`s. A `ListNode` holds a `Student`, but it is not a `Student`. Here `studentList` is a `ListNode` and the `new Student` operator returns a `Student`, so the assignment won't work. Choice B makes a similar mistake: a `ListNode` holds a `Student` object as a whole, not its individual data members, and `ListNode` does not have a constructor with three parameters. Choice D <u>replaces</u> the value in the first node (or throws a `NullPointerException` if the list is empty) — rather than create a new node. Choice E either throws an exception (if `studentList` is `null`) or cuts off the first node of the list and attaches the new node to it. The new list will have only two nodes; the rest of the nodes will be lost. Choice C first creates a `Student` object with the given name and GPA, then creates a new node that holds this student and a link to the old head of the list, which in effect appends the new node at the head of the list. The answer is C. ☜

50

Consider a method that appends a given student at the end of a list of students:

```
// precondition:  list is null or points to a list of students
// postcondition: student is added at the end of the list;
//                returns the new list
public ListNode insert(ListNode list, Student student)
{
  ListNode tail = list;
  < code >
  return list;
}
```

Which of the following code segments may be substituted for < *code* > so that the
insert method works as intended?

```
I.   if (list == null)
     {
         list = new ListNode(student, null);
     }
     else
     {
       while (tail.getNext() != null)
       {
         tail = tail.getNext();
       }
       tail = new ListNode(student, null);
     }
```

```
II.  while (tail != null && tail.getNext() != null)
     {
       tail = tail.getNext();
     }
     if (tail == null)
       list = new ListNode(student, null);
     else
       tail.setNext(new ListNode(student, null));
```

```
III. ListNode newNode = new ListNode(student, null);
     if (tail != null)
     {
       while (tail.getNext() != null)
       {
         tail = tail.getNext();
       }
       tail.setNext(newNode);
     }
     else
     {
       list = newNode;
     }
```

(A)   I only
(B)   II only
(C)   I and II
(D)   II and III
(E)   I, II, and III

☞ This is too much code for a typical multiple-choice question, but it gives us a chance to review some common mistakes.

Segment I may look straightforward at first, but the last statement has a bug: it sets `tail`, a local variable, to the new node, instead of replacing `null` in the `tail`'s next link with a new node by calling `tail.setNext(new ListNode(student, null))`.

In Segment II, the condition

```
tail != null && tail.getNext() != null
```

may look suspicious at first, but it works due to short-circuit evaluation. If `studentList` is empty at the beginning, then `tail` is `null` and the `while` loop is not executed. Otherwise `tail` advances until it points to the last node of the list. The following `if-else` statement correctly sets either `tail`'s next or `studentList` to the new node. So, Segment II works.

Segment III takes a step-wise approach: it first allocates a new node, then appends it to the list. It works, and perhaps this approach is actually cleaner. The answer is D.

The step-wise approach of Segment III may be helpful in answering free response questions. Credit is often given for each completed step, and you may be able to write code for some of the steps (e.g., allocating the node) even if you do not know the rest. ☜

5.3. Stacks and Queues

Stacks

A stack is a storage structure that implements the last-in-first-out (LIFO) storage method. A stack is controlled by two operations: *push* places an item at the top of the stack and *pop* removes and returns the top item. Stacks are used for untangling hierarchical nested structures and branching processes.

The AP Development Committee's `Stack` interface has four methods:

```
public interface Stack
{
  boolean isEmpty();
  void push(Object x);
  Object pop();
  Object peekTop();         // Returns the top item without
                            //   removing it from the stack
}
```

It is easy to implement a stack using an `ArrayList`. For example:

```
public class ArrayStack implements Stack
{
  // Constructor:
  public ArrayStack()  { items = new java.util.ArrayList(); }

  public boolean isEmpty() { return items.size() == 0; }
  public void push(Object obj) { items.add(obj); }
  public Object pop() { return items.remove(items.size() - 1); }
  public Object peekTop() { return items.get(items.size() - 1); }

  private java.util.ArrayList items;
}
```

51

What is the output from the following code segment?

```
Stack s1 = ... < create an empty stack >;
s1.push(new Integer(1));
s1.push(new Integer(2));

Stack s2 = ... < create an empty stack >;
s2.push(new Integer(3));
s2.push(new Integer(4));
s2.push(new Integer(5));

Stack s3 = ... < create an empty stack >;
while (!s1.isEmpty() && !s2.isEmpty())
{
  s3.push(s1.pop());
  s3.push(s2.pop());
}
while (!s3.isEmpty())
{
  System.out.print(s3.pop() + " ");
}
```

(A) 4 2 3 1
(B) 2 5 1 4
(C) 4 1 5 2
(D) 5 2 4 1 3
(E) 2 3 1 4 5

☞ This question is not as difficult as it might seem. s1 gets 2 on top, so 2 gets pushed onto s3 first and ends up at the bottom of s3. Therefore, 2 will be the last number printed. The answer is C. ☜

Queues

A queue is a storage structure that implements the first-in-first-out (FIFO) storage method. A queue is controlled by two operations: *enqueue* adds an item at the rear of the queue and *dequeue* removes and returns the item in front. Queues are used for processing events in the order of their arrival.

The Development Committee's Queue interface has four methods:

```
public interface Queue
{
  boolean isEmpty();
  void enqueue(Object x);
  Object dequeue();
  Object peekFront();    // Returns the first item without
                         //    removing it from the queue
}
```

It is easy to implement a queue using a `LinkedList`. For example:

```
public class ListQueue implements Queue
{
  // Constructor:
  public ListQueue()  { items = new java.util.LinkedList(); }

  public boolean isEmpty() { return items.size() == 0; }
  public void enqueue(Object obj) { items.addLast(obj); }
  public Object dequeue() { return items.removeFirst(); }
  public Object peekFront() { return items.getFirst(); }

  private java.util.LinkedList items;
}
```

52

Consider the following method:

```
public void parse(String exp)
{
  Stack s = ... < create an empty stack >;
  Queue q = ... < create an empty queue >;
  int j, k;

  for (k = 0; k < exp.length(); k++)
  {
    String kth = exp.substring(k, k+1);
    if (kth.equals("("))
    {
      s.push(new Integer(k));
    }
    else if (kth.equals(")"))
    {
      if (s.isEmpty())
      {
        System.out.println("*** Syntax error ***");
        return;
      }
      j = ((Integer)s.pop()).intValue();
      q.enqueue(exp.substring(j+1, k));
    }
  }

  if (!s.isEmpty())
  {
    System.out.println("*** Syntax error ***");
  }
  else
  {
    while (!q.isEmpty())
    {
      System.out.println(q.dequeue());
    }
  }
}
```

What is the output when `parse("Evaluate(((a+b)*(a-b))/2)")` is called?

(A) `a+b`
     `a-b`
     `(a+b)*(a-b)`
     `((a+b)*(a-b))/2`

(B) `Evaluate(((a+b)*(a-b))/2)`
     `((a+b)*(a-b))/2`
     `(a+b)*(a-b)`
     `a+b`
     `a-b`

(C) `((a+b)*(a-b))/2`
     `(a+b)*(a-b)`
     `a+b`
     `a-b`

(D) `a+b`
     `a-b`

(E) `*** Syntax error ***`

☞ This example is longer than a typical multiple-choice question, but it allows us to review stacks and queues in a more realistic setting. In this method a stack is used to untangle an expression with nested parentheses and a queue is used for storing parenthesized subexpressions when they are extracted. This is a reasonable example of what stacks and queues might be used for. As soon as an opening parenthesis is found, its position is saved on the stack; when a closing parenthesis is found, the saved opening position is popped from the stack and the substring between them (excluding the parentheses themselves) is added to the queue. The use of a stack automatically assures that the opening and closing parentheses for a substring are indeed a matching pair. The stack must be empty at the end; otherwise a syntax error is reported because the parentheses do not match.

In this example, exp is `"Evaluate(((a+b)*(a-b))/2)"`. The parentheses do match, so E is not the right answer. Their contents are printed for each pair of matching parentheses, so D is not the right answer either. There are four matching pairs, so the output must contain exactly four lines, as in A and C. The inner expressions end up closer to the top of the stack, so they will be queued and printed first. The answer is A.
↵

5.4.   Sets and Maps

java.util.Set

A *set* holds unique values. The `java.util.Set` interface methods in the AP subset are:

```
int size();                     // Returns the number of elements
                                //   in the set
boolean add (Object x);         // Adds x to the set
boolean contains (Object x);    // Returns true if the set contains x
boolean remove (Object x);      // Removes x from the set;
Iterator iterator();            // Returns an Iterator for this set
```

> **The elements of a set are not indexed and an iterator, returned by the `iterator` method, traverses the elements in an order that depends on a particular implementation.**

What constitutes "unique" (not equal) values is not a simple question: it also depends on the particular implementation. `java.util` offers two classes that implement `Set`: `TreeSet`, which uses a binary search tree, and `HashSet`, which uses a hash table. These data structures are discussed in Sections 5.5 and 5.6.

In the AP subset, objects placed into a `TreeSet` are assumed to be `Comparable`, and `TreeSet` uses the `compareTo` method for comparing them. `x` is deemed to be "equal" to `y` if `x.compareTo(y)` returns 0. An iterator returns the `TreeSet`'s values in ascending order. A `HashSet` does not assume that its elements are `Comparable`; it uses the `hashCode` method and the `equals` method to decide whether two objects are equal. So objects placed into a `HashSet` must have a decent `hashCode` method. An iterator returns the `HashSet`'s values in no particular order.

java.util.Map

A *map* holds pairs of objects: (key, value) and establishes a relation between keys and the values associated with the keys. The keys form a set, so they are all different. Only one value is associated with each key. However, different keys can be mapped onto the same value. A map provides a convenient way of looking up a value when we know its key. For example, a phone company customer database may use a map with the phone number as a key and a customer record associated with that key.

The `java.util.Map` interface methods in the AP subset are:

```
int size();                         // Returns the number of keys
                                    //   in the map
Object put(Object key,
              Object value);        // Associates value with key
                                    //   (returns the old value associated
                                    //   with key, or null if key was not
                                    //   yet in the map)
Object get(Object key);             // Returns the value associated
                                    //   with key, or null if key is not
                                    //   in the map
boolean containsKey(Object key);    // Returns true if key is in the set
                                    //   of keys
Object remove(Object key);          // Removes key and from the map; returns
                                    //   the value previously associated
                                    //   with key, or null
Set keySet();                       // Returns the set of all keys
```

To iterate over a map, you need to get the set of all the keys and then iterate over that set. For example:

```
Map map = ... < create an empty map >;
map.put(...);
...
Iterator it = map.keySet().iterator();
while (it.hasNext())
{
  Object key = it.next();
  System.out.println(key + " ==> " + map.get(key));
}
```

`java.util` offers two classes that implement `Map`: `TreeMap`, which uses a binary search tree for the keys, and `HashMap`, which uses a hash table for the keys.

A course registration database holds information about students' sign-ups for courses in a given semester and must be able to quickly tell whether a particular student is in a given course. It must also be able to quickly generate a list of all the students in a given course. Which of the following data organization methods is the most appropriate for these tasks?

(A)   A map that uses students as keys and a course as a value associated with a key
(B)   A map that uses courses as keys and a student as a value associated with a key
(C)   A two-dimensional array of Boolean values with rows corresponding to courses and columns corresponding to students; the element at the intersection of course and student is set to true if the student is taking the course
(D)   A map that uses courses as keys; a value associated with the key is a set of all students taking this course
(E)   A map that uses students as keys; a value associated with the key is a list of all courses taken by the student

☞ Note that sets and lists are objects in Java, so choices D and E are entirely plausible. A student can take several courses and several students can be in the same course, so mappings in A and B do not work. The table approach in C could potentially work if you kept students and courses sorted and used binary searches to find the appropriate row and column. Still, you would need to scan the whole row to find all the students taking the corresponding course. Also the table would waste a lot of space. Choice E could tell you quickly whether a student is taking a given course (because the list of courses must be relatively short), but it would be difficult to list all the students in a given course: you would have to iterate over all the students. In choice D, both operations are relatively quick because finding a key in a map and finding an element in a set (`TreeSet` or `HashSet`) are both quick operations. If you use a `TreeSet` for all students in a course, a `TreeSet` iterator will list all the students in the specified order (e.g. alphabetically, if names are used as keys). The answer is D. ⮐

5.5.   Binary Trees

In a binary tree, each node, except the *root*, has one parent. Each node contains references to its left and right children; a `null` value indicates that the corresponding child is not in the tree. A node that doesn't have any children is called a *leaf*. Each node is a root of a smaller binary tree, its *subtree* (Figure 5-3).

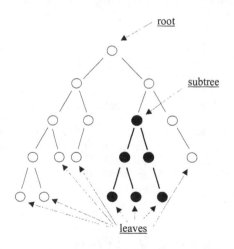

Figure 5-3.   Binary tree

For "do-it-yourself" projects and exam questions, the Development Committee has provided a class `TreeNode` that represents a node in a binary tree:

```
public class TreeNode
{

  // Constructor:
  public TreeNode(Object initValue, TreeNode initLeft, TreeNode initRight)
            { value = initValue; left = initLeft; right = initRight; }

  public Object getValue() { return value; }
  public TreeNode getLeft() { return left; }
  public TreeNode getRight() { return right; }
  public void setValue(Object theNewValue) { value = theNewValue; }
  public void setLeft(TreeNode theNewLeft) { left = theNewLeft; }
  public void setRight(TreeNode theNewRight) { right = theNewRight; }

  private Object value;
  private TreeNode left;
  private TreeNode right;
}
```

Trees are almost always handled recursively. Recursive code for trees doesn't use any loops.

Recursion can be readily applied because a tree is an inherently recursive structure: the subtree that grows from each node is a smaller binary tree. Recursive code is usually much more compact and readable. The following method, for example, returns the total number of nodes in a tree:

```
// precondition:  root refers to the root node of a binary tree
// postcondition: Returns the number of nodes in the tree
public int getNodeCount(TreeNode root)
{
  if (root == null)    // Base case: empty tree
    return 0;
  else                 // Recursive case: 1 for the root plus
                       //   count in left and right subtrees
    return 1 + getNodeCount(root.getLeft()) +
            getNodeCount(root.getRight());
}
```

Tree traversals

A process of visiting (e.g., printing the information in) each node of a tree is called *traversal*. The three common types of binary tree traversals are *inorder*, *preorder*, and *postorder*:

```
public void traverseInorder(TreeNode root)
{
  if (root != null)
  {
    traverseInorder(root.getLeft());
    System.out.println(root.getValue());  // Visit root in the middle
    traverseInorder(root.getRight());
  }
}

void traversePreorder(TreeNode root)
{
  if (root != null)
  {
    System.out.println(root.getValue());  // Visit root first
    traversePreorder(root.getLeft());
    traversePreorder(root.getRight());
  }
}

void traversePostorder(TreeNode * T)
{
  if (root != null)
  {
    traversePostorder(root.getLeft());
    traversePostorder(root.getRight());
    System.out.println(root.getValue());  // Visit root last
  }
}
```

54

Consider the following binary tree:

```
        1
      /   \
     2     3
      \   /\
       4 5  6
        /\
       7  8
```

Which of the following sequences describes the preorder traversal of this tree?

(A)   1 2 3 4 5 6 7 8
(B)   1 2 4 3 5 7 8 6
(C)   1 4 2 3 5 6 7 8
(D)   4 2 1 3 6 5 8 7
(E)   2 4 1 7 5 8 3 6

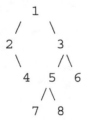 In preorder traversal we visit the root first, then the left subtree, and then the right subtree. So the correct sequence should begin with 1, followed by 2, and it should end with 6. The answer is B.

55

Consider the following incomplete implementation of a method `isEqual` that compares two trees:

```
// postcondition:  Returns true if the trees referred to by root1
//                 and root2 have the same shape and contain
//                 the same information in the corresponding nodes,
//                 false otherwise
public boolean isEqual (TreeNode root1, TreeNode root2)
{
  if (root1 == null && root2 == null)
  {
    return true;
  }
  else if (root1 == null || root2 == null)
  {
    return false;
  }
  else
  {
    return < expression >;
  }
}
```

Consider the following two replacements for *< expression >* :

I. "Preorder":

```
root1.getValue().equals(root2.getValue()) &&
isEqual(root1.getLeft(), root2.getLeft()) &&
isEqual(root1.getRight(), root2.getRight())
```

II. "Postorder":

```
isEqual(root1.getLeft(), root2.getLeft()) &&
isEqual(root1.getRight(), root2.getRight()) &&
root1.getValue().equals(root2.getValue())
```

Suppose `root1` and `root2` point to the following trees:

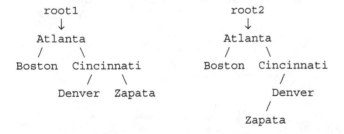

How many times will `String`'s `equals` method execute in each of the two implementations when `isEqual(root1, root2)` is called?

	Preorder	Postorder
(A)	1	0
(B)	3	2
(C)	3	1
(D)	4	1
(E)	4	4

☞ This is not an easy question because you have to approach it in just the right way. Also you have to keep short-circuit evaluation in mind. The preorder implementation compares all nodes in corresponding places, starting at the root, then the left subtree and right subtree, and proceeds for as long as they match. So it will verify the match for "Atlanta," "Boston," "Cincinnati," and "Denver." This eliminates A, B, and C. In the postorder implementation we compare <u>only the nodes in corresponding places whose left and right subtrees match</u>. There is only one such node here, "Boston" (a leaf). The answer is D. ☜

56

Consider an incomplete implementation of the following method:

```
// precondition:  root refers to the root of a binary tree;
// postcondition: Returns an array with two elements:
//                info[0] is set to the count of all nodes
//                in the tree that match target; info[1]
//                is set to the sum of the lengths of paths
//                from the root to such nodes
public int[] totalPaths(TreeNode root, Object target)
{
  int[] info = new int[2];  // info[0] = 0; info[1] = 0; by default

  if (root != null)
  {
    int[] infoLeft = totalPaths(root.getLeft(), target);
    int[] infoRight = totalPaths(root.getRight(), target);
    int count, pathsSum;

    < missing code >

    info[0] = count;
    info[1] = pathsSum;
  }
  return info;
}
```

Which of the following code segments completes the method so that it works as specified?

I.
```
count = infoLeft[0] + infoRight[0];
if (root.getValue().equals(target))
{
  count++;
}
pathsSum = infoLeft[1] + infoRight[1] + 2;
```

II.
```
count = infoLeft[0] + infoRight[0];
if (root.getValue().equals(target))
{
  count++;
}
pathsSum = infoLeft[1] + infoLeft[0] +
           infoRight[1] + infoRight[0];
```

III.
```
count = 0;
pathsSum = 0;
if (infoLeft[0] > 0)
{
  count += infoLeft[0];
  pathsSum += (infoLeft[1] + infoLeft[0]);
}
if (infoRight[0] > 0)
{
  count += infoRight[0];
  pathsSum += (infoRight[1] + infoRight[0]);
}
if (root.getValue().equals(target))
{
  count++;
}
```

(A) I only
(B) II only
(C) III only
(D) I and II
(E) II and III

☞ You might be asked to write something like the `totalPaths` method in the free-response section of the exam.

In this method, the values returned from the recursive step have to be adjusted in order to work for the top level. We find the sum of the lengths of all paths that start in the root's left child, but now these paths have to be extended to the root. So we have to add 1 to the length of each path, and we can achieve that by adding the number of matching nodes, `infoLeft[0]`, to the total length of the paths, `infoLeft[1]`. We do the same, of course, for the right subtree. Hence

```
pathsSum = infoLeft[1] + infoLeft[0] + infoRight[1] + infoRight[0];
```

Segment I should be rejected because it adds 2 to `pathsSum` whether or not any matching nodes are found in the subtrees; it fails, for instance, if the tree has just one node. This eliminates A and D. It is possible to verify formally that Segments II and III give the same result. Indeed, after a call to `totalPaths`, if `info[0]` is 0 then `info[1]` is 0, too. Therefore, the `if (info...[0] > 0)` statements in Segment III are redundant, though the code still works. The answer is E.

Binary Search Trees

Binary Search Trees (BSTs) are structures that organize information for rapid searching. They directly implement the divide and conquer method, similar to Binary Search in sorted arrays, but they also allow relatively fast insertions and removals of elements (the time is roughly proportional to log *n*, where *n* is the total number of nodes). The nodes of a BST contain values for which an order relation (less than, greater than, equals to) is established. In the AP subset, BSTs hold `Comparable` objects and all nodes contain different values.

> **The following is the defining property of a BST: each node is greater than all the nodes in its left subtree and smaller than all the nodes in its right subtree.**

This property allows us to write a simple and quick search method. For example:

```
// precondition:  root points to a BST; target is not null
// postcondition: Returns the node that contains target or null
//                if target is not in the tree
public TreeNode find(TreeNode root, Object target)
{
  if (root == null)
    return null;
  int compResult = ((Comparable)target).compareTo(root.getValue());
  if (compResult == 0)
    return root;
  else if (compResult < 0)    // target is less than root
    return find(root.getLeft(), target);
  else // if (compResult > 0)
    return find(root.getRight(), target);
}
```

> **Inorder traversal of a BST produces the sequence of its nodes in ascending order.**

The `java.util.TreeSet` and `java.util.TreeMap` classes use BSTs.

57

A binary search tree is built by inserting the following values in this order:

```
"F" "L" "O" "R" "I" "D" "A"
```

The nodes are appended as leaves in the appropriate places as determined by their alphabetical ordering. Which of the following sequences corresponds to the preorder traversal of the resulting binary search tree?

(A)   F L O R I D A
(B)   A D F I L O R
(C)   F D A L I O R
(D)   R O L I F D A
(E)   I D A F O L R

 Since "F" is inserted first, it becomes the root and will be the first in preorder traversal. This eliminates B, D, and E. Choice A would work if it were a queue, not a binary search tree. The answer is C.

Note that if you were asked to arrange the letters of "FLORIDA" into a binary search tree with the smallest possible number of levels —

```
        I
       / \
      D   O
     /\   /\
    A  F L  R
```

— then the answer would be E.

The average search time in a BST is approximately proportional to the average length of a path from the root to a node.

> If a BST tree is "bushy," with all its levels almost filled with nodes, the search time is roughly proportional to log n (where n is the number of nodes). But in the worst case, when a tree deteriorates into an almost linear structure, with only a few nodes in each level, then the search time may become proportional to n.

5.6. Hashing

Hashing is a method for storing information in which the value of an item (or the value of the key of an item) translates directly into its location in a *hash table*. Ideally, hashing provides instantaneous access to data (more precisely, the search time is constant regardless of the number of elements).

A typical hash table is a one-dimensional array of fixed size. Some elements of the array contain stored information, others may be empty. A *hash method* is provided that translates the value of an element into an integer in the range from 0 to *size* - 1, which serves as an index into the array.

Hash tables are similar to lookup tables, but not quite the same. In a lookup table, the function that converts values into indices is always a one-to-one mapping, so each value is mapped onto a unique index into the table and therefore can be found without any ambiguity.

> **In hash tables, different values can be mapped into the same location in the table (i.e., the same index). These situations are called *collisions*.**

Hash tables are used when lookup tables would take too much space to be practical. A good hashing method spreads the values uniformly in the table, minimizing the number of collisions. Still, some way to resolve collisions is needed.

A common way to resolve collisions is by *chaining*. In *chaining*, each element of the hash table is not just one value, but a *bucket*, something that has <u>its own storage</u>. For example, a bucket may be a list. Finding a value in such a table involves first computing the index for the bucket, then finding the target value in the bucket. In a good hash table the buckets remain small, containing just a few elements.

The `java.util.HashSet` and `java.util.HashMap` classes use a hash table to implement `Set` and `Map`, respectively. These classes assume that objects in a set (or keys in a map) have a reasonable `hashCode` method. In Java, the `Object` class has a generic `hashCode` method, so every object has this method. More specific types of objects (`Strings`, `Integers`, etc.) have their own `hashCode` methods defined. It is a good idea to appropriately redefine the generic `hashCode` method for your class. Usually this is accomplished by combining calls to `hashCode` for some of the data members of the class. A `hashCode` method returns an integer from the whole integer range. That value is further mapped for a particular hash table to the range from 0 to table size - 1.

To resolve collisions, `HashSet` and `HashMap` rely on the `equals` method. (Recall that `TreeSet` relies on the `compareTo` method.) In order for `HashSet` and `TreeSet` to treat their elements the same way, all three methods, `compareTo`, `equals`, and `hashCode`, must agree with each other:

> `x.compareTo(y) == 0` if and only if `x.equals(y) == true`;
> If `x.equals(y)` then `x.hashCode() == y.hashCode()`

58

A class `SSN` has a data member `String ssn` that represents a nine-digit social security number as a string. The method `getDigit(k)` returns the *k*-th decimal digit of the number as an `int`. Which of the following would be the most appropriate code for `SSN`'s `hashCode` method?

(A)
```
return ssn.hashCode();
```

(B)
```
return 100 * ssn.hashCode();
```

(C)
```
Random gen = new Random();
return gen.nextInt(1000) * ssn.hashCode();
```

(D)
```
int i;
int sum = 0;
for (i = 0; i < ssn.length(); i++)
{
   sum += getDigit(k);
}
return sum;
```

(E)
```
int i;
int sum = 0;
Random gen = new Random();
for (i = 0; i < ssn.length(); i++)
{
   sum += gen.nextInt(100) * getDigit(k);
}
return sum;
```

☞ A `hashCode` method may seem to do "random" things with an object, but using random numbers in the calculation is a bad idea because the method must be predictable: it must always return the same result for the same object. Choices C and E test your understanding of that. Choice B results in hash codes that are too sparse: they may only fall on multiples of 100. In D, the range of all possible results is from 0 to 81 — not enough to cover the `int` range. We have to believe that the experts who wrote the `String` class knew what they were doing. The answer is A. ☜

5.7. Priority Queues, Heaps, and Heapsort

A priority queue is a storage structure that allows you to retrieve items in order of their priority or rank. A priority queue is controlled by two operations: *add* adds an item and *removeMin* removes and returns the smallest item. In this convention, the smallest item has the highest priority or rank. Priority queues are used for processing events (messages, orders, bids) in order of their priority. A priority queue can hold several items of the same priority.

The Development Committee's PriorityQueue interface has four methods:

```
public interface PriorityQueue
{
  boolean isEmpty();
  void add(Object x);
  Object removeMin();
  Object peekMin();        // Returns the smallest item without
                           //   removing it from the priority queue
}
```

A standard implementation is not provided.

It is not hard to implement a priority queue using an ArrayList. For example:

```
public class ArrayPriorityQueue implements PriorityQueue
{
  private List items;

  public ArrayPriorityQueue()  { items = new ArrayList(); }

  public boolean isEmpty() { return items.size() == 0; }
  public void add(Object x) { items.add(x); }
  public Object removeMin() { return items.remove(findMin()); }
  public Object peekTop() { return items.get(findMin()); }

  private int findMin()
  {
    int i, iMin = 0;
    for (i = 1; i < items.size(); i++)
      if (((Comparable)items.get(i)).compareTo(items.get(iMin)) < 0)
        iMin = i;
    return iMin;
  }
}
```

However, the removeMin and peekMin methods in this implementation are not very efficient: you have to scan through the whole list to find the minimum value. A more efficient implementation of a priority queue uses a particular type of binary tree called a *heap*.

A heap is a binary tree with two additional properties:

1. **Completeness — each level, except perhaps the bottom one, is filled with nodes. The last level may have nodes missing on the right side.**

2. **Ordering — each node is smaller than or equal to all the nodes in its left and right subtrees.**

For example:

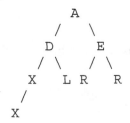

It is easy to find the smallest node in a heap — it is at the root.

The completeness property allows us to store a heap in an array. The nodes are simply stored in order of scanning all levels top to bottom, left to right. In Java implementations, it is convenient to leave the first element of the array unused, because in algorithms that handle heaps it is easier to have the root of the heap in the element of the array with the subscript 1. The above tree, for example, may be stored as

```
<empty> A D E X L R R X
```

In this scheme, `a[1]` is the root. If `a[i]` is a node, its parent is found in `a[i/2]` and its left and right children, if present, are found in `a[2*i]` and `a[2*i+1]`.

In the heap implementation, `removeMin` removes the root of the heap and returns its value. After the root is removed, the heap is repaired by moving its last leaf (that is, the rightmost node in the bottom row) to the root and then "reheaping it down" until the ordering property is restored. "Reheaping down" is swapping the node that is out of order with its smallest child until it falls into place.

A node is inserted by adding it as a new leaf to the bottom row, then "reheaping it up" until the ordering is restored. "Reheaping up" is swapping the node that is out of order with its parent until it falls into place.

The time of both removal and insertion operations, on average as well as in the worst case, is roughly proportional to log *n*, where *n* is the number of nodes in the heap.

Heapsort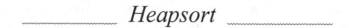

Another application of heaps is *Heapsort*.

> **Heapsort is an *n* log *n* sorting method. Heapsort does not require a temporary array.**

Suppose we have a list of values. In the first phase of the Heapsort we can start with an empty heap and insert all the values from the list into it. In the second phase we remove the values one by one from the top of the heap and store them back into the list. We will end up with a list sorted in ascending order.

If a list is stored in an array, there is an efficient algorithm that reorders its elements in the same space in such a way that the array becomes a representation of a heap (in this case, a "maximum" heap with the largest element in the root). We then remove the elements from the top of this heap and store them starting at the end of the same array in reverse order. This algorithm eliminates the need for an additional temporary array.

59

Suppose Heapsort is used to sort an array of nine elements in ascending order in the same place without additional space. The first phase of the algorithm rearranges the elements of the array to form a maximum heap (with the largest value at the root). In the second phase the elements are removed one by one from the top of the heap and placed in order starting at the end of the array. Suppose the following sequence represents a heap built after the first phase of Heapsort:

   9 6 8 3 4 7 5 2 1

Which of the following sequences may represent the elements of the array after two iterations through the second phase of Heapsort?

(A) 6 3 4 7 5 2 1 8 9
(B) 7 5 1 2 6 3 4 8 9
(C) 8 9 6 3 4 7 5 2 1
(D) 9 6 8 5 4 7 1 2 3
(E) 7 6 5 3 4 1 2 8 9

☞ After two iterations, the two largest elements, 9 and 8, must be in place at the end of the array. This eliminates C and D. The next largest element, 7, must be at the top of the heap, that is, at the beginning of the array. This eliminates A. To decide between B and E we have to find out which one represents a heap in its first seven elements. It has to be E because in a maximum heap the smallest element, 1, must be a leaf, and all the leaves have to be clustered in the second half of the array. The answer is E. If you find this solution too tricky, you can get the same answer by running the data through the actual Heapsort algorithm, but that may require more work. ☜

5.8.   Big-O Analysis

In previous chapters we have several times said things like "the number of required comparisons is approximately proportional to n^2" or "the running time is roughly proportional to log n." What exactly does "approximately" or "roughly" mean? "Big-O" provides a formal definition and notation for the concept of *order of growth*.

A formal definition of "Big-O" can be found in many textbooks. Here we only give a practical rule:

> **If we have two functions, $f(n)$ and $g(n)$, and the ratio $f(n)/g(n)$ approaches a positive constant as n increases without bound, then we can say that f and g have the same order of growth, and we can write:**
>
> $f(n) = O(g(n))$

The order of growth definition disregards a constant factor: $f(n) = O(k \cdot f(n))$ for any constant $k > 0$.

In the analysis of algorithms, an integer n defines the size of a task: the number of elements in an array to be sorted; the number of nodes in a list or a set, and so on. The time or space requirements for an algorithm can be expressed in terms of $O(f(n))$. We use several standard reference functions to which we compare the rates of growth. The most common reference functions are:

1	(constant)	n log n	("n log n")
log n	(logarithmic)	n^2	(quadratic)
n	(linear)		

> **If $f(n)$ is a polynomial of degree k, then $f(n) = O(n^k)$.**

For example,

$$\frac{n(n-1)}{2} = \frac{n^2}{2} - \frac{n}{2} = O(n^2)$$

Most often we are interested in the running time. Table 5-2 shows big-O time requirements for some of the common algorithms discussed earlier. The table assumes that the algorithm is implemented in an optimal way and lists the <u>average</u> big-O performance. There may be best-case and worst-case scenarios whose big-O is different. Table 5-3 shows the average, best, and worst cases for common algorithms. The worst case, in general, assumes that the algorithm is running on the data that takes the longest time to process.

There are also rules of thumb, but <u>you have to use them with caution</u>.

- If an algorithm uses a single loop, it's either $O(n)$ for straightforward sequential processing or $O(\log n)$ for divide and conquer methods.

- If an algorithm uses nested loops, it's either $O(n^2)$ for straightforward sequential iterations over a square or a triangle or $O(n \log n)$ for an algorithm with a divide and conquer component. The only "$n \log n$" algorithms that are specifically named in the AP program are Mergesort, Quicksort, and Heapsort.

Big-O	Algorithm
$O(1)$ — "constant"	<ul><li>Appending an element at the end of an array</li><li>Appending a node at the head of a linked list or at the head or tail of a doubly-linked list</li><li>Push and pop operations for a stack</li><li>Enqueue and dequeue operations for a queue</li><li>Retrieval/insertion in a hash table</li></ul>
$O(\log n)$ — "logarithmic"	<ul><li>Binary Search in a sorted array</li><li>Search and insertion in a binary search tree</li><li>Retrieval/insertion in a heap</li></ul>
$O(n)$ — "linear"	<ul><li>Sequential Search in an array</li><li>Traversals of lists or trees with n nodes</li><li>Calculating sums or products of n elements, e.g. $n!$</li></ul>
$O(n \log n)$ — "n-log-n"	<ul><li>Mergesort</li><li>Quicksort</li><li>Heapsort</li></ul>
$O(n^2)$ — "quadratic"	<ul><li>Selection Sort and Insertion Sort</li><li>Traversals of n-by-n 2-D arrays</li><li>Algorithms that take "triangular" nested loops</li></ul>

Table 5-2. Big-O Examples for Common Algorithms

	Best case	Average case	Worst case
Sequential Search	$O(1)$ — found right away	$O(n)$ — found on average in the middle	$O(n)$
Binary Search	$O(1)$ — found right away	$O(\log n)$	$O(\log n)$
Hash table search	$O(1)$ — found right away	$O(1)$ — small fixed-length buckets	$O(n)$ — table degenerated into one or two buckets
Search in a binary search tree	$O(1)$ — found right away	$O(\log n)$	$O(n)$ — tree degenerated into nearly a list
Selection Sort	$O(n^2)$	$O(n^2)$	$O(n^2)$
Insertion Sort	$O(n)$ — array already sorted	$O(n^2)$	$O(n^2)$
Mergesort	$O(n \log n)$, or $O(n)$ in a slightly modified version when the array is sorted	$O(n \log n)$	$O(n \log n)$
Quicksort	$O(n \log n)$	$O(n \log n)$	$O(n^2)$ — pivot is consistently chosen far from the median value, e.g., the array is already sorted and the first element is chosen as pivot
Heapsort	$O(n \log n)$	$O(n \log n)$	$O(n \log n)$
Insert a value into a heap	$O(1)$ — the value is the largest in the heap	$O(\log n)$	$O(\log n)$

Table 5-3. Best, Average, and Worst Case Big-O

60

The following method eliminates consecutive nodes with duplicate values from a linked list. For example, A→B→B→B→C→A→A becomes A→B→C→A.

```
public void skipDuplicates(ListNode head)
{
  ListNode p = head;
  ListNode p2;

  while (p != null)
  {
    p2 = p.getNext();
    while (p2 != null && p2.getValue().equals(p.getValue()))
    {
      p2 = p2.getNext();
    }
    p.setNext(p2);
    p = p.getNext();
  }
}
```

Which of the following best describes the best-case and worst-case running time for skipDuplicates on a list with *n* nodes?

        Best case: Worst case:

(A) $O(1)$ $O(n)$
(B) $O(n)$ $O(n)$
(C) $O(1)$ $O(n^2)$
(D) $O(n)$ $O(n^2)$
(E) $O(n^2)$ $O(n^2)$

No matter what exactly the "best case" is, the method has to examine every node of the list. The running time cannot possibly be constant; therefore, A and C are wrong answers. There is a case when all the nodes are different. In that case the inner loop is simply skipped, and we end up with a simple traversal of the list in one sequential loop. The running time in that case is $O(n)$, so E is not the right answer, either. We are left with B and D. This example is an exception to the rule of thumb: it has nested loops, so you might think the worst time might be $O(n^2)$. But this method eliminates <u>consecutive</u> duplicate values, not all duplicate values. The trick is that the outer loop doesn't necessarily go to the next node, but can jump over all the removed nodes. Even when all the nodes of the list are the same, each node is visited only once. We did warn you to use the rules of thumb with caution, didn't we? The answer is B.

Chapter 6. *Marine Biology Simulation* Case Study

6.1. Introduction

The *Marine Biology Simulation* (*MBS*) case study is a teaching and testing tool developed specifically for the AP Computer Science program. The case study involves a fairly large software project for modeling a population of fish in an environment. The case study materials include a narrative (150 pages), Java source code and class libraries, HTML documentation, and sample data files. All these materials are posted at the AP Central web site (click on A Guide to AP Central at http://www.skylit.com).

MBS models the environment as a rectangular grid in which each cell may be empty or may hold one fish. A fish can move to a vacant neighboring cell. One of the fish's attributes is its direction; a fish can only move forward and to the sides, but not backward. Fish also get a chance to breed and a chance to die. The simulation proceeds in discrete "timesteps." At each step all fish "act": each fish may move or breed, and may die. The later enhancements include different types of fish that "act" in different ways.

The MBS software includes several "visible" classes, provided with complete source code, and several "black-box" classes, provided in jar libraries. You need to be familiar with the implementations of some of the visible classes and the documentation for some of the black-box classes. These materials will be included in the reference booklet provided to you at the exam. Table 6-1 shows the MBS components tested on the A exam.

Implementation	Documentation only
`Simulation`	`Environment` (interface)
`Fish`	`Locatable` (interface)
`DarterFish`	`Location`
`SlowFish`	`Direction`
	`EnvDisplay` (interface)
	`RandNumGenerator`
	`Debug`

Table 6-1. MBS classes tested on the AP CS A-level exam

⌐ In addition, <u>for the AB exam</u>, you need to know the `Environment` interface and two classes that implement it: `BoundedEnv` and `UnboundedEnv`. ⌐

The "visible" classes also include three different classes with a `main` method (MBS calls them "drivers") : `SimpleMBSDemo1`, `SimpleMBSDemo2`, and `MBSGUI`.

The "driver" classes are not tested on the exams.

Chapter 2 of the MBS narrative provides an overview of the (A-level) required classes and interfaces using a top-down approach: it starts from the "core" classes and interfaces (`Fish`, `Simulation`, `Environment`) then proceeds to the low-level "utility" classes and interfaces (`Location`, `Locatable`, `Direction`, `RandNumGenerator`, `EnvDisplay`, and `Debug`). We take a complementary "bottom-up" approach: first take a look at the utility classes to get them out of the way, then review the core classes.

6.2. The Utility Classes and Interfaces

Location

A `Location` object represents a location on a two-dimensional grid (with integer coordinates). The `Location` class has one constructor —

```
public Location (int row, int col)
```

— and two accessor methods:

```
public int row()            //  Returns the row for this location
public int col()            //  Returns the column for this location
```

`Location` implements `Comparable` and provides a `compareTo` method, something like this (adapted from the actual code):

```
public int compareTo(Object other)
{
  Location otherLoc = (Location)other;
  if (row() == otherLoc.row())
    return col() - otherLoc.col();
  else
    return row() - otherLoc.row();
}
```

If *this* and *other* are in the same row, the one to the left is considered "smaller." Otherwise a location is considered "smaller" than any location in a row below it.

`Location` also provides the `equals` method, something like this:

```
public boolean equals(Object other)
{
  Location otherLoc = (Location)other;
  return row() == otherLoc.row() && col() == otherLoc.col();
}
```

`Location`'s `toString` method converts a location into a string:

```
public String toString()
{
  return "(" + row() + ", " + col() + ")";
}
```

The Locatable interface

The `Locatable` interface specifies one method,

```
Location location();
```

In MBS, `Fish` are `Locatable` objects. In general, a class may implement `Locatable` if its objects are to be placed on a two dimensional grid.

Direction

The `Direction` class represents a compass direction. Directions are measured in degrees, starting from 0 for the "North" direction and going clockwise (90 degrees corresponds to "East," etc.). The class has three constructors:

```
public Direction()            // Creates a default direction -- North
public Direction(int degrees) // Creates a direction for degrees
public Direction(String str)  // Creates a direction named in str:
                              //   "north", "northeast", "east", etc.
                              //   (uses case-blind comparison of strings)
```

The methods are:

```
public int inDegrees()          // Returns this direction in degrees
public Direction toRight()      // Returns a direction obtained by rotating
                                //   this 90 degrees clockwise
public Direction
       toRight(int degrees)     // Returns a direction obtained by rotating
                                //   this by degrees clockwise
public Direction toLeft()       // Returns a direction obtained by rotating
                                //   this 90 degrees counterclockwise
public Direction
       toLeft(int degrees)      // Returns a direction obtained by rotating
                                //   this by degrees counterclockwise
public Direction reverse()      // Returns the opposite direction
public Direction
       equals(Object other)     // Returns true if this is equal to other
public String toString()        // Returns either the name or "x degrees"
```

The `Direction` class also provides eight public static `Direction` constants: NORTH, NORTHEAST, EAST, and so on, which you can use in client classes. For example:

```
Direction dir = Direction.SOUTH;
```

Finally, `Direction` supplies a static method `randomDirection`, which returns a random direction from 0 to 359 degrees.

> **Note that both `Location` and `Direction` objects are immutable.**

In MBS, a `Fish` object has `Location` and `Direction` attributes; the `Fish` class implements the `Locatable` interface.

The `EnvDisplay` interface

`EnvDisplay` isolates the model from a particular implementation of the display class. It specifies one method:

```
void showEnv();
```

A class that implements `EnvDisplay` has a constructor that takes an `Environment` object as a parameter — that's how `showEnv()` knows what to show.

RandNumGenerator

This class has only one method,

```
static Random getInstance()
```

Its purpose is to give us the same `Random` object whenever we need random numbers. Recall that `java.util.Random` is a library class, which has `nextInt(n)` and `nextDouble` methods. If we created a different `Random` object in every method that needs a few random numbers —

```
Random gen = new Random();
...
int x = gen.nextInt(3);
```

— the behavior of the program would be hard to control. `RandNumGenerator` is a helper "singleton" class in which a `Random` object is constructed only once, when a `RandNumGenerator` is created; then its `getInstance` method returns the same `Random` object and the application draws random numbers from the same sequence:

```
public class RandNumGenerator
{
  private static Random theRandNumGenerator = new Random();

  public static Random getInstance()
  {
    return theRandNumGenerator;
  }
}
```

`Random`'s no-args constructor "seeds" the sequence of random numbers using the system clock as a parameter. This results in a different sequence of random numbers for each run of the program. We can provide a "seed" parameter to `Random`'s constructor or call the `Random`'s `setSeed` method. For example:

```
...
private static Random theRandNumGenerator = new Random(2010);
...
```

With this change, the program will use the same sequence of random numbers on each run — a useful trick for getting reproducible test results.

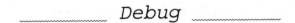

Debug

This class provides static `print` and `println` methods, similar to the ones in `System.out`. However, these printouts can be easily turned on or off by calling `Debug`'s `turnOn` and `turnOff` methods. All `Debug`'s methods are static. The full list is as follows:

```
static boolean isOn()
static boolean isOff()
static void turnOn()
static void turnOff()
static void restoreState()      // Restores the state in effect before
                                //   the last call to turnOn or turnOff
static void print(String msg)
static void println(String msg)
```

Call `Debug.turnOn()` to print diagnostic messages throughout the program.

6.3. The `Environment` Interface

`Environment` represents a two-dimensional grid that can hold `Locatable` objects. `Environment` is an interface; it is designed to shield `Fish` and `Simulation` classes from a particular implementation of the environment. `Environment` is somewhat abstract, but it clearly has the underlying model of a rectangular grid. It would not be very easy to extend it to an arbitrary shape.

A direct implementation (as in `BoundedEnv`) implements it as a two-dimensional array of `Locatable` objects, but `Environment` can also be implemented as a list of `Locatable` objects, as in `UnboundedEnv`. ⌈ Only <u>the AB exam</u> deals with specific implementations of `Environment`. ⌋

The `Environment` interface is shown in Figure 6-1. It has sixteen methods that roughly fall into three groups: "global geography," "topography," and "population." In fact, if you peek under the hood, you will find that the "topography" methods are implemented in a separate abstract class `SquareEnvironment`. (It is named "SquareEnvironment" not because it represents a square, but because it is an environment of squares: each cell has four sides.) "Global geography" and "population" methods are grouped in a subclass of `SquareEnvironment`: either `BoundedEnv` or `UnboundedEnv`. Figure 6-2 illustrates this design.

```
public interface Environment
{
  // "Global geography" methods:

  int numRows();                    // Returns -1 for unbounded environment
  int numCols();                    // Returns -1 for unbounded environment
  boolean isValid(Location loc);    // Returns true if loc is valid in this
                                    //    environment
  // "topography" methods:

  int numCellSides();               // Returns 4
  int numAdjacentNeighbors();       // Returns the number of adjacent
                                    //    neighbors around each cell: 4 or 8

  Direction randomDirection();      // Returns a random direction

  Direction getDirection(Location loc1, Location loc2);
                                    // Returns the direction from loc1 to loc2

  Location getNeighbor(Location loc, Direction dir);
                                    // Returns the adjacent neighbor of loc
                                    //    in the direction dir

  ArrayList neighborsOf(Location loc);
                                    // Returns a list of locations,
                                    //    neighbors of loc

  // "Population" methods:

  int numObjects();                 // Returns the total number of objects
                                    //    in this environment

  Locatable[] allObjects();         // Returns an array of all objects
                                    //    in this environment

  boolean isEmpty(Location loc);    // Returns true if loc is empty

  Locatable objectAt(Location loc);
                                    // Returns the object in loc or null
                                    //    if loc is empty

  void add(Locatable obj);          // Adds obj to this environment
  void remove(Locatable obj);       // Removes obj from this environment

  void recordMove(Locatable obj, Location oldLoc);
                                    // Updates this environment to reflect
                                    //    the move of obj from oldLoc
                                    //    to obj.location()
}
```

Figure 6-1. The Environment interface

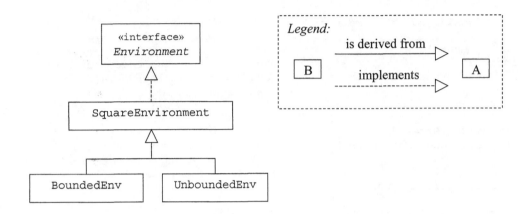

Figure 6-2. Environment and its implementations

"Global geography" methods

The three "global geography" methods define the dimensions of the environment and what is a valid location. `numRows` and `numCols` return the number of rows and columns in the grid, respectively, for a bounded environment, and -1 for an unbounded environment. `isValid(Location loc)` returns `true` if `loc` is a valid location. Like this:

```
public class BoundedEnv extends SquareEnvironment
{
    ...
  public boolean isValid(Location loc)
  {
    return loc != null && loc.row() >= 0 && loc.row() < numRows() &&
                          loc.col() >= 0 && loc.col() < numCols();
  }
    ...
}
```

Or:

```
public class UnboundedEnv extends SquareEnvironment
{
    ...
  public boolean isValid(Location loc)
  {
    return loc != null;
  }
    ...
}
```

"Topography" methods

The six "topography" methods deal with the neighbors of a cell. numCellSides returns 4, reassuring us that a cell is a square. numAdjacentNeighbors returns either 4 or 8 — it tells us whether diagonally touching cells are considered neighbors or not. This is defined by a parameter passed to SquareEnvironment's constructor. The no-args constructor creates an environment with no diagonal neighbors: each cell has 4 neighbors. The other constructor takes a boolean parameter (true for allowing the diagonal neighbors) and is apparently reserved for exercises (and perhaps exam questions).

getDirection(Location loc1, Location loc2) returns a Direction corresponding to a vector from loc1 to loc2, rounded to the nearest multiple of 45 degrees (for 8 neighbors) or 90 degrees (for 4 neighbors).

randomDirection returns a randomly chosen direction to an adjacent cell. Something like this:

```
public Direction randomDirection()
{
  Random gen = RandNumGenerator.getInstance();
  int count = numAdjacentNeighbors();
  int n = gen.nextInt(count);
  return new Direction(n * 360 / count);
}
```

getNeighbor(Location loc, Direction dir) returns a neighboring location obtained by going from loc in the direction dir.

Finally, neighborsOf(Location loc) returns an ArrayList of all the valid neighboring locations of loc. Something like this:

```
public ArrayList neighborsOf(Location loc)
{
  ArrayList nbrs = new ArrayList();

  Direction dir = Direction.NORTH;
  int count = numAdjacentNeighbors();

  for (int i = 0; i < count; i++)
  {
    Location nbrLoc = getNeighbor(loc, dir);
    if (isValid(nbrLoc))
      nbrs.add(nbrLoc);
    dir = dir.toRight(360 / count);
  }
  return nbrs;
}
```

The above code segments are <u>not</u> required for the exam. We show them only to give you a feel for how the "topography" methods work and how `RandNumGenerator` and `ArrayList` are used.

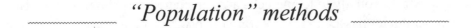

"Population" methods

An environment holds `Locatable` objects. `isEmpty(Location loc)` returns `true` if `loc` is a valid location that does not hold an object. `objectAt(Location loc)` returns the object stored in `loc`, or `null` if `loc` is empty. `numObjects` returns the total number of objects in this environment. `allObjects` returns an <u>array</u> (not an `ArrayList`!) of all the objects in this environment. Something like this:

```
public Locatable[] allObjects()
{
  Locatable[] objects = new Locatable[numObjects()];
  ... // etc.
  return objects;
}
```

`add(Locatable obj)` adds `obj` to the environment. `obj` is placed at its appropriate location, `obj.location()`, which must be empty. `remove(Locatable obj)` removes `obj` from its location. `obj` must be the exact object currently stored in `obj.location()`. If it isn't, `remove` throws an exception:

```
if (objectAt(obj.location()) !=  obj)
   throw new IllegalArgumentException("Cannot remove " +
                                      obj + "; not there");
```

`recordMove(Locatable obj, Location oldLoc)` updates the environment when `obj` "moves" from `oldLoc` to its new location. This method assumes that only `obj` knows it has moved: its new location is `obj.location()`, but `obj`'s environment still doesn't know that. As far as the environment is concerned, `obj == objectAt(oldLoc)` while `obj.location()` is empty. If any of these conditions is false, the method throws an exception. If all is in order, the method makes `oldLoc` empty and places `obj` where it belongs, in `obj.location()`. Calling `recordMove` is like filing a change-of-address form for `obj` with the environment.

61

Consider the following method:

```
// precondition:   loc1 and loc2 are both valid locations in env
// postcondition:  Returns true if loc1 and loc2 are neighbors;
//                 false otherwise
public boolean areNeighbors(Environment env, Location loc1, Location loc2)
{
  return < expression >;
}
```

Which of the following replacements for *< expression >* will make this method work as specified?

I. ```
    env.getNeighbor(loc1,
          env.getDirection(loc1, loc2)) == loc2;
    ```

II. ```
    env.getNeighbor(loc1,
          env.getDirection(loc1, loc2)).equals(loc2);
    ```

III. ```
     env.neighborsOf(loc1).contains
                  (env.getDirection(loc1, loc2));
     ```

(A)  I only
(B)  II only
(C)  III only
(D)  I and II
(E)  II and III

The idea in Options I and II is to first get the direction from loc1 to loc2, then create a neighboring location from loc1 in that direction and compare it to loc2. If loc2 is a neighbor, these locations must be equal. But they won't be the same object! So Option II is correct while Option I is wrong, because == compares addresses of objects. In Option III, neighborsOf returns a list of <u>locations</u>, and a list of locations cannot contain a direction. (An ArrayList does have a method contains, but it is not in the AP subset.) The answer is B.
     ```

62

Suppose a class `Checker` is defined as shown below:

```
public class Checker implements Locatable
{
  public Checker (Color color, Location loc)
         { myLoc = loc, myColor = color; }
  public Color getColor() { return myColor; }
  public Location location() { return myLoc; }
  public void move(Location newLoc) { myLoc = newLoc; }

  private Color myColor;
  private Location myLoc;
}
```

Another class, `CheckerBoard`, implements `Environment`. Consider the following method in a client class `CheckersGame`:

```
public boolean jump(CheckerBoard board, Location loc, direction dir)
{
  if (dir.inDegrees() % 45 != 0)  // only diagonal jumps are allowed
    return false;
  if (dir.inDegrees() % 90 == 0)
    return false;
  if (!board.isValid(loc) || board.isEmpty(loc))
    return false;
  Location loc2 = board.getNeighbor(loc, dir);
  if (!board.isValid(loc2) || board.isEmpty(loc2))
    return false;
  Location loc3 = board.getNeighbor(loc2, dir);
  if (!board.isValid(loc3) || !board.isEmpty(loc3))
    return false;

  Checker chk1 = (Checker)board.objectAt(loc);
  Checker chk2 = (Checker)board.objectAt(loc2);
  if (chk1.getColor().equals(chk2.getColor()))
    return false;

  // chk1 is moved from loc to loc3; loc2 is emptied:

  board.remove(chk2);
  < missing statements >

  return true;
}
```

Which of the following replacements for < *missing statements* > will make this method work as specified?

(A) `chk1.move(loc3);`

(B) `board.recordMove(chk1, loc3);`

(C) `board.recordMove(chk1, loc3);`
     `chk1.move(loc3);`

(D) `chk1.move(loc3);`
     `board.recordMove(chk1, loc);`

(E) `board.remove(chk1);`
     `board.add(new Checker(chk1, loc3));`

☞ This is not a real multiple-choice question, of course, just some practice in reading MBS-type code and using MBS utility classes and `Environment` methods. Note how general and reusable the `Environment` interface and classes are: we can use them to hold fish or to program a checkers game.

Choices A through D attempt to move `chk1` from `loc` to `loc3`, while Choice E tries to remove `chk1` and create an identical object in `loc3`. The latter approach could potentially work, but it is not in the spirit of MBS. Also, the wrong argument is passed to the constructor: it should be

```
add(new Checker(chk1.getColor(), loc3));
```

Choices A through D clearly hinge on the right way to move and "record" a move. Choice A doesn't call `recordMove` at all, so it can't be right: we move `chk1` but the board doesn't know about it! Choice B forgets to move `chk1` before recording the move and also passes the wrong argument (the new location instead of the old one) to `recordMove`. It pretends that `recordMove` itself moves the object. Choice C does things in reverse order: you have to move the object first, then record the move in the environment. The answer is D. ☜

6.4. The `Fish` Class

_____ *Attributes and constructors* _____

A `Fish` object has the following attributes: ID, color, location, and direction. A fish also holds a reference to its environment. All of the above are represented as private instance variables:

```
private Environment theEnv;     // environment in which the fish lives
private int myId;               // unique ID for this fish
private Location myLoc;         // fish's location
private Direction myDir;        // fish's direction
private Color myColor;          // fish's color
```

The `Fish` class has three constructors:

```
public Fish (Environment env, Location loc)
public Fish (Environment env, Location loc, Direction dir)
public Fish (Environment env, Location loc, Direction dir, Color col)
```

A constructor sets the fish's ID to the next sequential number. The `Fish` has a *class* (static) variable —

```
private static int nextAvailableID = 1;   // next avail unique identifier
```

— initially set to 1. All fish share this variable, and it is incremented whenever a new fish is created.

A constructor that does not receive a color parameter sets the fish's color to `randomColor()`, a `Color` object with random RGB components. Something like this:

```
protected Color randomColor()
{
    // red, green, and blue intensities of a color range from 0 to 255
    Random gen = RandNumGenerator.getInstance();
    return new Color(gen.nextInt(256),    // amount of red
                     gen.nextInt(256),    // amount of green
                     gen.nextInt(256));   // amount of blue
}
```

Likewise, if a direction parameter is not provided, the constructor sets it to `env.randomDirection()`, a random direction.

To avoid duplication of code in `Fish`'s constructors, `Fish` has a private method

```
private void initialize(Environment env, Location loc,
                                     Direction dir, Color col)
```

called from its constructors. Normally this wouldn't be necessary: the first two constructors could simply call the third one using `this`. For example:

```
public Fish (Environment env, Location loc)
{
   this (env, loc, env.randomDirection(), randomColor());
}
```

But calling one constructor from another using `this(...)` is not in the AP subset. Hence

```
public Fish (Environment env, Location loc)
{
   initialize (env, loc, env.randomDirection(), randomColor());
}
```

The constructors not only create a fish object, but also add it to the environment:

```
private void initialize(Environment env, Location loc,
                                     Direction dir, Color col)
{
  theEnv = env;
  myId = nextAvailableID;
  nextAvailableID++;
  myLoc = loc;
  myDir = dir;
  myColor = col;
  theEnv.add(this);
}
```

This is a somewhat unusual design decision. Normally a constructor does not modify other objects. Adding fish to the environment should probably have been done separately, after the fish is created. Here it happens as a side effect of creating the fish.

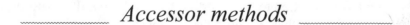

Accessor methods

`Fish` has five accessor methods:

```
public Environment environment() { return theEnv; }
public int id() {return myId; }
public Location location() { return myLoc; }
public Direction direction() {return myDir; }
public Color color() { return myColor; }
```

`Fish` implements `Locatable`.

Fish's toString method combines all the attributes in one String:

```
public String toString()
{
  return id() + location().toString() + direction().toString();
}
```

The Fish class also has a boolean method isInEnv that checks whether this fish is indeed in the right place in the environment:

```
public boolean isInEnv()
{
  return environment().objectAt(location()) == this;
}
```

As we have seen, when a fish is created it is added to its environment. When a fish moves, it updates its environment (by calling recordMove). But in theory a fish may be removed from the environment without its knowledge (by calling the environment's remove method). isInEnv checks whether this fish and its environment are in a consistent state (mainly for debugging purposes).

 *Action methods*

Initially (in Chapter 2 of the MBS Narrative), the only action a fish can take is move, but later (in Chapter 3, called "Dynamic Population"), fish also breed and die. We will proceed with this enhanced Fish class and consider all fish actions together. To support a dynamic population, two instance variables are added to the Fish class:

```
private double probOfBreeding;
private double probOfDying;
```

They define the probability of breeding or dying, respectively, in each "timestep" (i.e., each call to act). initialize sets probOfBreeding to 1/7 and probOfDying to 1/5.

In this model, when a fish is called to "act," it first tries to breed. If unsuccessful, it tries to move. Finally it checks whether it should die. Something like this:

```
public void act()
{
  if (!isInEnv())
    return;

  if (!breed())
    move();

  Random gen = RandNumGenerator.getInstance();
  if (gen.nextDouble() < probOfDying)
    die();
}
```

According to the specs provided by "marine biologists," a fish moves to a randomly chosen vacant neighboring location, but not backward. It breeds by placing offspring into all vacant neighboring locations.

This functionality calls for a helper method emptyNeighbors that returns a list (an ArrayList) of all vacant neighboring locations of this fish. This method is declared protected, which makes it still accessible in Fish's subclasses. protected methods are supposed to be inaccessible outside of the hierarchy of subclasses, but, for some reason, this is not the case in the current implementation of the Java compiler. Strictly speaking, protected class members are not in the AP subset, but you are supposed to know to call protected methods only from the same class and its subclasses and never from clients.

emptyNeighbors works like this:

```
protected ArrayList emptyNeighbors()
{
  ArrayList allNbrs = environment().neighborsOf(location());
  ArrayList emptyNbrs = new ArrayList();

  for (int i = 0; i < allNbrs.size(); i++)
  {
    Location loc = (Location) allNbrs.get(i);
    if (environment().isEmpty(loc))
      emptyNbrs.add(loc);
  }
  return emptyNbrs;
}
```

The breed and die methods

The breed method (with comments and debugging printouts removed) looks like this:

```
protected boolean breed()
{
  Random gen = RandNumGenerator.getInstance();
  if (gen.nextDouble() >= probOfBreeding )
    return false;

  ArrayList emptyNbrs = emptyNeighbors();
  if (emptyNbrs.size() == 0)
    return false;

  for (int i = 0; i < emptyNbrs.size(); i++)
  {
    Location loc = (Location)emptyNbrs.get(i);
    generateChild(loc);
  }
  return true;
}


protected void generateChild(Location loc)
{
  Fish child = new Fish(environment(), loc,
                    environment().randomDirection(), color());
}
```

Note that the new fish is added to the environment as a <u>side effect</u> of Fish's constructor. As we said earlier, it would be more appropriate to add a new fish to the environment explicitly: theEnv.add(this) should be removed from the constructor and a corresponding statement should be added here:

```
Fish child = new Fish(environment(), loc,
                  environment().randomDirection(), color());
environment().add(child);
```

Which of the following is the most compelling reason for having a separate generateChild method as opposed to integrating its code directly into breed?

(A)   A separate generateChild method improves code readability
(B)   generateChild is also called from Fish's constructors
(C)   generateChild may be called from other Fish's methods
(D)   generateChild may be called from Fish's subclasses
(E)   generateChild may be redefined in Fish's subclasses

A is simply false: it is easier to see right away what the statement does rather that go looking for it in another method. B is false and C is unlikely: why would we want to generate a child of a fish outside the `breed` method? D is unlikely too: if we define a different type of fish, why would its offspring revert to the more generic type `Fish`? It is the last option that is important: if `SpecialFish` extends `Fish`, we want `SpecialFish`'s `generateChild` to create a new instance of `SpecialFish`, not `Fish`. (A special fish will have special children.) What we want is this:

```
public class SpecialFish extends Fish
{
    ...
  protected void generateChild(Location loc)
  {
    Fish child = new SpecialFish(environment(), loc,
                        environment().randomDirection(), color());
  }
    ...
}
```

If `generateChild`'s code were integrated directly into `breed`, we would have to redefine the whole `breed` method in `SpecialFish`, duplicating most of its code. The answer is E.

That's all there is to breeding. Dying is much easier, though. Something like this:

```
protected void die()
{
  environment().remove(this);
}
```

The move method

Moving is the trickiest thing a fish does. A move involves the following steps:

1. Get a list of empty neighboring locations;

2. Remove from this list the one that would require moving backward;

3. Choose a random location from the list as the fish's new location;

4. Move the fish to the new location and record the move with the environment;

5. Set the fish's new direction to the direction of the move.

The `move` method accomplishes these tasks by calling helper methods: `nextLocation`, `changeLocation`, and `changeDirection`. `nextLocation` takes care of Steps 1-3, `changeLocation` takes care of Step 4, and `changeDirection` takes care of Step 5:

```
protected void move()
{
  Location oldLoc = location();
  Location newLoc = nextLocation();
  if (!newLoc.equals(oldLoc))
  {
    changeLocation(newLoc);
    Direction newDir = environment().getDirection(oldLoc, newLoc);
    changeDirection(newDir);
  }
}
```

The helper methods look like this:

```
protected Location nextLocation()
{
  ArrayList emptyNbrs = emptyNeighbors();
  Direction oppositeDir = direction().reverse();
  Location locationBehind = environment().getNeighbor(location(),
                                                      oppositeDir);
  emptyNbrs.remove(locationBehind);
  if (emptyNbrs.size() == 0)
    return location();  // Can't move, stay in the same place

  Random randNumGen = RandNumGenerator.getInstance();
  int randNum = randNumGen.nextInt(emptyNbrs.size());
  return (Location)emptyNbrs.get(randNum);
}

protected void changeLocation(Location newLoc)
{
  Location oldLoc = location();
  myLoc = newLoc;
  environment().recordMove(this, oldLoc);
}

protected void changeDirection(Direction newDir)
{
  myDir = newDir;
}
```

64

Suppose we want to define a new type of fish, `LonerFish`, which dies not due to random chance, but due to overcrowding (too many fish in neighboring locations). `LonerFish` is a subclass of `Fish`. Which of `Fish`'s methods must be redefined in `LonerFish` to achieve the desired dying behavior?

(A) act only
(B) die only
(C) act and die
(D) act, die, and move
(E) act, die, move, and breed

☞ In the MBS implementation of act and its helper methods, it is the act method that gives the fish a certain chance of dying at every timestep. The die method itself is a one-liner that just removes a fish from the environment. Note how this is different from breeding: here the random chance is tested in the breed method, not in act. Thus we'll have to change act to remove the test for a random chance of dying from it. Choice A could be a possible answer, but a more appropriate answer is C, because the new logic for dying (testing the number of non-empty neighbors of the loner fish) does not belong in act. ☜

6.5. The Simulation Class

A simulation puts together an environment and a display and provides the step method for running one "timestep" in the simulation (Figure 6-3). A "timestep" allows each fish in the environment to "act" once.

Simulation's constructor saves an Environment object and an EnvDisplay object in the instance variables. step receives a list of all fish from the environment, then iterates through the list, calling act for each fish. Note that Environment's allObjects method returns an array of Locatable objects, so the name theFishes for this array is a little misleading. It would be better to call it simply envObjects. We know that each object in this array is actually a Fish and we need to cast it to Fish to be able to call its act method.

```
public class Simulation
{
  private Environment theEnv;
  private EnvDisplay theDisplay;

  public Simulation(Environment env, EnvDisplay display)
  {
    theEnv = env;
    theDisplay = display;
    theDisplay.showEnv();
  }

  public void step()
  {
    Locatable[] theFishes = theEnv.allObjects();
    for (int i = 0; i < theFishes.length; i++ )
    {
      ((Fish)theFishes[i]).act();
    }
    theDisplay.showEnv();
  }
}
```

Figure 6-3. The Simulation class

6.6. `DarterFish` and `SlowFish`

As we have seen above, the `Fish` class is the most involved. The code complexity comes from the decision to make fish "smart": a fish knows its location, knows how to act (breed, move, die), and holds a reference to its own environment. In an alternative design, we could make fish "dumb" and let the environment take care of moving or acting on all the fish. This way we would be able to eliminate the `Locatable` interface, take out the `allObjects` and `recordMove` methods, and make other simplifications. However, we would have lost flexibility. The primary reason for doing things the way they are done is the ability to accommodate different species of fish in the same environment. Due to polymorphism, each species of fish would act appropriately. This is the subject of Chapter 4 in the MBS Narrative.

In Chapter 4, the MBS proceeds to define two subclasses of `Fish`, `DarterFish` and `SlowFish`. These types of fish move differently from the base `Fish`, but they `breed` and `die` the same way and the `act` method remains the same. So most of `Fish`'s code can be reused and only a few methods have to be redefined.

Even if we didn't take advantage of reusing any of `Fish`'s code, we still must derive all species of fish from `Fish`. Otherwise, the statement

```
((Fish)theFishes[i]).act();
```

in `Simulation`'s `step` method would throw a `ClassCastException`.

The constructors are not inherited, but a `Fish` constructor can be called from a subclass constructor. For example:

```
public class DarterFish extends Fish
{
  public DarterFish(Environment env, Location loc)
  {
    super(env, loc, env.randomDirection(), Color.yellow);
  }
  ...
}
```

—————— *DarterFish* ——————

A `DarterFish` moves two squares forward (along its current direction) if both squares are vacant. If only the square immediately in front is vacant, the darter moves there. If there is another fish in front of a darter and nowhere to move, the darter stays in place and reverses its direction.

Here OOP begins to pay off. In implementing `DarterFish` we can reuse most of `Fish`'s code through inheritance. The only methods that need to be redefined are `move`, `nextLocation`, and `generateChild`. Something like this:

```
protected void generateChild(Location loc)
{
  DarterFish child = new DarterFish(environment(), loc,
                        environment().randomDirection(), color());
}


protected Location nextLocation()
{
  Environment env = environment();
  Location oneInFront = env.getNeighbor(location(), direction());
  Location twoInFront = env.getNeighbor(oneInFront, direction());
  if (env.isEmpty(oneInFront) && env.isEmpty(twoInFront))
    return twoInFront;
  else if (env.isEmpty(oneInFront))
    return oneInFront;
  else
    return location();
}

protected void move()
{
  Location newLoc = nextLocation();

  if (!nextLoc.equals(location()))
    changeLocation(newLoc);
  else
    changeDirection(direction().reverse());
}
```

How does `act` in `Fish` know which `move` to call, `Fish`'s or `DarterFish`'s? A fish itself "knows" exactly what kind of fish it is and the appropriate method is called automatically. This is polymorphism, achieved through a technique called *dynamic method binding*: which method to call is decided not at compile time but at run time and each object itself holds a table of entry points for its methods.

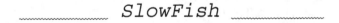

SlowFish

A `SlowFish` moves the same way as a normal fish, but its probability of moving on any step is only 1 out of 5; 4 out of 5 times, on average, it stays in the same place.

The case study author decided to put the random chance check into the `nextLocation` method, although it could also have gone into the `move` method. So `nextLocation` is redefined in `SlowFish`. The code for the `SlowFish` class may look something like this:

```java
public class SlowFish extends Fish
{
  private double probOfMoving = 1.0 / 5.0;

  public SlowFish(Environment env, Location loc)
  {
    super(env, loc, env.randomDirection(), Color.red);
  }

  public SlowFish(Environment env, Location loc, Direction dir)
  {
    super(env, loc, dir, Color.red);
  }

  public SlowFish(Environment env, Location loc, Direction dir, Color col)
  {
    super(env, loc, dir, col);
  }

  protected void generateChild(Location loc)
  {
    SlowFish child = new SlowFish(environment(), loc,
                      environment().randomDirection(), color());
  }

  protected Location nextLocation()
  {
    Random gen = RandNumGenerator.getInstance();
    if (gen.nextDouble() < probOfMoving)
      return super.nextLocation();       // call Fish's nextLocation
    else
      return location();
  }
}
```

Note that the code for choosing the next location randomly among vacant neighbors remains the same. We can reuse it by calling the superclass's nextLocation method from a subclass's nextLocation, as in

```java
return super.nextLocation();
```

(Strictly speaking, this use of super is not in the A-level AP subset, but you must understand it in the context of MBS.)

> **It is likely that a free-response question may ask you to derive another class from Fish and redefine some of the methods.**

6.7. AB Topic: Environment Implementations

⌈ All the material in this section is needed only for the <u>AB exam</u>. ⌋

The case study includes two implementations of the environment. The BoundedEnv class implements the environment as a two-dimensional array of locatable objects. The UnboundedEnv class implements the environment as a list of objects. In the bounded environment, it is easy to find the object at a given location and easy to find neighbors of a cell. The advantages of the unbounded environment are that it can be as big as you want, no memory is wasted for empty cells, and it is easy to put all its objects into an array without scanning through all the rows and columns.

As we have mentioned earlier, both BoundedEnv and UnboundedEnv extend the abstract class SquareEnvironment. The latter implements "topographic" methods (to deal with directions between locations, etc.) that are common to both bounded and unbounded implementations. It is called "square" not because its shape is square, but because each cell is a square. This is a black-box class — don't even try to read its code!

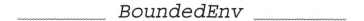

BoundedEnv

The BoundedEnv class is really very straightforward. Objects are stored in a 2-D array theGrid; empty cells hold null. (When theGrid is created, all its elements are set to null by default.) The class also maintains a total count of objects stored in theGrid; the add method increments the count and the remove method decrements it. Something like this:

```
public void add(Locatable obj)
{
  Location loc = obj.location();
  if (!isEmpty(loc))
    throw new IllegalArgumentException("Location " + loc +
                              " is not a valid empty location");
  theGrid[loc.row()][loc.col()] = obj;
  objectCount++;
}

public void remove(Locatable obj)
{
  Location loc = obj.location();
  if (objectAt(loc) != obj)
    throw new IllegalArgumentException("Cannot remove " +
                                  obj + "; not there");
  theGrid[loc.row()][loc.col()] = null;
  objectCount--;
}
```

The `allObjects` method scans the whole grid to find all objects and collect them in an array:

```
public Locatable[] allObjects()
{
  Locatable[] objects = new Locatable[numObjects()];
  int count = 0;

  for (int r = 0; r < numRows(); r++)
  {
    for (int c = 0; c < numCols(); c++)
    {
      Locatable obj = theGrid[r][c];
      if (obj != null)
      {
        objects[count] = obj;
        count++;
      }
    }
  }
  return objects;
}
```

The `recordMove` method looks like this:

```
public void recordMove(Locatable obj, Location oldLoc)
{
  Location newLoc = obj.location();
  if (newLoc.equals(oldLoc))
    return;       // not moved

  if (!isEmpty(newLoc) || objectAt(oldLoc) != obj))
    throw new IllegalArgumentException("Precondition violation moving "
            + obj + " from " + oldLoc);

  theGrid[newLoc.row()][newLoc.col()] = obj;
  theGrid[oldLoc.row()][oldLoc.col()] = null;
}
```

UnboundedEnv

The unbounded environment still conceptually represents a rectangular grid of cells, but it holds objects in a list, more precisely an `ArrayList`. The `numRows` and `numCols` methods return -1 — there are no specific bounds. The `objectAt` method needs to scan the whole list to find the object at a given location. The class provides a protected helper method `indexOf` for this purpose. Something like this:

```
public class UnboundedEnv extends SquareEnvironment
{
  private ArrayList objectList;    // list of Locatable objects in environment

  public UnboundedEnv()
  {
    super();
    objectList = new ArrayList();
  }

  ...

  protected int indexOf(Location loc)
  {
    for (int i = 0; i < objectList.size(); i++)
    {
      Locatable obj = (Locatable) objectList.get(i);
      if (obj.location().equals(loc))
        return i;
    }
    return -1;
  }

  ...

}
```

The add and remove methods rely directly on ArrayList's add and remove:

```
public void add(Locatable obj)
{
  Location loc = obj.location();
  if (!isEmpty(loc))
    throw new IllegalArgumentException("Location " + loc +
                                " is not a valid empty location");
  objectList.add(obj);
}

public void remove(Locatable obj)
{
  int i = indexOf(obj.location());
  if (i == -1)
    throw new IllegalArgumentException("Cannot remove " +
                                  obj + "; not there");
  objectList.remove(i);
}
```

Unbounded environment — other implementations

The case study exercises mention other implementations of the unbounded environment using more advanced data structures, such as TreeMap or HashMap. These would be likely exam questions.

Note that the Location class has hashCode and compareTo methods. This is a clear indication that at some point Location objects will be stored in a TreeSet or

HashSet, or, more likely, serve as keys in a TreeMap or HashMap, associating a location with a fish stored in it. For example:

```
public class UnboundedMapEnv extends SquareEnvironment
{
  private Map objectMap;    // a map of Locatable objects, location is key

  public UnboundedMapEnv()
  {
    super();
    objectMap = new TreeMap();
  }

  ...

  public Locatable objectAt(Location loc)
  {
    return (Locatable)objectMap.get(loc);
  }

  public void add(Locatable obj)
  {
    Location loc = obj.location();
    if (!isEmpty(loc))
      throw new IllegalArgumentException("Location " + loc +
                                " is not a valid empty location");
    objectMap.put(loc, obj);
  }

  ...
```

6.8.   Tips for the Case Study Questions

To answer case study questions successfully, you need to be familiar both with the relevant code and concepts behind it. For the A exam, look very carefully at the code for the Simulation, Fish, DarterFish, and SlowFish classes. ⌈ For the AB exam, also look at the Environment interface and the BoundedEnv and UnboundedEnv classes. ⌋ Figure 6-4 shows the "big picture."

Several multiple-choice questions are likely to focus on concepts: why certain design decisions were made, what the alternatives and tradeoffs are, what certain methods do, how inheritance and polymorphism work in the case study, and so on. Don't panic; most of it is common sense, especially if you have read the case study narrative.

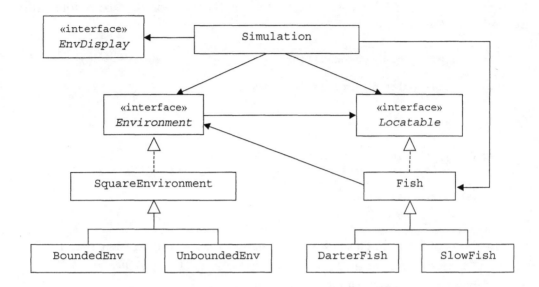

(All environment and fish classes use `Location` and `Direction`)

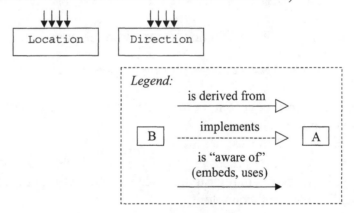

Figure 6-4. The core MBS classes and interfaces

Free-response questions will ask you to write variations on the case-study code. The key here is to find a similar code segment in the case study and adapt it — not to improvise your code from scratch. Pay attention to the following:

- `equals` vs. `==`: use `equals` for comparing locations; use `==` for comparing fish.

- **ArrayLists vs. arrays:** Environment's `neighborsOf` returns an `ArrayList` — use `....get(index)`; but `allObjects` returns an array, `Locatable[]` — use `...[index]`.

- Casting: an `ArrayList` holds objects. `allObjects` returns an array of `Locatables`. You need to cast the element into the appropriate type before calling its methods. For example:

```
ArrayList emptyNbrs = emptyNeighbors();
...
return (Location)emptyNbrs.get(randNum);
```

Or:

```
Locatable[] theFishes = theEnv.allObjects();
for (int index = 0; index < theFishes.length; index++)
{
   ((Fish)theFishes[index]).act();
}
```

- Call methods of the right class. For example, `reverse` is in `Direction`, but `randomDirection` and `getDirection(fromLoc, toLoc)` are in `Environment`. To reverse a fish's direction, use:

```
changeDirection(direction().reverse());
```

To change a fish's direction to a random direction, use:

```
changeDirection(environment().randomDirection());
```

- `protected`: never call protected methods from client classes (even though your code may compile in Java).

- `private`: never access private instance variables from other classes. It is preferable to use accessors to refer to instance variables within the same class, as the case study code does. For example:

```
environment().remove(this);
```

as opposed to:

```
theEnv.remove(this);
```

Chapter 7. Annotated Solutions to Past Free-Response Questions

The material for this chapter is on our web site:

http://www.skylit.com/beprepared/fr.html

That page includes links to free-response questions from recent years and one or several annotated solutions for each question.

Practice Exam A-1

Time — 1 hour and 15 minutes
Number of questions — 40
Percent of total grade — 50

1. Given the declarations

   ```
   int p = 5, q = 3;
   ```

   which of the following expressions evaluate to 7.5?

   I.   `(double)p * (double)q / 2;`
   II. `(double)p * (double)(q / 2);`
   III. `(double)(p * q / 2);`

   (A)   I only
   (B)   II only
   (C)   I and II
   (D)   I, II, and III
   (E)   None of the above

2. Consider the following method:

   ```
   public void mystery(int a, int b)
   {
     System.out.print(a + " ");
     if (a <= b)
       mystery(a + 5, b - 1);
   }
   ```

   What is the output when `mystery(0, 16)` is called?

   (A)   0
   (B)   0 5
   (C)   0 5 10
   (D)   0 5 10 15
   (E)   0 5 10 15 20

3.   Assuming that c and d are Boolean variables, the expression

```
!c || d
```

is equivalent to which of the following?

(A)   `!(c && d)`
(B)   `!(c && !d)`
(C)   `c && !d`
(D)   `!(c || !d)`
(E)   `!(!c && d)`

4.   Suppose method fun2 is defined as:

```
public int fun2(int x, int y)
{
  y -= x;
  return y;
}
```

What are the values of variables a and b after the following code is executed?

```
int a = 3, b = 7;
b = fun2(a, b);
a = fun2(b, a);
```

(A)   a is -1 and b is 4
(B)   a is -4 and b is 7
(C)   a is -4 and b is 4
(D)   a is 3 and b is 7
(E)   a is 3 and b is 4

5.   Assuming that a and b are Boolean variables, when is the following expression true?

```
!(!a || b) || (!a && b)
```

(A)   If and only if a and b have different values
(B)   If and only if a and b have the same value
(C)   If and only if both a and b are true
(D)   If and only if both a and b are false
(E)   Never

6. Suppose a, b, and c are positive integers under 1000 and x satisfies the formula

$$\frac{a}{b} = \frac{c}{x}$$

The integer value d is obtained by truncating x to an integer. Which of the following code segments correctly calculates d?

    I.   `d = c * b / a`

    II.   `int temp = c * b;`
                 `d = temp / a;`

    III.   `int temp = b / a;`
                 `d = c * temp;`

(A) I only
(B) II only
(C) I and II
(D) II and III
(E) I, II, and III

7. Given two classes, `Animal` and `Mammal`, which of the following situations would make the statement

```
Animal a = new Mammal("Elephant");
```

valid?

(A) `Mammal` extends `Animal` and `Mammal` has a constructor with one parameter of the `String` type.
(B) `Mammal` extends `Animal` and `Animal` has a constructor with one parameter of the `String` type.
(C) `Animal` has a method `Mammal` that takes one parameter of the `String` type.
(D) `Animal` has a public data member `String Mammal`.
(E) None of the above

8. What is the value of v[4] after the following code is executed?

```
int i;
int d = 1;
int[] v = {1, 1, 1, 1, 1};

for (i = 0; i < v.length; i++)
{
  d *= 2;
  v[i] += d;
}
```

(A) 16
(B) 32
(C) 33
(D) 64
(E) 65

9. Which of the following is NOT a good reason to use comments in programs?

(A) To document the names of the programmers and the date of the last change
(B) To document requirements for correct operation of a method
(C) To document which methods of a class are private
(D) To describe parameters of a method
(E) To explain a convoluted piece of code

10. *Top-down* program development methodology is best characterized by:

(A) Defining a class's methods and class variables first and instance variables and constructors later
(B) Coding classes and methods that implement higher-level tasks first, using temporary "stubs" for lower-level classes and methods
(C) Having a project leader design the software and then divide the work among programmers
(D) Assembling the program from reusable components
(E) Designing data structures first and classes and objects later

11. Suppose a class `Particle` has the following variables defined:

```
public class Particle
{
   public static final int STARTPOS = 100;
   private double velocity;
   < other code not shown >
}
```

Which of the following is true?

(A) `velocity` can be passed as an argument to one of `Particle`'s methods, but `STARTPOS` cannot.

(B) Java syntax rules wouldn't allow us to use the name `startPos` instead of `STARTPOS`.

(C) A statement `double pos = STARTPOS + velocity;` in one of `Particle`'s methods would result in a syntax error.

(D) Java syntax rules wouldn't allow us to make `velocity` public.

(E) A statement `STARTPOS += velocity;` in one of `Particle`'s methods would result in a syntax error.

12. What is the output of the following code segment?

```
String s = "ban";
ArrayList words = new ArrayList();
words.add(s);
words.add(s.substring(1));
words.add(s.substring(1,2));
String w = "";
for (int k = 0; k < words.size(); k++)
{
   w += (String)words.get(k);
}
System.out.print(w.indexOf("an"));
```

(A) 1
(B) 2
(C) 3
(D) ana
(E) banana

13. Consider the following code segment, intended to find the position of an integer `targetValue` in `int[] a`:

```
int i = 0, position;
while (a[i] != targetValue)
{
   i++;
}
position = i;
```

When will this code work as intended?

(A) Only when `0 <= targetValue < a.length`
(B) Only when `targetValue == a[0]`
(C) Only when `targetValue == a[i]` for some i, `0 <= i < a.length`
(D) Only when `targetValue != a[i]` for any i, `0 <= i < a.length`
(E) Always

14. Which of the following statements about Java's platform independence are true?

I.   The number of bytes used by an `int` variable is the same on any computer.

II. Java source code is compiled into bytecodes, which may then be run on any computer that has a Java Virtual Machine installed.

III. Overflow in arithmetic operations occurs at the same values regardless of the platform on which the Java program is running.

(A) I only
(B) II only
(C) I and II
(D) II and III
(E) I, II, and III

15. Given two initialized `String` variables, `str1` and `str2`, which of the following conditions correctly tests whether the value of `str1` is greater than or equal to the value of `str2` (in lexicographical order)?

(A) `str1.compareTo(str2) == true`
(B) `str1.compareTo(str2) >= 0`
(C) `str1 >= str2`
(D) `str1.equals(str2) || str1.compareTo(str2) == 1`
(E) `str1.length() > str2.length() || str1 >= str2`

Questions 16-17 refer to the method `smile` below:

```
public static void smile(int n)
{
  if (n == 0)
    return;
  for (int k = 1; k <= n; k++)
    System.out.print("smile!");
  smile(n-1);
}
```

16. What is the output when `smile(4)` is called?

    (A)   smile!
    (B)   smile!smile!
    (C)   smile!smile!smile!
    (D)   smile!smile!smile!smile!
    (E)   smile!smile!smile!smile!smile!smile!smile!smile!smile!smile!

17. When `smile(4)` is called, how many times will `smile` actually be called, including the initial call?

    (A)   2
    (B)   3
    (C)   4
    (D)   5
    (E)   10

18. Consider the following method from `ClassX`:

```
private int modXY(int x, int y)
{
  r = x / y;
  return x % y;
}
```

    If `ClassX` compiles with no errors, which of the following statements must be true?

    I.   `modXY` has a side effect since `r` is not a local variable in `modXY`.
    II.   `r` must be an instance variable in the superclass of `ClassX`.
    III. `r` must have the type `double`.

    (A)   I only
    (B)   II only
    (C)   III only
    (D)   I and II
    (E)   None

19. Consider the following three code segments:

I.
```
int  i = 1;
while (i <= 10)
{
   System.out.println(i);
   i += 2;
}
```

II.
```
for (int i = 0; i < 5; i++)
{
   System.out.println(2*i + 1);
}
```

III.
```
for (int i = 0; i < 10; i++)
{
   i++;
   System.out.println(i);
}
```

Which of the three segments produce the same output?

(A)   I and II only
(B)   II and III only
(C)   I and III only
(D)   I, II, and III
(E)   All three outputs are different.

20. Consider the following class definitions:

```
public class Country
{
   public String toString() { return "Country"; }
}

public class Brazil extends Country
{
   public String toString() { return "Brazil"; }
}
```

What is the output of the following code segment?

```
Country country1 = new Country();
Country country2 = new Brazil();
System.out.print(country1 + " " + country2 + " ");
country1 = country2;
System.out.print(country1);
```

(A)   Country Country Country
(B)   Country Country Brazil
(C)   Country Brazil Country
(D)   Country Brazil Brazil
(E)   Brazil Brazil Brazil

21. Classes `Salsa` and `Swing` implement an interface `Dance`. If both calls

```
perform(new Salsa());
perform(new Swing());
```

are valid, which of the following could serve as definitions of the `perform` method(s)?

I. Two methods:

```
public void perform(Salsa dance) { < code not shown > }
public void perform(Swing dance) { < code not shown > }
```

II.   `public void perform(Dance dance) { < code not shown > }`

III.   `public void perform(Object dance) { < code not shown > }`

(A) I only
(B) II only
(C) I and II only
(D) II and III only
(E) I, II, and III

22. Consider the following method with two missing statements:

```
// precondition:  1 <= n <= arr.length
// postcondition: returns the sum of all positive odd values
//                among the first n elements of arr
public static int addPositiveOddValues(int[] arr, int n)
{
    int i, sum = 0;
    < statement1 >
    {
        < statement2 >
            sum += arr[i];
    }
    return sum;
}
```

Which of the following are appropriate replacements for < *statement1* > and < *statement2* > so that the method works as specified?

	< *statement1* >	< *statement2* >
(A)	`for (i = 1; i < n; i += 2)`	`if (arr[i] > 0)`
(B)	`for (i = 0; i < n; i++)`	`if (arr[i] > 0 && arr[i] % 2 != 0)`
(C)	`for (i = 1; i <= n; i += 2)`	`if (arr[i] > 0)`
(D)	`for (i = 0; i <= n; i++)`	`if (arr[i] % 2 != 0)`
(E)	None of the above	

23. What is the output from the following code segment?

```
double pi = 3.14159;
int r = 100;
int area = (int)(pi * Math.pow(r, 2));
System.out.println(area);
```

   (A)   30000

   (B)   31415

   (C)   31416

   (D)   314159

   (E)   Depends on the particular computer system

Questions 24-26 involve reasoning about classes and objects used in an implementation of a library catalog system. An object of the class BookInfo represents information about a particular book, and an object of the class LibraryBook represents multiple copies of a book on the library's shelves:

```
public class BookInfo
{
  private String myTitle;
  private String myAuthor;
  private int myNumPages;

  < Constructors not shown >

  public String toString()
  {
    return myTitle + " by " + myAuthor;
  }

  public String getTitle() { return myTitle; }
  public int getNumPages() { return myNumPages; }
}

public class LibraryBook
{
  private BookInfo myInfo;
  private int myNumCopies;   // Number of copies on shelf

  < Constructors not shown >

  public int getNumCopies() { return myNumCopies; }
  public void setNumCopies(int numCopies)
                        { myNumCopies = numCopies; }
  public BookInfo getInfo() { return myInfo; }

  // postcondition: if there are copies on shelf, decrements
  //                the number of copies left and returns true;
  //                otherwise returns false
  public boolean checkOut() { < code not shown > }
}
```

24. If `catalog` is declared in a client class as

    ```
    LibraryBook [] catalog;
    ```

    which of the following statements will correctly display *title* by *author* of the third book in `catalog`?

    I.   `System.out.println(catalog[2]);`

    II. `System.out.println(catalog[2].getInfo());`

    III. `System.out.println(catalog[2].getInfo().toString());`

    (A) I only
    (B) II only
    (C) I and II
    (D) II and III
    (E) I, II and III

25. Which of the following code segments will correctly complete the `checkOut()` method of the `LibraryBook` class?

    I.
    ```
    if (getNumCopies() == 0)
       return false;
    else
    {
       setNumCopies(getNumCopies() - 1);
       return true;
    }
    ```

    II.
    ```
    int n = getNumCopies();
    if (n == 0)
       return false;
    else
    {
       setNumCopies(n - 1);
       return true;
    }
    ```

    III.
    ```
    if (myNumCopies == 0)
       return false;
    else
    {
       myNumCopies--;
       return true;
    }
    ```

    (A) I only
    (B) II only
    (C) I and II
    (D) I and III
    (E) I, II, and III

26. Consider the following method from another class, a client of `LibraryBook`:

```
// postcondition: returns the total number of pages in
//                 all books in catalog that are on the shelves
public int totalPages(LibraryBook [] catalog)
{
  int count = 0;
  int k;

  for (k = 0; k < catalog.length; k++)
  {
    < statement >
  }
  return count;
}
```

Which of the following replacements for *< statement >* completes the method as specified?

(A) `count += catalog[k].myNumCopies * catalog[k].myInfo.numPages;`
(B) `count += catalog[k].getNumCopies() * catalog[k].getNumPages();`
(C) `count += catalog[k].(myNumCopies * myInfo.getNumPages());`
(D) `count += catalog[k].getNumCopies() *`
          `catalog[k].getInfo().getNumPages();`

(E) None of the above

27. An `ArrayList list` contains `Integer` objects. The following method is intended to remove from `list` all objects whose value is less than zero:

```
public void removeNegatives(ArrayList list)
{
  int i = 0, n = list.size();

  while (i < n)
  {
    Integer x = (Integer)list.get(i);
    if (x.intValue() < 0)
    {
      list.remove(i);
      n--;
    }
    i++;
  }
}
```

For which lists of `Integer` values does this method work as intended?

(A) Only an empty list
(B) All lists that do not contain negative values in consecutive positions
(C) All lists where all the negative values occur before all the positive values
(D) All lists where all the positive values occur before all the negative values
(E) All lists

28. Consider the following interface and class:

```
public interface Student
{
  double getGPA();
  int getSemesterUnits();
}

public class FullTimeStudent
    implements Student, Comparable
{
  < required methods go here >
}
```

What is the minimum set of methods that a developer must implement in order to successfully compile the FullTimeStudent class?

(A) None: you would not be required to implement any methods
(B) getGPA, getSemesterUnits
(C) getGPA, getSemesterUnits, compareTo
(D) getGPA, getSemesterUnits, equals, toString
(E) getGPA, getSemesterUnits, compareTo, equals, toString

29. Brad has derived his class from a library class JPanel. JPanel's paintComponent method displays a blank picture in a panel. Brad redefined JPanel's paintComponent to display his own picture. Brad's class compiles with no errors, but when he runs the program, only a blank background is displayed. Which of the following hypotheses CANNOT be true in this situation?

(A) Brad misspelled "paintComponent" in his method's name.
(B) Brad specified an incorrect return type for his paintComponent method.
(C) Brad chose the wrong type for a parameter in his paintComponent method.
(D) Brad specified two parameters for his paintComponent method, while JPanel's paintComponent takes only one parameter.
(E) Brad has a logic error in his paintComponent code which prevents it from generating the picture.

30. Consider the following method:

```
// precondition:  a[0] ... a[a.length - 1] are
//                sorted in ascending order
// postcondition: Returns the location of the target
//                value in the array a, or -1 if not found
public static int search(int[] a, int target)
{
  int first = 0;
  int middle;
  int last = a.length - 1;

  while (first <= last)
  {
    middle = (first + last) / 2;
    if (target == a[middle])
      return middle;
    else if (target < a[middle])
      last = middle;
    else
      first = middle;
  }
  return -1;
}
```

This method fails to work as expected under certain conditions. If the array has five elements with values 3 4 35 42 51, which of the following values of target would make this method fail?

(A)   3
(B)   4
(C)   35
(D)   42
(E)   51

31. Which of the following best describes the return value for the method `propertyX` below?

```
// precondition: v.length >= 2
public boolean propertyX(int[] v)
{
  boolean flag = false;
  int i;

  for (i = 0; i < v.length - 1; i++)
  {
     flag = flag || (v[i] == v[i+1]);
  }

  return flag;
}
```

(A) Returns `true` if the elements of `v` are sorted in ascending order, `false` otherwise
(B) Returns `true` if the elements of `v` are sorted in descending order, `false` otherwise
(C) Returns `true` if `v` has two adjacent elements with the same value, `false` otherwise
(D) Returns `true` if `v` has two elements with the same value, `false` otherwise
(E) Returns `true` if all elements in `v` have different values, `false` otherwise

Questions 32-34 refer to the following `SortX` class:

```
public class SortX
{
  public static void sort(Comparable[] items)
  {
    int n = items.length;
    while (n > 1)
    {
      sortHelper(items, n - 1);
      n--;
    }
  }

  private static void sortHelper(Comparable[] items, int last)
  {
    int k, m = last;
    for (k = 0; k < last; k++)
    {
      if (items[k].compareTo(items[m]) > 0)
        m = k;
    }
    Comparable temp = items[m];
    items[m] = items[last];
    items[last] = temp;
  }
}
```

32. The sorting algorithm implemented in the sort method can be best described as:

    (A) Selection Sort
    (B) Insertion Sort
    (C) Quicksort
    (D) Mergesort
    (E) Incorrect implementation of a sorting algorithm

33. Suppose names is an array of String objects:

    ```
    String[] names = {"Dan", "Alice", "Claire", "Evan", "Boris"};
    ```

    If SortX.sort(names) is running, what is the order of the values in names after two complete iterations through the while loop in the sort method?

    (A) "Boris", "Alice", "Claire", "Dan", "Evan"
    (B) "Alice", "Claire", "Boris", "Dan", "Evan"
    (C) "Alice", "Boris", "Claire", "Evan", "Dan"
    (D) "Alice", "Claire", "Dan", "Evan", "Boris"
    (E) None of the above

34. If items contains five values and SortX.sort(items) is called, how many times, total, will items[k].compareTo(items[m]) be called in the sortHelper method?

    (A) 5
    (B) 10
    (C) 15
    (D) 25
    (E) Depends on the values in items

Questions 35-40 refer to the code from the Marine Biology Simulation case study.

35. The picture below shows two Fish objects (regular fish with breeding and dying abilities) in a bounded environment.

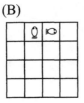

    Which of the following fish configurations is NOT possible after one simulation step?

    (A)   (B)   (C)   (D)   (E)

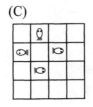

36. Given

```
int row = 2, col = 3;
Location loc = new Location(row, col);
```

which of the following conditions check if `loc` is equal to (2, 3)?

I. `loc.row() == 2 && loc.col() == 3`

II. `loc.equals(new Location(2, 3))`

III. `loc == new Location(2, 3)`

(A) I only
(B) II only
(C) I and II
(D) II and III
(E) I, II, and III

37. Suppose a class `SchoolFish` extends `Fish`. In addition to dying with the same specified probability as a normal fish, a `SchoolFish` dies if it has no neighbors. To implement this behavior, the `act` method is redefined in the `SchoolFish` class and the statement

```
if (randNumGen.nextDouble() < probOfDying)
  die();
```

is replaced by

```
if (randNumGen.nextDouble() < probOfDying || < condition >)
  die();
```

Which of the following could replace < *condition* > for `SchoolFish`'s act method to work as intended?

(A) `neighborsOf(this).size() == emptyNeighbors().size()`

(B) `neighborsOf(location()).size() == emptyNeighbors().size()`

(C) `environment().numAdjacentNeighbors() == emptyNeighbors().size()`

(D) `environment().neighborsOf(location()).size() == 0`

(E) `environment().neighborsOf(location()).size() ==`
                                        `emptyNeighbors().size()`

38. In order for the statements

```
Environment env = new BoundedEnv();
env.add(new Oyster(env, new Location(0, 0)));
```

to work, which of the following features must the Oyster class have?

   I.   It must implement Locatable and have a method location that returns a Location object.

   II.   It must have a constructor with two parameters: an Environment and a Location.

   III.   It must be a subclass of the Fish class.

(A)   I only
(B)   II only
(C)   III only
(D)   I and II
(E)   II and III

39. Which of the following is NOT a useful test data file for the MBS program running in a 10-by-10 bounded environment?

(A)   A file with no fish
(B)   A file with one fish in the corner
(C)   A file with two fish in the same location
(D)   A file with a fish outside of the environment grid
(E)   All of the above are useful tests

40. Consider an alternative MBS design in which the Simulation class is eliminated, its step method moved into the classes that implement Environment (with

```
Locatable[] theFishes = allObjects();
```

replacing

```
Locatable[] theFishes = theEnv.allObjects();
```

in step's code), and the EnvDisplay parameter passed to the environment's constructor. Which of the following is the primary reason for staying with the current design?

(A)   The Simulation class can be reused in other projects.
(B)   The environment classes can be reused in projects not related to fish.
(C)   step's code is not duplicated in the BoundedEnv and UnboundedEnv classes.
(D)   The recordMove method would become more complicated in the alternative design.
(E)   Calling showEnv() from an environment object won't work in the alternative design.

Practice Exam A-1

Time — 1 hour and 45 minutes
Number of questions — 4
Percent of total grade — 50

1. A parking garage consists of several levels with many parking spaces on each level. A garage management program keeps track of the number of cars parked in the garage and helps to find the location of a car with a given ID. Consider the following three Java classes used in this program. The class Car represents an individual car:

```java
public class Car
{
  // postcondition: returns the id of this Car
  public String getID() { < code not shown > }

  // ... constructors, other methods, and fields not shown
}
```

The class ParkingLevel represents one level of the garage. It keeps track of the cars parked within its spaces as well as empty spaces. The parking spaces on each level are numbered by consecutive integers, starting from 0. Assume that the following methods in the ParkingLevel class work as specified:

```java
public class ParkingLevel
{
  // postcondition: returns the number of parking spaces on this
  //                level
  public int numSpaces() { < code not shown > }

  // postcondition: returns the car parked in the space number
  //                spaceNum or null if that space is empty
  public Car getCar(int spaceNum) { < code not shown > }

  // postcondition: returns the smallest space number of an
  //                available space; returns -1 if the level is
  //                full and there are no empty spaces
  public int findEmptySpace() { < code not shown > }

  // precondition:  space number spaceNum is empty
  // postcondition: car v has been placed in space number
  //                spaceNum on this level; if v == null
  /                 the space is marked as empty
  public void setCar(int spaceNum, Car v) { < code not shown > }

  // ... constructors, other methods, and fields not shown
}
```

The `ParkingGarage` class keeps track of all the levels in the garage. It keeps the information about the levels in an array of `ParkingLevel` objects.

```
public class ParkingGarage
{
  private int totalCars;    // Total number of cars in this
                            // garage

  private ParkingLevel[] levels;

  // pre- and postconditions are shown below, in Part (a)
  public boolean isFull() { < code not shown > }

  // postcondition: returns true if a car with a given ID is
  //                already parked somewhere in the garage,
  //                false otherwise
  public boolean isCarAlreadyParked(String id)
  { < code not shown > }

  // pre- and postconditions are shown below, in Part (b)
  public boolean parkCar(Car v) { < code not shown > }

  // pre- and postconditions are shown below, in Part (c)
  public Car removeCar(String id) { < code not shown > }

  < constructors and other public and private members
     not shown >
}
```

(a) Write the `isFull` method of the `ParkingGarage` class, as started below. `isFull` returns `true` if there are no available spaces on any level within the parking garage, `false` otherwise.

```
  // postcondition: returns true if there are no available
  //                spaces on any level within the garage,
  //                false otherwise
  public boolean isFull()
```

(b) Write the `parkCar` method of the `ParkingGarage` class, as started below. If the parking garage is not full and if the car is not already in the garage, then the car should be parked in an empty space, the number of cars in the garage should be updated, and the method should return `true`, indicating successful parking. Otherwise, the garage data should remain unchanged and the method should return `false`, indicating that the car was not parked. Assume that the method `isFull` works as specified, regardless of what you wrote in Part (a).

```
// postcondition: if the garage is not full and no car
//                with the same ID as v's ID is in the
//                garage yet, parks Car v into the garage,
//                updates the number of cars parked in the
//                garage, and returns true; otherwise, leaves
//                the garage unchanged and returns false
public boolean parkCar(Car v)
```

(c) Write the `removeCar` method of the `ParkingGarage` class, as started below. The method looks for a car that matches a given ID string. If it finds a car with a matching ID, the car is removed from its space and the method returns that car; otherwise the method returns `null`.

```
// precondition:   id is not null and is a non-empty string
// postcondition:  if a car with a given ID String id is
//                 found, removes that car, updates
//                 the number of cars parked in the garage
//                 and returns the found car; otherwise,
//                 leaves the garage unchanged and
//                 returns null
public Car removeCar(String id)
```

2. Millions of web pages on the Internet are formatted in HTML, the HyperText Markup
    Language. HTML text contains embedded tags — formatting instructions enclosed in
    angular brackets < and >. The formatting tags often come in pairs where the opening tag
    indicates the beginning of some formatting (e.g., italics, bold, underline) and the closing tag
    indicates the end of the formatting. The closing tag contains the same keyword or
    instruction as the opening tag, but preceded by a slash (the "/" character). The following
    example shows a line of HTML text and illustrates the way it might be displayed on the
    screen:

    ```
    The <i>quick</i> <b>brown</b> fox <b>jumps
    <u>over</b> the lazy</u> dog
    ```

    > The *quick* **brown** fox **jumps <u>over** the lazy</u> dog

    Processing HTML text may involve such tasks as removing HTML tags from the text or
    verifying that opening and closing tags come in matching pairs.

    In this question we deal with text represented as a `String` object. We assume that this
    HTML text contains only complete tags: all "<" and ">" characters properly delimit tags
    and do not otherwise occur inside tags or anywhere else in the text. The segments of text
    formatted with different tags may overlap. In the above example, the word "**<u>over</u>**" falls into
    the overlapping bold and underscored segments. You will write a few methods of the
    `HTMLProcessor` class for processing HTML text.

    (a) Write the `findFirstTag` method of the `HTMLProcessor` class as started below. The
         method finds and returns the first tag in a given HTML text string. The method returns
         `null` if no tags were found.

         ```
         // precondition:   text is a segment of HTML text which may
         //                  contain complete HTML tags; a tag is any
         //                  substring starting with < and ending with
         //                  the closest >
         // postcondition:  returns the first HTML tag found in text
         //                  (including the < and > brackets) or null
         //                  if no tags are found
         public static String findFirstTag(String text)
         ```

(b) Write a method `remove` for the `HTMLProcessor` class, as started below. The method finds the first occurrence of a given substring in a given `String text` and returns `text` with that substring removed. If the given substring is not found, the method returns `text` unchanged.

```
// precondition:  str is a non-empty string
// postcondition: if str is found in text, its first
//                occurrence is removed from text and
//                the new string is returned; otherwise
//                the original string text is returned
public static String remove(String text, String str)
```

(c) Write a method `removeAllTags` for the `HTMLProcessor` class. The method deals only with a subset of HTML tags: it assumes that a given text contains only complete simple tags, such as `<u>` and `</u>` or `<cite>` and `</cite>`, where a closing tag differs from the corresponding opening tag only by the `"/"` character after `"<"`. The closing tag must come after the opening tag. The method returns the text with all tags removed (or the original text if no tags were found). The method should throw an `IllegalArgumentException` if the tags in `text` do not match (no closing tag found after an opening tag). You can assume that the methods `remove` and `findFirstTag` work as specified, regardless of what you wrote in Parts (a) and (b).

Write `removeAllTags` as started below.

```
// precondition:  text is a segment of HTML text which may
//                contain complete HTML tags
// postcondition: if all HTML tags in text come in matching
//                opening-closing pairs, then all the tags are
//                removed from text and the new text string
//                is returned; if text has no tags, the
//                original string text is returned;
//                throws an IllegalArgumentException if the
//                tags do not match
public static String removeAllTags(String text)
```

3. This question refers to the code from the Marine Biology Simulation case study. Many
    species of tropical fish spend their whole lives within a few feet of the coral reef where they
    were born. Our goal is to add a new type of fish to the project, `CoralReefFish`. This type
    of fish shares many attributes and methods with a regular `Fish`. In particular, it breeds and
    dies the same way. But a coral reef fish moves differently: it never ventures far from its
    place of birth. `CoralReefFish`'s constructors save the fish's initial location in an instance
    variable, `Location placeOfBirth`. Then `CoralReefFish`'s `nextLocation` method
    removes all locations from the list of empty neighbors whose distance from the
    `placeOfBirth` location exceeds a given constant (e.g., 4).

    (a) Implement a constructor for `CoralReefFish` that takes two parameters, an
         `Environment` object and a `Location` object. The new fish should get a random
         direction and a `Color.yellow` color. Your constructor should save the initial location
         of this fish in an instance variable, `Location placeOfBirth`.

```
// precondition: loc is a valid location in env
// postcondition: a coral reef fish is constructed at the
//                specified location in env with a random
//                direction and the Color.yellow color;
//                the initial location of this fish is saved
//                in placeOfBirth
public CoralReefFish(Environment env, Location loc)
```

    (b) Implement a private helper method `distanceFromHome` that returns the distance from
         a given location to `placeOfBirth`. The distance between `loc1 = (r1,c1)` and
         `loc2 = (r2,c2)` should be calculated using the formula

$$d = \sqrt{(r2 - r1)^2 + (c2 - c1)^2}$$

    Implement the `distanceFromHome` method as started below.

```
// postcondition:  returns the distance from loc to
//                 placeOfBirth
protected double distanceFromHome(Location loc)
```

(c) Redefine the nextLocation method for the CoralReefFish class. The next location to move to should be chosen randomly from all the empty neighboring locations of this fish whose distance from placeOfBirth does not exceed 4. A CoralReefFish <u>can move backward</u> (in the direction opposite to its current direction), so this restriction should be removed. In writing this method, assume that the distanceFromHome method works as specified, regardless of what you wrote in Part (b). Debugging statements are not required. Implement the nextLocation method as started below.

```
// postcondition: returns this fish's next location;
//                if this fish cannot move, returns its
//                current location; the fish may move
//                to any empty adjacent location
//                (including the location behind) except
//                those whose distance from placeOfBirth
//                is greater than 4
protected Location nextLocation()
```

4.   Consider the class `APExam` that represents an AP exam taken by a student:

```
public class APExam
{
    // postcondition: constructs an APExam with the specified
    //                subject, level, and grade
    public APExam(String subject, int level, int grade)
    { < code not shown > }

    // postcondition: returns this exam's subject
    public String getSubject() { < code not shown > }

    // postcondition: returns this exam's level: 1 for
    //                half year, 2 for full year
    public int getLevel() { < code not shown > }

    // postcondition: returns this exam's grade:
    //                from 1 to 5
    public int getGrade() { < code not shown > }
}
```

The class `APStudent` represents a student's participation in the AP program. An `APStudent` object holds the name of the student and a list of all the AP exams taken by that student. The list of exams is represented by an `ArrayList` that holds `APExam` objects. The class should have a constructor that takes a student name as a parameter and initializes the list of exams to an empty list. The class provides accessor methods for the name and the list of exams, a method that adds an AP exam to the list, and a method that returns the student's average grade on all exams.

(a)   Write a class definition for `APStudent`, putting only "..." in the bodies of its constructor and methods. In writing this definition you must:

- choose appropriate names for methods, data members, and parameters;

- provide the functionality specified above;

- make data representation consistent with the above specification;

- make design decisions that are consistent with information-hiding principles.

Comments are not required but may be used if desired.

DO NOT write the implementations of the constructors or the member methods of the `APStudent` class.

(b)   The College Board offers an AP Scholar award to students with grades of 3 or higher on three or more AP Exams for full-year courses. Half-year courses are counted as half of a full-year course. The College Board also grants an AP Scholar with Honor award to students with grades of 3 or higher on four or more full-year-course exams (or the equivalent mix of full- and half-year courses) and an average AP Exam grade of at least 3.25 on all exams taken. Students may have low grades on some AP exams and still meet the requirements for either award. This is summarized in the table below:

	AP Scholar	AP Scholar with Honor
Minimum grade that counts	3	3
Required number courses not below min grade	3 years	4 years
Average grade on <u>all</u> AP exams taken	no effect	3.25
Number of exams below min grade	no effect	no effect

Suppose the class `APStats` keeps track of the AP exam statistics. Write a method `getAwardLevel` of the `APStats` class that returns the level of award earned by a given AP student: 0 for no award, 1 for the AP Scholar award, and 2 for the AP Scholar with Honor award. You may assume that all the methods of the `APStudent` class that you have designed in Part (a) work as specified. Complete the `getAwardLevel` method as started below.

```
// postcondition: the award level is computed and returned,
//                as follows: 0 for no award, 1 for AP Scholar
//                and 2 for AP Scholar with Honor
public int getAwardLevel(APStudent student)
```

(c)   Write a method `getStats` of the `APStats` class that takes a non-empty list of AP program participants and calculates the percentages of students with no award, AP Scholars, and AP Scholars with Honor. For example, if a list holds 10 AP students of whom 6 received no award, 3 are AP Scholars, and 1 is an AP Scholar with Honor, then `getStats` returns an array with values 60.0, 30.0, and 10.0. In writing `getStats`, assume that the method `getAwardLevel` works as specified, regardless of what you wrote in Part (b). Complete `getStats` below the following header:

```
// precondition:  list contains APStudent objects;
//                list.size() > 0
// postcondition: returns an array percents of length 3;
//                percents[0], percents[1], and percents[2]
//                are filled with percentages of all students
//                from the list with no award, AP Scholars,
//                and AP Scholars with Honor, respectively
public double[] getStats(ArrayList list)
```

Practice Exam A-2

COMPUTER SCIENCE A
SECTION I

Time — 1 hour and 15 minutes
Number of questions — 40
Percent of total grade — 50

1. What is the output of the following program segment?

```
int num = 5;
while (num >= 0)
{
   num -= 2;
}
System.out.print(num);
```

(A) -2
(B) -1
(C) 0
(D) 2
(E) 21

2. Assuming that x and y are int variables, the expression

```
!(x > y && y <= 0)
```

is equivalent to which of the following?

(A) !(x <= y) || (y > 0)
(B) x > y && y <= 0
(C) x <= y || y > 0
(D) x > y || y < 0
(E) x <= y && y <= 0

3. Which of the following could serve as a postcondition in the following method?

```
// precondition: amt represents a positive value in dollars
//                and cents (for example, 1.15 represents
//                one dollar and fifteen cents)
private int process(double amt)
{
   return (int)(amt * 100 + 0.5) % 100;
}
```

(A) Returns the cent portion in amt.
(B) Returns the number of whole dollars in amt.
(C) Returns amt converted into cents.
(D) Returns amt rounded to the nearest integer.
(E) Returns amt truncated to the nearest integer.

4. What is the output of the following code segment?

```
int sum = 0, count, d = -1;
for (count = 10; count > 0; count--)
{
  sum += d;
  if (d > 0)
    d++;
  else
    d--;
  d = -d;
}
System.out.println(sum);
```

(A) 0
(B) 5
(C) -5
(D) 10
(E) -10

5. The following code segment is supposed to calculate and display $1 + 2 + ... + 20$:

```
int count = 0, sum = 0;
while (count < 20)
{
  sum += count;
}
System.out.println(sum);
```

Which statement best describes the result:

(A) The total displayed will be correct.
(B) The total displayed will be 20 too small.
(C) The output will be the number 0.
(D) The output will be the number 20.
(E) There will be no output because the program goes into an infinite loop.

6.   Consider the following class:

```
public class Rectangle
{
  private int width, height;

  public Rectangle(int w, int h) { width = w; height = h; }
  public int getHeight() { return height; }
  public int getWidth() { return width; }
  public int getArea() { return width * height; }
}
```

Suppose we want to modify this class to make it implement the Comparable interface.
Rectangle objects should be compared based on their area: the rectangle with the smaller
area should be deemed smaller. Which of the following methods do we have to add?

(A)
```
public boolean compareTo(int area)
{
  return getArea() < area;
}
```

(B)
```
public int compareTo(int area)
{
  return getArea() - area;
}
```

(C)
```
public boolean compareTo(Rectangle other)
{
  return getArea() < other.getArea();
}
```

(D)
```
public int compareTo(Rectangle other)
{
  return getArea() - other.getArea();
}
```

(E)
```
public int compareTo(Object other)
{
  return getArea() - ((Rectangle)other).getArea();
}
```

7. Which of the following Boolean expressions properly implement a comparison for equality of two `String` objects `str1` and `str2` and evaluate to `true` if and only if `str1` and `str2` hold the same values?

    I.   `str1 == str2`

    II. `str1.equals(str2)`

    III. `str1.compareTo(str2) == 0`

    (A) I only
    (B) II only
    (C) I and II
    (D) II and III
    (E) I, II, and III

8. What is the output of the following code segment?

    ```
    int a = 3;
    int b = 4;
    int c = 0;

    if (a == b && b/c == 1)
    {
      c = a * b;
    }
    else
    {
      c = a + b * c;
      System.out.println(c);
    }
    ```

    (A) Run-time division-by-zero error
    (B) 0
    (C) 3
    (D) 6
    (E) 12

9. Which of the following statements about overloaded methods is FALSE?

    (A) Overloaded methods must be made either all public or all private.
    (B) Overloaded methods are defined in the same class and have the same name.
    (C) Overloaded methods may have the same number of parameters.
    (D) One of the overloaded methods may take no parameters.
    (E) Overloaded methods cannot be differentiated based only on the names chosen for their parameters.

10. Consider the following class:

```
public class Sphere
{
  public static final double pi = 3.14159;

  public static double volume(int r)
  {
    return 4 / 3 * pi * Math.pow(r, 3);
  }
}
```

Which of the following statements about this code is true?

(A)   The class will not compile because no constructors are defined.
(B)   The class will not compile because `pi` cannot be declared `public`.
(C)   The class will not compile because the `volume` method is declared `static`.
(D)   `Math.pow(r, 3)` cannot be used because `r` is an `int`.
(E)   The class compiles with no errors but the `volume` method returns a significantly smaller value than the expected $\frac{4}{3}\pi r^3$.

11. Consider the following method:

```
// precondition: a != null; a.length > 0
private static void doIt(double[] a)
{
  double temp;

  for (int k = 0; k < a.length / 2; k++)
  {
    temp = a[k];
    a[k] = a[a.length - 1 - k];
    a[a.length - 1 - k] = temp;
  }
}
```

Which of the following best describes the task performed by this method?

(A)   Sorts an array in ascending order
(B)   Sorts an array in descending order
(C)   Swaps the first and last elements of an array
(D)   Reverses the order of elements in an array
(E)   None of the above tasks is implemented correctly.

12. Consider the following method:

```
public String filter(String str, String pattern)
{
  int pos = str.indexOf(pattern);
  if (pos == -1)
    return str;
  else
    return filter(str.substring(0, pos) +
            str.substring(pos + pattern.length()), pattern);
}
```

What is the output of

```
System.out.print(filter("papaya", "pa"));
```

(A)   p
(B)   pa
(C)   ya
(D)   aya
(E)   paya

13. Consider the following code segment:

```
int n = IO.readInt();   // read an int value
n = Math.abs(n);

while (n >= 2)
{
  n = n/2 - 1;
}
System.out.print(n);
```

Which of the following is the list of all possible outputs?

(A)   0
(B)   -1, 0
(C)   0, 1
(D)   -1, 1
(E)   -1, 0, 1

14. Which of the following recommendations for testing software is NOT good advice?

(A)   Test a program with all possible values of input data.
(B)   When testing a large program, test the smaller pieces individually before testing the entire program.
(C)   If possible, use automated testing procedures or read test data from files so that you can re-run the tests after corrections have been made.
(D)   Design test data that exercises as many different paths through the code as is practical.
(E)   Test on data that is at the boundary of program conditionals to check for "off by one" errors.

15. Whitney is a cheerleader and a programmer. She has written the following recursive method that is supposed to generate the cheer "2 4 6 8 Who do we appreciate!":

```
public void cheer(int i)
{
  if (i != 8)                                    // Line 1
  {                                              // Line 2
    i = i + 2;                                   // Line 3
    cheer(i);                                    // Line 4
    System.out.print(i + " ");                   // Line 5
  }                                              // Line 6
  else                                           // Line 7
  {                                              // Line 8
    System.out.print("Who do we appreciate!");   // Line 9
  }                                              // Line 10
}
```

However, Whitney's method doesn't work as expected when she calls `cheer(0)`.
To get the right cheer, Whitney should

(A) replace `if (i != 8)` with `if (i <= 8)` on Line 1
(B) replace `if (i != 8)` with `if (i == 8)` on Line 1
(C) replace `if (i != 8)` with `while (i != 8)` on Line 1
(D) swap Line 4 and Line 5
(E) move Line 3 after Line 5

16. What is displayed when the following method is called with `splat("**")`?

```
public static void splat(String s)
{
  if (s.length() < 8)
    splat(s + s);
  System.out.println(s);
}
```

(A) **

(B) ****

(C) ********

(D) ********
     **

(E) ********
     ****
     **

Questions 17-18 refer to the following `sort` method:

```
public void sortX(int[] a)
{
  int i, j, k;                       // Line 1

  for (i = 1; i < a.length; i++)     // Line 2
  {
    int current = a[i];              // Line 3
    j = 0;                           // Line 4

    while (a[j] < current)           // Line 5
    {
      j++;                           // Line 6
    }
    for (k = i; k > j; k--)          // Line 7
    {
      a[k] = a[k-1];                 // Line 8
    }
    a[j] = current;                  // Line 9
  }
}
```

17. The sorting algorithm implemented in the `sortX` method can be best described as:

    (A)   Selection Sort
    (B)   Insertion Sort
    (C)   Quicksort
    (D)   Mergesort
    (E)   Incorrect implementation of a sorting algorithm

18. Given

        `int[] a = {24, 16, 68, 56, 32};`

what will be the result after the statement on Line 9 in `sortX` completes for the second time?

    (A)   The values in a are 16, 24, 68, 56, 32
    (B)   The values in a are 16, 24, 32, 56, 68
    (C)   The values in a are 24, 16, 32, 56, 68
    (D)   The code has failed with an `ArrayIndexOutOfBoundsException` on Line 5
    (E)   The code has failed with an `ArrayIndexOutOfBoundsException` on Line 9

19. Consider the following class:

```
public class BuddyList
{
   private ArrayList buddies;   // contains Strings --
                                //    the names of buddies

   < Constructors and other methods and variables not shown >

   public ArrayList getBuddies() { return buddies; }
}
```

If `BuddyList myFriends` is declared and initialized in some other class, a client of `BuddyList`, which of the following correctly assigns to `name` the name of the first buddy in the `myFriends` list?

   I.   `String name = (String)myFriends.buddies[0];`

   II. `String name = (String)myFriends.buddies.get(0);`

   III. `String name = (String)myFriends.getBuddies().get(0);`

   (A)   I only
   (B)   II only
   (C)   III only
   (D)   I and II
   (E)   II and III

20. The class `PlayList` provides methods that allow you to represent and manipulate a list of tunes, but you are not concerned with how these operations work or how the list is stored in memory. You only know how to initialize and use `PlayList` objects and have no direct access to the implementation of the `PlayList` class or its private data members. This is an example of:

   (A)   encapsulation
   (B)   overriding
   (C)   inheritance
   (D)   dynamic binding
   (E)   method overloading

21. Which of the following statements about constructors is NOT true?

   (A)   All constructors must have the same name as the class they are in.
   (B)   Constructors' return type must be declared `void`.
   (C)   A class may have a constructor that takes no parameters.
   (D)   A constructor is called when a program creates an object with the `new` operator.
   (E)   A constructor of a subclass can call a constructor of its superclass using the Java reserved word `super`.

22. Consider the following method, intended to use Binary Search to find the location of `target` within an `ArrayList a`:

```java
public int findLocation(ArrayList a, String target)
{
  int first = 0, last = a.size() - 1;
  while (first <= last)
  {
    int middle = (first + last) / 2;
    int compResult = target.compareTo(a.get(middle));
    if (compResult == 0)
      return middle;
    if (compResult < 0)
      last = middle - 1;
    else
      first = middle + 1;
  }
  return -1;
}
```

This method may fail if it is applied to a list that is not sorted. For which of the following lists will `findLocation(a, "C")` return -1?

(A)   "A", "B", "C", "D", "E", "F", "G"

(B)   "G", "F", "E", "D", "C", "B", "A"

(C)   "A", "C", "D", "G", "E", "B", "F"

(D)   "B", "A", "D", "C", "F", "E", "G"

(E)   "D", "F", "B", "A", "G", "C", "E"

Questions 23 and 24 refer to the following class:

```java
public class Sample
{
  private double[] amps;

  public Sample(int n) { < missing statements > }
  public double get(int k) { return amps[k]; }
}
```

23. Which of the following code segments can replace < *missing statements* > in `Sample`'s constructor so that it initializes `amps` to hold n values and fills them with random values $0.0 \leq \text{amps}[i] < 1.0$?

(A)
```
        amps = new double[n];
```

(B)
```
        amps = new double[n];
        for (int k = 0; k < n; k++)
          amps[k] = new Random();
```

(C)
```
        amps = new double[n];
        for (int k = 0; k < n; k++)
          amps[k] = Random.nextDouble();
```

(D)
```
        amps = new double[n];
        Random randGen = new Random();
        for (int k = 0; k < n; k++)
          amps[k] = randGen.nextDouble();
```

(E)
```
        amps = new Double[n];
        Random randGen = new Random();
        for (int k = 0; k < n; k++)
          amps[k] = new Double(randGen.nextDouble());
```

24. Given

```
        int size = 100;
        Sample s = new Sample(size);
```

which of the following statements assigns to x the last value in `amps` from `s`:

(A)   `double x = s[99];`
(B)   `double x = s.amps[amps.length - 1];`
(C)   `double x = s.get(amps.length - 1);`
(D)   `double x = s.get(size - 1);`
(E)   `double x = s.get[s.length - 1];`

25. A project needs two related classes, *X* and *Y*. A programmer has decided to provide an abstract class *A* and derive both *X* and *Y* from *A* rather than implementing *X* and *Y* completely independently of each other. Which of the following is NOT a valid rationale for this design decision?

    (A) Being able to use some common code accessible in classes *X* and *Y* without duplication
    (B) Being able to cast objects of type *X* into *Y* and vice-versa.
    (C) Being able to pass as a parameter an object of either type, *X* or *Y*, to the same constructor or method in place of a parameter of the type *A*.
    (D) Being able to place objects of both types, *X* and *Y*, into the same array of type `A[]`.
    (E) Making it easier to implement in the future another class that reuses some code from *A*.

26. Suppose `ArrayList` objects `names` and `numbers` are created as follows:

```
ArrayList numbers = new ArrayList();
Integer x = new Integer(1);
numbers.add(x);
numbers.add(x);

ArrayList names = new ArrayList();
names.add(0, "Anya");
names.add(0, "Ben");
names.add(0, "Cathy");
```

    What is the result of the following code segment?

```
int k;
for (k = 0; k < numbers.size(); k++)
{
    Integer index = (Integer)numbers.get(k);
    names.remove(index.intValue());
}
for (k = 0; k < names.size(); k++)
{
    System.out.print(names.get(k) + " ");
}
```

    (A) `Cathy`
    (B) `Cathy Anya`
    (C) `Anya Cathy`
    (D) `IndexOutOfBoundsException`
    (E) `NoSuchElementException`

27. When does a class have to be declared `abstract`?

    (A) When it has no constructors
    (B) When it has no public methods
    (C) When the class has no public or private instance variables
    (D) When you need to derive another class from this class
    (E) When one or more methods in the class are declared abstract

28. Consider the following interface TV and class MyTV:

```
public interface TV
{
  void tuneTo(String channel);
}

public class MyTV implements TV
{
  private ArrayList myFavoriteChannels;

  public MyTV(ArrayList channels) { < code not shown > }
  public void tuneTo(int k) { < code not shown > }
  public void tuneTo(int k, String name) { < code not shown > }
}
```

One of them has one or more errors and won't compile properly. Which of the following best describes the compiler errors reported for the statements that are shown?

(A)   In the TV interface, the tuneTo declaration is missing the keyword public

(B)   MyTV should be declared abstract; it does not define tuneTo(String) in MyTV

(C)   tuneTo is defined more than once in MyTV

(D)   Cannot convert int to String in the tuneTo method in MyTV

(E)   Two errors: (1) tuneTo is defined more than once and (2) cannot convert int to String in the tuneTo(int) method in MyTV

29. Consider the following code segment:

```
if (!somethingIsFalse())
  return false;
else
  return true;
```

Which of the following replacements for this code will produce the same result?

(A)   return true;

(B)   return false;

(C)   return !somethingIsFalse();

(D)   return somethingIsFalse();

(E)   none of the above

30. Consider the following class definitions:

```
public class Airplane
{
  private int fuel;

  public Airplane() { fuel = 0; }
  public Airplane(int g) { fuel = g; }

  public void addFuel() { fuel++; }
  public void display() { System.out.print(fuel + " "); }
}

public class Jet extends Airplane
{
  public Jet(int g) { super(2*g); }
}
```

What is the result when the following code is compiled and run?

```
Airplane plane = new Airplane(4);
Airplane jet = new Jet(4);
plane.display();
plane.addFuel();
plane.display();
jet.display();
jet.addFuel();
jet.display();
```

(A)   A syntax error, "undefined addFuel," is reported for the `jet.addFuel();` statement.

(B)   A run-time error, `ClassCastException`, occurs when `jet.addFuel()` is attempted.

(C)   The code compiles and runs with no errors; the output is 4 5 5 6

(D)   The code compiles and runs with no errors; the output is 4 5 8 9

(E)   The code compiles and runs with no errors; the output is 8 9 9 10

31. A programmer wants to create a swap method that swaps two integer values. Which of the following three ways of representing the values and corresponding methods successfully swap the values?

    I.

```
// a and b are Integer objects that represent the values
// to be swapped
public static void swap(Integer a, Integer b)
{
    Integer temp = a; a = b; b = temp;
}
```

    II.

```
// a[0] and a[1] contain the values to be swapped
public static void swap(int[] a)
{
    int temp = a[0]; a[0] = a[1]; a[1] = temp;
}
```

    III.

```
// a[0] and b[0] contain the values to be swapped
public static void swap(int[] a, int[] b)
{
    int temp = a[0]; a[0] = b[0]; b[0] = temp;
}
```

(A)   I only
(B)   II only
(C)   I and II
(D)   II and III
(E)   I, II, and III

32. Suppose an interface Solid specifies the getVolume() method. Two classes, Cube and Pyramid, implement Solid. Which technique makes it possible for the following code segment to print the correct values for the volume of a pyramid and a cube?

```
Solid[] solids = new Solid[2];
solids[0] = new Cube(100);
solids[1] = new Pyramid(150, 100);
System.out.println("Cube: " + solids[0].getVolume());
System.out.println("Pyramid: " + solids[1].getVolume());
```

(A)   abstraction
(B)   encapsulation
(C)   dynamic method binding
(D)   Just-In-Time compilation
(E)   method overloading

33. Consider the following code segment:

```
ArrayList list = new ArrayList();
list.add("One");
list.add("Two");
String msg;
list.add(msg);
< another statement >
```

Which of the following choices for < *another statement* > will cause a `NullPointerException`?

(A)   `msg = "Three";`
(B)   `msg = (String)list.get(list.size());`
(C)   `if (!"Three".equals(list.get(2))) msg = "Three";`
(D)   `list.add(2, msg);`
(E)   `msg = msg.substring(0, 2);`

34. A programmer is trying to choose between an `ArrayList` and a standard one-dimensional array for representing data. Which of the following is NOT a correct statement?

(A)   Both an `ArrayList` and a standard array allow direct access to the *k*-th element.
(B)   A standard array may hold elements of a primitive data type, such as `int` or `double`; an `ArrayList` may only hold objects.
(C)   An `ArrayList` may hold objects of different types, such as `Integer` and `Double`, simultaneously.
(D)   An `ArrayList` has a convenient method for inserting a value at a specified location in the middle.
(E)   Both an `ArrayList` and a standard array are expanded automatically when the number of values stored exceeds their size.

Questions 35-40 refer to the code from the Marine Biology Simulation case study.

35. Suppose a simulation starts with two `Fish` objects (regular fish with breeding and dying) located close to the center of a large bounded environment. Which of the following describes all possible numbers of fish after one step?

(A)   Any number from 0 to 10
(B)   Any number from 0 to 10, except 3
(C)   Any number from 0 to 10, except 3 and 7
(D)   0, 2, or 10
(E)   0, 1, 2, 6, or 10

36. Assuming that `loc1` and `loc2` are `Location` objects that represent valid locations in the `Environment env`, which of the following conditions verifies that `loc2` lies to the north of `loc1` in env?

    (A)   `loc1.getDirection(env, loc2) == 0`
    (B)   `loc1.getDirection(loc1) == env.Direction.NORTH`
    (C)   `env.getDirection(loc1, loc2).equals(Direction.NORTH)`
    (D)   `loc1.getDirection(loc2, env).equals(Direction.NORTH)`
    (E)   `env.getDirection(loc1, loc2) == new Direction(Direction.NORTH)`

37. Which method in MBS contains code that prevents fish from moving backward?

    (A)   `emptyNeighbors` in the `Fish` class
    (B)   `nextLocation` in the `Fish` class
    (C)   `move` in the `Fish` class
    (D)   `getNeighbor` in the class that implements `Environment`
    (E)   `getDirection` in the class that implements `Environment`

38. Which of the following implementation features rely on dynamic binding?

    I.   `DarterFish` constructors call `Fish` constructors

    II.   `nextLocation` in `SlowFish` calls `nextLocation` in `Fish`

    III.   `breed` in `Fish` calls `generateChild` in `Fish` or in `Fish`'s subclass

    (A)   I only
    (B)   II only
    (C)   III only
    (D)   I and II
    (E)   II and III

39. While experimenting with the interactive MBS program, Pat placed only one red fish at the (0, 0) location, facing east. Pat then chose "Use fixed seed..." from the "Seed" menu and entered 90001 for the seed. When Pat pressed "Step" for the first time, the fish disappeared. Pat suspected that the fish might have died of "natural causes." Which of the following tests will confirm this hypothesis?

    I.   Place the fish in the southeast corner of the environment, instead of the northwest corner.

    II.   Temporarily set `probOfDying` in Fish to 0

    III.   Enable `Debug` printouts and examine the console output

    (A)   I only
    (B)   II only
    (C)   I and II
    (D)   II and III
    (E)   I, II, and III

40. The diagram below shows the interactions between some of the MBS classes and interfaces. A solid-end arrow from *A* to *B* indicates that the code in *A* explicitly calls a method or a constructor in *B*, so that *A* cannot compile without *B*. The arrow with a dotted line from *C* to *I* indicates that *C* implements *I*.

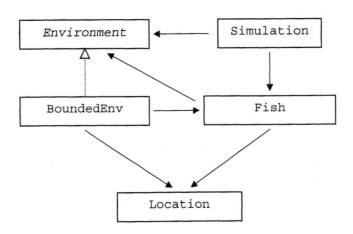

This diagram has a mistake: one arrow should not be in the diagram. Which arrow should be removed?

    (A)   `Simulation --> Fish`
    (B)   `Fish --> Environment`
    (C)   `BoundedEnv --> Fish`
    (D)   `BoundedEnv --> Location`
    (E)   `Fish --> Location`

Practice Exam A-2

COMPUTER SCIENCE A
SECTION II

Time — 1 hour and 45 minutes
Number of questions — 4
Percent of total grade — 50

1. Consider a class `Story` that represents a list of words as an array of words. Each word is a `String` object. The following is a partial definition of the `Story` class:

```
public class Story
{
  private String[] storyWords;

  // postcondition: Creates an array storyWords of the same
  //                length as wordsArray and copies all the
  //                strings from wordsArray to storyWords
  public Story(String[] wordsArray)
  { < code not shown > }

  // pre- and postconditions are shown below, in Part (a)
  private int printWord(String nextWord, int cursorPos,
                                          int lineWidth)
  { < code not shown > }

  // pre- and postconditions are shown below, in Part (b)
  public void print(int lineWidth)
  { < code not shown > }
}
```

(a) Write the `printWord(nextWord, cursorPos, lineWidth)` method that prints `nextWord` to `System.out`. `cursorPos` indicates the number of characters already printed on the current line. The word must fit on the line so that the total width of the line does not exceed `lineWidth`. If the word doesn't fit, the line is ended and the word is printed on the next line, starting at cursor position 0. If `nextWord` is too long to fit on a line by itself, it is truncated. You can use the following algorithm:

1. If this is not the first word on the line (i.e., if `cursorPos > 0`) and the word does not fit on this line, call `System.out.println()` and reset `cursorPos` to 0.

2. If the word is not the first on the line, print a single space and increment `cursorPos`.

3. If `nextWord` fits on this line, print it and add its length to `cursorPos`; otherwise print the longest substring of `nextWord` that fits and set `cursorPos` to `lineWidth`.

4. Return the new cursor position.

Complete `printWord` as started below.

```
// precondition:  cursorPos indicates the number of characters
//                already printed on the current output line.
//                lineWidth is the maximum allowed width of
//                the line.
// postcondition: nextWord is printed to System.out.
//                If this word is not the first one on the
//                current line (cursorPos > 0), one space is
//                printed before the word.  If the word does
//                not fit on the current line, it is printed
//                on the next line.  If nextWord is too long
//                to fit on a line by itself, it is truncated.
//                Returns the cursor position (the total
//                number of characters) in the current
//                line) after nextWord has been printed.
private int printWord(String nextWord, int cursorPos,
                                       int lineWidth)
```

(b) Write the method `print` that prints all the words in `storyWords` so that the lines do not exceed a given line width. Assume that `printWord` works as specified, regardless of what you wrote in Part (a).

```
// postcondition: All the words from storyWords are printed
//                to System.out.  Consecutive words on the
//                same line are separated by one space.
//                The lengths of all lines do not exceed
//                lineWidth
public void print(int lineWidth)
```

2. The Chinese calendar associates an animal and an element with each year. There are 12 animals, associated with successive years, that rotate in a twelve-year cycle. The five elements, wood, fire, earth, metal, and water, combined with an "elder" or "younger" attribute, rotate in a ten-year cycle. The class ChineseZodiac below defines the names of the animals and the elements and provides static methods for determining the Zodiac description for a given year and for finding a year that matches the given animal and element:

```
public class ChineseZodiac
{
  private static final int startYear = 1924;

  private static final String[] animals =
      {"rat", "ox", "tiger", "rabbit", "dragon", "snake",
       "horse", "sheep", "monkey", "chicken", "dog", "pig"};

  private static final String[] elements =
      {"elder wood (fir)", "younger wood (bamboo)",
       "elder fire (burning wood)", "younger fire (lamp flame)",
       "elder earth (hill)", "younger earth (plain)",
       "elder metal (weapon)", "younger metal (kettle)",
       "elder water (wave)", "younger water (brook)"};

  // precondition:  year >= startYear
  // postcondition: returns the zodiac string in the form
  //                "animal, element description"
  //                that corresponds to year
  public static String toZodiacString(int year)
  { < code not shown > }
}
```

The year startYear = 1924 was the year of the animal "rat" and the element "fir" as indicated by the values of animals[0] and elements[0]. The following year, 1925, was the year of the animal "ox" and the element "bamboo" as indicated by animals[1] and elements[1]. Note that in the past 60 years there were several years that were "the year of the dragon" but only one year that was both "dragon" and "elder earth (hill)".

A public class ChineseCalendar is a client of the ChineseZodiac class:

```
public class ChineseCalendar
{
  public String shortZodiac(int year) { < code not shown > }

  public int getYear(int year, String animal, String element)
  { < code not shown > }

  < constructors, other methods and instance variables
    not shown >
}
```

(a)   Write a method `toZodiacString` of the `ChineseZodiac` class that returns a string that combines the animal name with the full element name for a given year, separated by a comma and a space. For example, `toZodiacString(1925)` should return the string

```
"ox, younger wood (bamboo)"
```

Complete the method `toZodiacString` below.

```
// precondition:  year >= startYear
// postcondition: returns the zodiac string in the form
//                "animal, element description"
//                that corresponds to year
public static String toZodiacString(int year)
```

(b)   Write a method `shortZodiac` of the class `ChineseCalendar`. `shortZodiac` returns a zodiac string for a given year in the "colloquial" format: a string that combines the animal name and the informal element name, removed from parentheses, separated by a slash character. For example, `shortZodiac(1925)` returns the string

```
"ox/bamboo"
```

Assume that `toZodiacString` in the `ChineseZodiac` class works as specified, regardless of what you wrote in Part (a). Complete method `shortZodiac` below.

```
// precondition:  year meets the precondition of the
//                toZodiacString method of the ChineseZodiac
//                class
// postcondition: returns the zodiac string in the form
//                "animal/informal element" that corresponds
//                to year
public String shortZodiac(int year)
```

(c)   Write a method `getYear` of the class `ChineseCalendar`. `getYear` returns the year of the first occurrence of a given animal and element (described by its full or informal name) since the specified year. For example,
`getYear(1924, "ox", "younger wood (bamboo)")` and
`getYear(1924, "ox", "bamboo")` both return 1925. The method should throw an `IllegalArgumentException` if either the animal or the element string is invalid. Assume that methods described in Parts (a) and (b) work as specified, regardless of what you wrote. Complete the `getYear` method below.

```
// precondition:  year meets the precondition of the
//                toZodiacString method of the
//                ChineseZodiac class
// postcondition: returns the year of the first occurrence
//                of animal and element in the Chinese
//                calendar, since year (year included);
//                throws IllegalArgumentException if such
//                year is not found
public int getYear(int year, String animal, String element)
```

3. This question refers to the code from the Marine Biology Simulation case study. Our goal is to add to the project a new type of fish, AgingFish. An aging fish shares many attributes and methods with a regular Fish. In particular, it moves the same way as a regular fish, and when it breeds, it breeds the same way, producing new AgingFish objects as its offspring. What is different is that an aging fish keeps track of its "age" (the number of timesteps since its "birth") . An aging fish can breed only when its age is from 3 to 10 (with the same probability as a regular fish). An aging fish's probability of dying increases with age. Since the probOfDying is a private instance variable in Fish and there are no accessors or modifiers for it, the AgingFish class uses its own instance variable to hold its probability of dying.

(a) Write a class definition for AgingFish, putting only "..." in the bodies of constructors and methods. In writing this definition you must:

- provide the functionality specified above;

- provide a complete set of constructors consistent with the Fish class;

- reuse the existing MBS code to the fullest possible degree without duplicating it;

- choose appropriate names for variables and parameters;

- make data representation consistent with the above specification;

- make design decisions that are consistent with information-hiding principles.

Comments are not required but may be used if desired.

DO NOT write the implementations of the constructors or methods of the AgingFish class in this part of the question.

(b) Implement an AgingFish constructor that takes two parameters, an Environment object and a Location object. The new fish should get a random direction and the Color.blue color. Your constructor should set the initial probability of dying for this fish to 1/7; its age should be set to 0.

```
// precondition:  env != null; loc != null; loc is valid
//                for env
// postcondition: constructs an AgingFish at the
//                specified location in a given environment
//                with a random direction and Color.blue color
public AgingFish(Environment env, Location loc)
```

(c) Implement `AgingFish`'s `act` method. An aging fish acts in a way similar to a regular fish. But the following aspects of the aging fish's behavior are different:

- At the end of each timestep, the age of the fish is incremented by 1.

- An aging fish cannot breed when its age (the number of timesteps since its "birth") is less than 3 or greater than 10. If its age is within the breeding age, it breeds with the same probability as a regular fish.

- Once an aging fish reaches the age of 3, its probability of dying increases by 0.1 at each timestep. The probability of dying should be adjusted <u>before</u> the fish gets a random chance to die.

Implement the act method as started below.

```
// postcondition: acts for one step in the simulation.
//                Increments the age of this fish at the
//                end.  The fish attempts to breed
//                only if its age is from 3 to 10.
//                If this fish's age is 3 or greater,
//                its probability of dying is increased
//                by 0.1; this adjustment is done before
//                this fish gets a random chance to die.
public void act()
```

4. In searching for extra-terrestrial intelligence, data packets are assembled from radio-telescope telemetry data. A data packet describes the position in the sky, the intelligence factor, signal strength, and duration. For example, the data packet

```
Cygnus 5027 6.9 80 75
```

indicates the source in the constellation "Cygnus," quadrant 5027, with an intelligence factor of 6.9, signal strength 80, and signal duration of 75 milliseconds. The intelligence factor is measured on a scale from 0.0 to 10.0.

An object of the DataPacket class represents one data packet:

```
public class DataPacket
{
  // constructor: creates a data packet object with given
  //              parameters
  public DataPacket (String src, int quad, double intel,
                                        int strgth, int dur)
  { <... code not shown > }

  // postcondition: returns the source of this data packet
  public String getSource() { <... code not shown > }

  // postcondition: returns the quadrant of this data packet
  public int getQuadrant() { <... code not shown > }

  // postcondition: returns the intelligence factor of
  //                this data packet
  public double getIntelFactor() { <... code not shown > }

  // postcondition: returns the strength of this data packet
  public int getStrength() { <... code not shown > }

  // postcondition: returns the duration of this data packet
  public int getDuration() { <... code not shown > }

  // ... Other methods and instance variables not shown
}
```

A list of data packets forms an observation sample, represented by an object of the StarWatch class:

```
public class StarWatch
{
  private ArrayList dataPackets;

  public StarWatch() { dataPackets = new ArrayList(); }

  public DataPacket getBestPacket(double minIntelFactor)
  { < code not shown > }

  public int filterList(int minStrength, int minDuration)
  { < code not shown > }

  public ArrayList alienMessage(int minStrength,
          int minDuration, double minIntelFactor)
  { < code not shown > }

  // ... Other methods and instance variables not shown
}
```

(a) Write a method getBestPacket of the StarWatch class. getBestPacket finds the packet in the dataPackets list with the highest intelligence factor, greater than or equal to a given value minIntelFactor, and returns a reference to that packet. If no such packet is found, the method returns null. If more than one packet in the list has the same intelligence factor as the highest value, the method returns any one of them. Complete the getBestPacket method below.

```
// precondition:  dataPackets list is empty or
//                contains valid data packets
// postcondition: returns the data packet from the
//                dataPackets list with the highest
//                intelligence factor that is greater than
//                or equal to minIntelFactor.  If the list is
//                empty or no such packets are found,
//                returns null; if the list contains
//                several packets with an intelligence
//                factor equal to or above minIntelFactor
//                and equal to the highest value, returns
//                the first such packet in the list
public DataPacket getBestPacket(double minIntelFactor)
```

(b) Write a method `filterList` of the `StarWatch` class that deletes all the packets from the list whose signal is too weak and/or too short in duration. The minimum signal strength level and signal duration are passed as parameters. The method returns the number of removed packets. Complete method `filterList` below.

```
// postcondition: all the packets with strength less than
//                 minStrength and/or duration less than
//                 minDuration are removed from the
//                 dataPackets list; returns the number of
//                 removed packets
public int filterList(int minStrength, int minDuration)
```

(c) Write a method `alienMessage` of the `StarWatch` class. This method first filters the `dataPackets` list, removing all the packets that are too weak (with strength less than `minStrength`) and/or too short (with duration less than `minDuration`). Then it finds the "best" packet whose intelligence factor is not below `minIntelFactor`, as returned by the `getBestPacket` method described in Part (a), and, if not `null`, builds and returns an `ArrayList` of all packets from `dataPackets` that have the same source and quadrant settings as the best packet. The method returns `null` if no best packet is found. Assume that the `getBestPacket` and `filterList` methods work as specified, regardless of what you wrote in Part (a) and Part (b). Complete the `alienMessage` method below.

```
// postcondition: removes all packets with a strength
//                 less than minStrength and/or a duration less
//                 than minDuration from the dataPackets list;
//                 finds the best packet whose intelligence
//                 factor is greater than or equal to
//                 minIntelFactor and, if not null,
//                 builds and returns an ArrayList of all
//                 packets from dataPackets that have the same
//                 source and quadrant settings as the best
//                 packet; otherwise returns null
public ArrayList alienMessage(double minIntelFactor,
                    int minStrength, int minDuration)
```

Practice Exam AB-1

COMPUTER SCIENCE AB
SECTION I

Time — 1 hour and 15 minutes
Number of questions — 40
Percent of total grade — 50

1. Consider the following method:

```
public void change(double[] nums, int n)
{
  for (int k = 0; k < n; k++)
  {
    nums[k] = 5.4;
  }
  n = 2;
}
```

What will be stored in `samples` and `len` after the following statements are executed?

```
double[] samples = {1.0, 2.1, 3.2, 4.3};
int len = samples.length;
change(samples, len);
```

(A)   `samples` contains `5.4, 5.4, 5.4, 5.4` and `len` is `4`
(B)   `samples` contains `5.4, 5.4, 5.4, 5.4` and `len` is `2`
(C)   `samples` contains `1.0, 2.1, 3.2, 4.3` and `len` is `4`
(D)   `samples` contains `5.4, 5.4` and `len` is `2`
(E)   `samples` contains `1.0, 2.1` and `len` is `2`

2. At the county fair, prizes are awarded to the five heaviest pigs. More than 5,000 pigs are entered, and their records are stored in an array. Which of these would be the most efficient way of finding the records of the five heaviest pigs?

(A)   Selection Sort
(B)   Selection Sort terminated after the first five iterations
(C)   Insertion Sort
(D)   Insertion Sort terminated after the first five iterations
(E)   Quicksort

3. Consider the following code for a method that approximates the square root of a non-negative `double`:

```
public double squareRoot(double x)
{
    double x1 = 1, x2 = x;

    while (Math.abs(x1 - x2) > 0.001)
    {
        x2 = (x1 + x2) / 2;
        x1 = x / x2;
    }
    return x2;
}
```

Which of the following best describes the `while` loop invariant?

(A)   x1 times x2 is equal to x
(B)   x is the average of x1 and x2
(C)   x2 is the average of x and x1
(D)   The absolute value of x1 - x2 is less than or equal to 0.001
(E)   The absolute value of x1 - x2 is greater than 0.001

4. What is the output of the following code segment?

```
ArrayList list = new ArrayList();
int i;
for (i = 1; i <= 8; i++)
{
    list.add(new Integer(i));
}

for (i = 0; i < list.size(); i++)
{
    list.remove(i);
}

for (i = 0; i < list.size(); i++)
{
    System.out.print(list.get(i) + " ");
}
```

(A)   `IndexOutOfBoundsException`
(B)   No output because the resulting list is empty
(C)   1 3 5 7
(D)   2 4 6 8
(E)   1 2 3 4 5 6 7 8

5. Consider two different designs for a data structure to hold the total number of home runs hit in a season by baseball players. There are *n* players, and each total is in the range from 0 to 80.

    Design A: Use an array of length 81. Each index into the array corresponds to a number of home runs and each element of the array is a pointer to a linked list containing the names of the players who hit that many home runs.

    Design B: Use an array of length *n* so that each element of the array corresponds to one player. Each element of the array is an object that represents a player, holding his name and the number of home runs he has hit. The elements of the array are sorted alphabetically by player name.

    This data structure will be used to support three operations:

    Operation 1: Given a player's name, look up that player's home run total.

    Operation 2: Given the names of two players, determine whether they hit the same number of home runs.

    Operation 3: Print the names of all players who hit over 50 home runs.

    Which of the three operations could be performed more efficiently using Design A rather than Design B?

    (A)   Operation 1 only
    (B)   Operation 2 only
    (C)   Operation 3 only
    (D)   Operations 1 and 2
    (E)   Operations 2 and 3

6. The Binary Search algorithm is designed to work with an array sorted in ascending order. Under which of the following circumstances will the algorithm find a given target value even if the array is not sorted?

    I.   The array has an odd number of elements and the target value is located exactly in the middle of the array.

    II.   The array is partially sorted: the left third of the array has values all in ascending order and the target value is among them.

    III. The array is partially sorted: all the values to the left of the target are smaller than the target and all the values to the right of the target are larger than the target.

    (A)   I only
    (B)   I and II
    (C)   I and III
    (D)   II and III
    (E)   I, II, and III

7. In a certain card game, cards are distributed into seven separate piles. The rules of the game permit several cards to be moved from the top of one pile onto the top of another pile without changing their order, keeping the top card on top. Which of the following would be appropriate to simulate this aspect of the game without using additional data structures?

    I.   Seven linked lists
    II. Seven queues
    III. Seven stacks

    (A)   I only
    (B)   II only
    (C)   III only
    (D)   Either I or II
    (E)   Either II or III

8. Consider the following method:

```
public String encrypt(String word)
{
   int pos = word.length() / 2;
   if (pos >= 1)
   {
     word = encrypt(word.substring(pos)) +
            encrypt(word.substring(0, pos));
   }
   return word;
}
```

    What is the contents of the string returned by `encrypt("SECRET")`?

    (A)   TSECRE
    (B)   RETSEC
    (C)   TERCES
    (D)   CESTER
    (E)   ETRECS

9. Which of the following sorting algorithms runs in $O(n)$ time in the best case and $O(n^2)$ time in the worst case?

    (A)   Selection Sort
    (B)   Insertion Sort
    (C)   Quicksort
    (D)   Mergesort
    (E)   Heapsort

10. A UPC (Universal Product Code) is used to identify all goods sold. Suppose a class `GroceryItem` has a private instance variable `String upc` that represents this item's unique UPC:

```
public class GroceryItem
{
  private String upc;
  // other instance variables, constructors, and methods
  // not shown
}
```

Which of the following describes the set of methods that must be defined for `GroceryItem` objects if we want to hold them in a `HashSet`?

(A) `hashCode`
(B) `equals`
(C) `hashCode` and `equals`
(D) `equals` and `getUPC`
(E) `compareTo` and `equals`

11. Consider the following method:

```
public ListNode mince(ListNode head)
{
  ListNode r = null, p = null;

  while (head != null)
  {
    r = head.getNext();
    head.setNext(p);
    p = head;
    head = r;
  }
  return p;
}
```

If `head` refers to the first node of a linked list with five nodes, A → B → C → D → E, which of the following lists is returned by `mince(head)`?

(A) B → C → D → E
(B) E
(C) A → B → C → D
(D) A → B → C → D → E
(E) E → D → C → B → A

Questions 12-15 refer to the following classes:

```
public class Party
{
  private List theGuests;

  public Party() { theGuests = null; }

  public Party(List guests) { theGuests = guests; }

  public void setGuests(List guests) { theGuests = guests; }

  public String toString() { < code not shown > }
}

public class BDayParty extends Party
{
  private String theName;

  public BDayParty(String name, List guests)
  { < code not shown > }

  public String getName() { return theName; }

  // other methods not shown >
}
```

12. Given

```
        List guests = new LinkedList();
        guests.add("Alice");
        guests.add("Ben");
        guests.add("Candy");
```

which of the following declarations is NOT valid?

(A)   `Party[] celebrations = new Party[2];`

(B)   `Party[] celebrations =`
      `{new Party(guests), new Party()};`

(C)   `BDayParty[] celebrations =`
      `{new BDayParty("Malika", guests), new Party(guests)};`

(D)   `BDayParty[] celebrations =`
      `{new BDayParty("Lee", guests),`
      ` new BDayParty("Henry", guests)};`

(E)   All of the above are valid

13. Which of the following statements may replace < *missing statement* > in the following BDayParty constructor:

```
public BDayParty(String name, List guests)
{
  < missing statement >
  theName = name;
}
```

I.   theGuests = guests;

II.   super(guests);

III.   setGuests(guests);

(A) I only
(B) II only
(C) I and II
(D) II and III
(E) I, II, and III

14. Suppose we have decided to make the Party class abstract and have added the following methods to it:

```
public abstract String getOccasion();
public String getMessage() { return "Happy"; }
public String greetings() { return getMessage() + " "
                                        + getOccasion(); }
```

Which of the following is the smallest set of Party methods that would have to be overridden in the BDayParty class to make

```
BDayParty birthday = new BDayParty("Aaron", guests);
System.out.println(birthday.greetings());
```

display

```
Happy Birthday Aaron
```

(A) None
(B) getOccasion
(C) getMessage
(D) getOccasion and getMessage
(E) getOccasion, getMessage, and greetings

15. Party's toString method lists all the entries in the theGuests list. Should the programmer use an iterator or the list's get(i) method within a loop to traverse the list?

(A)   get(i), because it is always more efficient
(B)   get(i), because iterators are available only for linked lists
(C)   An iterator, because get(i) may be not available in the implementation of List passed to the constructor
(D)   An iterator, because it is more efficient when theGuests happens to be a LinkedList
(E)   Either method works and is equally efficient for all lists

16. Suppose we have found a compiled Java class, Fun.class, but we do not have its source code. We have discovered that a statement

```
Fun fun = new Fun(100);
```

compiles with no errors. Which of the following statements, if it compiles correctly, will convince us that Fun implements Comparable?

(A)   Comparable c = fun;
(B)   System.out.print(fun.compareTo(0));
(C)   System.out.print(fun.compareTo(fun));
(D)   System.out.print(fun.compareTo(new Fun(99)));
(E)   None of the above

17. What is the appropriate postcondition for the following method:

```
// precondition:  root refers to a non-empty
//                Binary Search Tree;
//                the left subtree is not empty and the
//                right subtree is not empty
// postcondition: < not shown >
public Object findX(TreeNode root)
{
  TreeNode node = root.getLeft();
  while (node.getRight() != null)
    node = node.getRight();
  return node.getValue();
}
```

(A)   Returns the largest value in the tree
(B)   Returns the smallest value in the tree
(C)   Returns the largest value in the tree's left subtree
(D)   Returns the smallest value in the tree's right subtree
(E)   Returns the value stored in the rightmost node on the level farthest from the root

18. Consider three versions of a code segment intended to fill a 3-by-5 two-dimensional array m with random integers from 1 to 100. Assume the array and a Random object rand are defined in each version as follows:

```
int rows = 3, cols = 5;
int row, col;
Random rand = new Random();
int m[][] = new int[rows][cols];
```

I.
```
for (row = 0; row < rows; row++)
{
  for (col = 0; col < cols; col++)
  {
    m[row][col] = rand.nextInt(100) + 1;
  }
}
```

II.
```
int k = rows * cols - 1;
while (k >= 0)
{
  row = k / cols;
  col = k % cols;
  m[row][col] = rand.nextInt(100) + 1;
  k--;
}
```

III.
```
for (int k = 0; k < rows * cols; k++)
{
  row = Math.abs(rand.nextInt(rows));
  col = Math.abs(rand.nextInt(cols));
  m[row][col] = rand.nextInt(100) + 1;
}
```

Which of these versions fill the array with random numbers?

(A)   I only
(B)   II only
(C)   I and II
(D)   II and III
(E)   I, II, and III

19. Suppose an empty stack is provided and an "input" queue contains the numbers
    1 2 3 4 5 6, with 1 at the front of the queue. The numbers are taken one by one from the
    input queue, and, depending on some criterion, either go directly into the "output" queue or
    are pushed onto the stack. After all the numbers from the input queue are processed, all the
    numbers from the stack are popped one by one and sent to the same output queue. Which of
    the following output queues would NOT be possible?

    (A)   1 2 3 4 5 6
    (B)   3 6 1 2 4 5
    (C)   1 2 3 6 5 4
    (D)   2 4 6 5 3 1
    (E)   1 6 5 4 3 2

20. Suppose the following three classes are defined and each has a "no-args" constructor (a
    constructor that takes no parameters):

    ```
    public class Vehicle {...}
    public class Car extends Vehicle {...}
    public class Buick extends Car {...}
    ```

    Which of the following is NOT a legal statement?

    (A)   Vehicle vehicle = new Car();
    (B)   Vehicle vehicle = new Buick();
    (C)   Car car = new Buick();
    (D)   Car car = new Vehicle();
    (E)   Buick buick = new Buick();

21. Suppose `ArrayStack` implements `Stack`. What is the output of the following code
    segment?

    ```
    Stack stk = new ArrayStack();
    LinkedList list = new LinkedList();
    list.add("One");
    stk.push(list);
    list.add("Two");
    stk.push(list);
    list.add("Three");
    while (!stk.isEmpty())
    {
      Iterator it = ((LinkedList)stk.pop()).iterator();
      while(it.hasNext())
        System.out.print(it.next() + " ");
    }
    ```

    (A)   Two One
    (B)   One Two One
    (C)   Two One One
    (D)   Three Two One
    (E)   One Two Three One Two Three

Questions 22-23 refer to the following class:

```
public class NumList
{
  private LinkedList list; // contains Integer objects

  public NumList() { list = new LinkedList(); }
  public void add(int value) { < code not shown > }
  public void remove(int value) { < code not shown > }
  public void shuffle() { < code not shown > }
  public String toString() { < code not shown > }
}
```

22. Suppose we plan to implement the NumList class by first coding and testing the constructor and two other methods. Which pair of methods can be conveniently chosen to be developed and tested first?

    (A) add and toString
    (B) toString and remove
    (C) add and remove
    (D) shuffle and remove
    (E) add and shuffle

23. Suppose remove is implemented as follows:

```
    //  postcondition: all the elements that contain an Integer
    //                 with a given value, if any, are removed
    //                 from the list
    public void remove(int value)
    {
      Iterator iter = list.iterator();
      Integer target = new Integer(value);

      while (iter.hasNext())
      {
        if (target.equals(iter.next()))
          iter.remove();
      }
    }
```

When does remove NOT work correctly?

    (A) Works correctly in all cases
    (B) When the list is empty
    (C) When the list contains null
    (D) When value occurs at the front of the list
    (E) When value occurs in two consecutive elements of the list

24. Consider the following classes:

```
public class APTestResult
{
  private String subject;
  private int score;

  public int getScore() { return score; }

  < constructors and other methods not shown >
}

public class APScholar
{
  private String name;
  private int id;
  private ArrayList exams; // holds APTestResult objects

  public ArrayList getExams { return exams; }

  < constructors and other methods not shown >
}
```

Given

```
        APScholar[] list = new APScholar[100];
```

which of the following expressions correctly represents the third AP score of the sixth AP Scholar in list?

(A)   `((APTestResult)(list[5].getExams().get(2))).getScore();`

(B)   `((APTestResult)((APScholar)list[5]).exams[2]).score;`

(C)   `((APScholar)list[5]).getExams(2).getScore();`

(D)   `((APTestResult)list[5].exams).getScore(2);`

(E)   `((APScholar)list[5]).exams[2].getScore();`

25. Consider designing a data structure for keeping track of student absences from school. Two designs are being considered:

Design A: A `HashMap` where an `Integer` key represents a day of the school year and the associated value is an `ArrayList` containing the names of absentees for that day, in alphabetical order.

Design B: A `TreeSet` of student records which are comparable by student ID. Each record contains a student's name and a `LinkedList` of that student's absence dates sorted by date in ascending order.

The following operations are to be implemented:

Operation 1: List alphabetically all students with perfect attendance.
Operation 2: List all days of the year with at least 30% more absentees than the average number of absentees for all school days.

Which of the following is true?

(A)   Operation 1 can be implemented more efficiently using Design A; Operation 2 can be implemented more efficiently using Design B.

(B)   Operation 1 can be implemented more efficiently using Design B; Operation 2 can be implemented more efficiently using Design A.

(C)   Both Operation 1 and Operation 2 can be implemented more efficiently using Design A than using Design B.

(D)   Both Operation 1 and Operation 2 can be implemented more efficiently using Design B than using Design A.

(E)   Both Operation 1 and Operation 2 can be implemented equally efficiently using either design.

26. Consider the following class `Athlete`:

```
public class Athlete implements Comparable
{
  private int numMedals;

  public int getRank() { return numMedals; }

  public int compareTo(Object obj)
  {
    Athlete other = (Athlete)obj;
    // return numMedals - other.numMedals;
    return getRank() - other.getRank();
  }
  < constructors and other methods not shown >
}
```

As you can see, the programmer has commented out direct references to `Athlete`'s instance variable `numMedals` in the `compareTo` code and replaced them with calls to the `getRank` method. What is the most compelling reason for doing this?

(A)   To correct a syntax error: being private, neither `numMedals` nor `other.numMedals` are directly accessible in the method's code.

(B)   To correct a syntax error: being private, `other.numMedals` is not directly accessible in the method's code (`numMedals` is replaced with `getRank()` for consistency).

(C)   To avoid possible problems later: if `other` happens to belong to a subclass of `Athlete` in which `numMedals` is not used in calculating the rank, the original code would fail.

(D)   To improve run-time efficiency.

(E)   To achieve better encapsulation.

27. Consider the following classes:

```
public class A
{
  private int myNum;

  public A (int x) { myNum = x; }
  public int getNumber() { return myNum; }
  public String getLetters() { return "A"; }
  public String getMessage()
          { return getLetters() + "-" + getNumber(); }
}

public class AB extends A
{
  public AB (int x) { super(x + 1); }
  public int getNumber() { return super.getNumber() + 1; }
  public String getLetters() { return "AB"; }
}
```

What is the output of the following code segment?

```
A test = new AB(0);
System.out.print(test.getMessage());
```

(A) A-0
(B) A-1
(C) A-2
(D) AB-1
(E) AB-2

28. Which of the following binary trees represent a (minimum) heap:

```
  I.                          II.                         III.
       3                           5                           3
      / \                         / \                         / \
     7   5                       3   7                       7   5
        / \                         / \                         / \
       6   9                       6   9                       6   9
      / \
     7   9
```

(A) I only
(B) II only
(C) I and II
(D) I and III
(E) None of the three

29. Yarong needs to write a method `hash(String word)` to be used in a hash table holding words (`String` objects). If `hash("lemon")` returns x, which of the following statements must be true?

    (A) `x = 5` (the number of letters in the word "lemon")
    (B) `hash("mango") > x`, since alphabetically "lemon" comes before "mango"
    (C) `hash("melon") = x`, since "lemon" and "melon" contain the same letters
    (D) `0 <= x < n/2`, where n is the maximum number of words that will ever be stored in the table
    (E) None of the above

Questions 30-32 refer to the class `ListPriorityQueue`, which implements the `PriorityQueue` interface. In this implementation, priority queue items are stored in a linked list in ascending order. It is assumed that items are `Comparable` objects.

```
public class ListPriorityQueue implements PriorityQueue
{
  private LinkedList items;

  public ListPriorityQueue() { items = new LinkedList(); }

  public boolean isEmpty() { return items.size() == 0; }
  public void add(Object x) { < code not shown > }
  public Object removeMin() { < code not shown > }
  public Object peekMin() { < code not shown > }

  // precondition:  x and y are Comparable objects
  // postcondition: returns the result of comparison of x and y
  //                as defined by their compareTo method
  private int compare(Object x, Object y) { < code not shown > }
}
```

30. Which of the following is a correct replacement for *< missing statement >* in the following `compare` method of `ListPriorityQueue`?

```
        private int compare(Object x, Object y)
        {
          < missing statement >
        }
```

    (A) `return x.compareTo(y);`
    (B) `return Comparable.compare(x, y);`
    (C) `return x.compareTo((Comparable)y);`
    (D) `return ((Comparable)x).compareTo(y);`
    (E) `return y.compareTo((Comparable)x);`

31. Consider the following code for the `removeMin` method:

```
public Object removeMin()
{
  if (!isEmpty())
    return items.remove(0);
  else
    < missing statement >
}
```

Which of the following is the most appropriate replacement for < *missing statement* >?

(A) `System.out.println("removeMin: NoSuchElementException");`
(B) `System.err.println("removeMin: NoSuchElementException");`
(C) `System.err.println("removeMin: " + NoSuchElementException);`
(D) `throw(NoSuchElementException);`
(E) `throw new NoSuchElementException();`

32. Consider the implementation of the `add` method:

```
public void add(Object x)
{
  ListIterator it = items.listIterator();
  while (it.hasNext())
  {
    if (compare(x, it.next()) < 0) // if x < it.next()
      {
        < missing statement >
        return;
      }
  }
  items.addLast(x);
}
```

Which of the following is an appropriate replacement for < *missing statement* >?

(A) `items.add(it, x);`
(B) `items.add(x);`
(C) `it.set(x);`
(D) `it.add(x);`
(E) None of the above

33. Consider the following method:

```
public TreeNode grow(TreeNode root)
{
  if (root == null)
    return null;
  else if (root.getLeft() != null && root.getRight() == null)
    return new TreeNode(root.getValue(),
               grow(root.getLeft()), grow(root.getLeft()));
  else if (root.getLeft() == null && root.getRight() != null)
    return new TreeNode(root.getValue(),
               grow(root.getRight()), grow(root.getRight()));
  else
    return new TreeNode(root.getValue(),
               grow(root.getLeft()), grow(root.getRight()));
}
```

What tree does grow(root) return when root refers to the following tree?

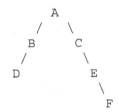

(A)

(B)

(C)

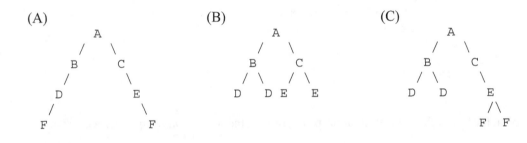

(D)

(E)

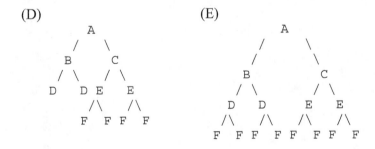

34. Consider the following method:

```
public boolean hasPropertyX(TreeNode root)
{
  if (root == null)
    return false;
  TreeNode left = root.getLeft();
  TreeNode right = root.getRight();
  return (left != null && right != null) ||
         hasPropertyX(left) || hasPropertyX(right);
}
```

hasPropertyX(root) returns true if and only if the binary tree rooted in root

(A) has non-empty left and right subtrees
(B) has at least one node with two children
(C) is not empty and its root is not a leaf
(D) is not empty and each node is either a leaf or has two children
(E) is a full tree

Questions 35-40 refer to the code from the Marine Biology Simulation case study.

35. Pat ran the MBS program with a dynamic population (including breeding and dying fish), starting with the following configuration in a 2-by-2 bounded environment (with no diagonal neighbors):

Which of the following configurations would NOT be possible after one timestep?

(A)   (B)   (C)   (D)   (E)

36. If fish1 and fish2 are two Fish objects in the same environment, which of the following expressions represents the direction (a Direction object) from fish1 to fish2?

(A) `fish1.location().getDirection(fish2.location())`

(B) `fish1.getDirection(fish1.location(), fish2.location())`

(C) `Fish.environment().getDirection(fish1.location(), fish2.location())`

(D) `fish1.environment().getDirection(fish1.location(), fish2.location())`

(E) `Fish.environment().getDirection(fish1.location(),`
`                                    fish2.location()).inDegrees();`

37. Suppose a class `AgingFish` extends `Fish`. Which of the following code segments would correctly implement `AgingFish`'s `growOld` method, which replaces this fish with a blue-colored `SlowFish` with the same location and direction?

(A)
```
environment().remove(this);
new SlowFish(environment(), location(),
                            direction(), Color.blue);
```

(B)
```
SlowFish f = new SlowFish(environment(), location(),
                                direction(), Color.blue);
environment().add(f);
```

(C)
```
environment().set(location(), new SlowFish(environment(),
                        location(), direction(), Color.blue);
```

(D)
```
Location oldLoc = location();
Environment env = environment();
Fish slowFish = new SlowFish(env, location(),
                                direction(), Color.blue);
env.recordMove(slowFish, oldLoc);
```

(E)
```
environment().remove(location());
Fish f = new SlowFish(environment(), location(),
                                direction(), Color.blue);
environment().add(f)
```

38. Given

```
Environment env = new BoundedEnv(10, 10);
int row = < read user input >;
int col = < read user input >;
Location loc = new Location(row, col);
```

when does the statement

```
env.add(new Fish(env, loc));
```

throw an `IllegalArgumentException`?

(A) Never
(B) If and only if `!env.isValid(loc)`
(C) If and only if `!env.isEmpty(loc)`
(D) If and only if `!env.isEmpty(loc) &&`
                    `(env.objectAt(loc).location() != loc)`
(E) Always

39. Which of the following are reasonable ways to test the move method of the SlowFish class?

   I.   Write a special test program that contains a loop that iterates 100 times. Each time through the loop, a new SlowFish is created in the middle of the environment with a random direction, its move method is called, and one of five counters is updated: one for no move and the other four for a move in a particular direction. At the end of the iteration, the fish's die method is called. The total number of moves should be around 20, and the values of the counters for the four directions should be roughly the same.

   II.   Create a data file that places 36 SlowFish with random directions in a regular grid pattern in a 20-by-20 environment:

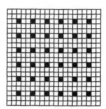

      Observe the actions of the fish in one timestep. Around one-third of the fish should breed or die (or both); of the remaining two-thirds, about 20% (around 5) should move to a new location. Repeat the experiment four times. The total number of fish moves in three runs should be around 20, with roughly the same number of moves in each direction.

   III.   Put one SlowFish in the middle of a 20-by-20 environment and observe its movements until it breeds or dies. Repeat this experiment 20 times. The fish should move about 20% of the time, with a roughly equal number of moves in each direction.

(A)   I only
(B)   II only
(C)   I and II
(D)   II and III
(E)   I, II, and III

40. Consider an alternative implementation of the unbounded environment that uses a
    `TreeMap objectMap` instead of an `ArrayList objectList`. In `objectMap`, the key is
    a location and the associated value is the object at that location. Our goal is to compare the
    big-O estimates for `Simulation`'s `step` method in the original design and this alternative
    design. In the alternative design, the `objectAt`, `add`, `remove`, and `recordMove` methods
    rely on `TreeMap`'s `get`, `put`, and `remove` methods, as shown below; `allObjects` uses an
    iterator. For example:

```
public Locatable objectAt(Location loc)
{ return (Locatable)objectMap.get(loc); }

public void add(Locatable obj)
{ objectMap.put(obj.location(), obj); }

public void remove(Locatable obj)
{ objectMap.remove(obj.location()); }

public void recordMove(Locatable obj, Location oldLoc)
{
  objectMap.remove(oldLoc);
  objectMap.put(obj.location(), obj);
}

public Locatable[] allObjects()
{
  Locatable[] objectArray = new Locatable[objectMap.size()];
  Iterator it = objectMap.keySet().iterator();
  int index = 0;
  while (it.hasNext())
  {
    objectArray[index] = (Locatable)it.next();
    index++;
  }
  return objectArray;
}
```

Assuming that `TreeMap`'s `put`, `get`, and `remove` methods have the same big-O efficiency,
what are the big-O estimates in terms of n (the total number of fish) for `Simulation`'s
`step` method in the original design and in this alternative design?

	Original: ArrayList	*Alternative: TreeMap*
(A)	$O(n)$	$O(n)$
(B)	$O(n^2)$	$O(n \log n)$
(C)	$O(n \log n)$	$O(n^2)$
(D)	$O(n^2)$	$O(n^2)$
(E)	$O(n^2)$	$O(4n^2)$

Practice Exam AB-1

COMPUTER SCIENCE AB
SECTION II

Time — 1 hour and 45 minutes
Number of questions — 4
Percent of total grade — 50

1. A barcode from a label or an ID tag is scanned and digitized by an electronic sensor and
    stored in a two-dimensional array containing zeros and ones. For better accuracy, a barcode
    is scanned by several sensors at once, and the data from each sensor form one row in the
    array. In a perfect scan, all the sensors produce the same readings, so all the values in one
    column are the same. For example, the scan array

    ```
    1 0 1 1 0 0
    1 0 1 1 0 0
    1 0 1 1 0 0
    1 0 1 1 0 0
    1 0 1 1 0 0
    1 0 1 1 0 0
    1 0 1 1 0 0
    ```

    represents a perfect scan for the barcode 101100.

    In an imperfect scan, some values may be off due to dirty sensors. Then the barcode value
    for a column is determined by the majority of zeros or ones in that column. For example, the
    scan array

    ```
    1 0 1 1 0 0
    1 0 1 0 0 1
    0 0 0 1 0 0
    1 0 1 1 0 0
    1 1 0 1 0 0
    0 0 1 0 0 0
    1 0 1 0 1 0
    ```

    will be converted into the barcode values 101100.

In addition to random errors, a sensor may occasionally get "stuck," producing the same value for all the elements in a code. For example, in the following scan array

```
1 0 1 1 0 0
1 1 1 1 1 1
1 0 1 1 0 0
1 0 1 1 0 0
1 0 1 1 0 0
1 0 1 1 0 0
1 0 1 1 0 0
```

the second sensor from the top is "stuck."

Barcodes have a built-in error-checking mechanism based on "parity": the number of ones in each barcode must be an odd number. Therefore, the array

```
0 0 1 0 0 1
0 0 1 0 0 1
0 0 1 0 0 1
0 0 1 0 0 1
0 0 1 0 0 1
0 0 1 0 0 1
0 0 1 0 0 1
```

represents an erroneous barcode because the parity check fails: the number of ones in the resulting code is not odd.

Barcode scan results are represented by an object of the following class `ScanData`:

```java
public class ScanData
{
  private static final int SCAN_HEIGHT = 7;
  private static final int SCAN_WIDTH = 6;
  private int[][] scan;

  public ScanData()
  {
    scan = new int[SCAN_HEIGHT][SCAN_WIDTH];
  }

  // pre- and postconditions are shown below, in Part (a)
  public boolean hasStuckSensor() { < code not shown > }

  // pre- and postconditions are shown below, in Part (b)
  public int getScanValue(int col) { < code not shown > }

  // pre- and postconditions are shown below, in Part (c)
  public int[] getBarCode() { < code not shown > }

  < other constructors and methods not shown >

}
```

(a)   Write a method `hasStuckSensor` of the `ScanData` class that returns `true` if the `scan` array indicates that a sensor is "stuck," `false` otherwise. Complete the `hasStuckSensor` method below.

```
// postcondition: returns true if a row is detected in scan
//                that contains all 1's or all 0's;
//                otherwise returns false
public boolean hasStuckSensor()
```

(b)   Write a method `getScanValue` of the `ScanData` class that returns 0 or 1, depending on the data in a given column. The method returns 1 if a majority of the values are 1; otherwise it returns 0. Assume that the number of rows is an odd number. Complete method `getScanValue` below.

```
// precondition:  SCAN_HEIGHT is an odd number;
//                scan contains 0's and 1's
// postcondition: returns 1 if a majority of data elements
//                in col are 1's; otherwise returns 0
public int getScanValue(int col)
```

(c)   Write a method `getBarCode` of the `ScanData` class that checks the scan data for errors and returns an `int` array that contains the barcode values extracted from the scan data. `getBarCode` returns `null` if the `scan` array indicates a "stuck" sensor or if the parity check fails. Otherwise the values placed in the resulting array are the values returned by the calls to `getScanValue` for the first SCAN_WIDTH - 1 columns. The value from the last column is used to check parity, but it is not stored in the resulting array. Therefore, the size of the returned array is SCAN_WIDTH - 1. Assume that `hasStuckSensor` and `getScanValue` work as specified, regardless of what you wrote in Parts (a) and (b).

```
// precondition:  scan contains barcode scan data:
//                1's and 0's
// postcondition: returns an array that contains
//                values from the first SCAN_WIDTH - 1
//                columns in the barcode; returns null
//                if scan indicates a stuck sensor
//                or if the parity check fails
public int[] getBarCode()
```

2.   This question involves a simulation of a production line for assembling pyramids made of disks. A disk is represented by an object of the class `Disk`. The `Disk` class has one constructor, which takes one `int` parameter, the radius of the disk. `Disk` objects are `Comparable`: a disk with a smaller radius is considered smaller. A `Tower` object represents a stack of disks (the class `Tower` implements the `Stack` interface). `Tower`'s no-args constructor creates an empty tower. In this application, all "towers" are "pyramids" of disks arranged by size. In a "regular" pyramid, the sizes of the disks increase from top to bottom; in an "inverted" pyramid the sizes decrease, as shown below:

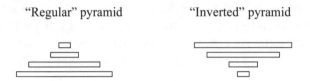

Disks arrive on an assembly line and are assembled into pyramids by a robot. The assembly line is represented by a `Queue` that contains `Disk` objects. The robot can temporarily build and hold an inverted pyramid of disks, represented by a `Tower` object. Eventually the robot "flips over" the pyramid it is holding and places it into the output assembly line, also represented by a `Queue`. This output queue contains regular pyramids, represented by `Tower` objects. This process is illustrated in the picture below.

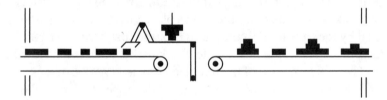

The simulation is implemented in the following class `ProductionLine`:

```
public class ProductionLine
{
    private Queue assemblyLineIn, assemblyLineOut;
    private Tower robotArm;

    // postcondition is shown below, in Part (a)
    public ProductionLine(int nDisks, int maxRadius)
    { < code not shown > }

    // pre- and postconditions are shown below, in Part (b)
    private void unloadRobot() { < code not shown > }

    // pre- and postconditions are shown below, in Part (c)
    public void process() { < code not shown > }

    < other constructors and methods not shown >
}
```

(a) Write a constructor of the `ProductionLine` class that takes two parameters, the number of disks, `nDisks`, and the maximum radius of a disk, `maxRadius`. The constructor should place `nDisks` with random radii, ranging from 1 to `maxRadius`, into the `assemblyLineIn` queue. Use the `RandNumGenerator` class from the Marine Biology Simulation case study to obtain random integers. The constructor should initialize `robotArm` to an empty tower and `assemblyLineOut` to an empty queue. Assume that the class `ListQueue` implements `Queue` and that its no-args constructor creates an empty queue; use a `ListQueue` object to initialize a queue. Finish the `ProductionLine` constructor as started below.

```
// postcondition: assemblyLineIn contains nDisks with
//                random radii ranging from 1 to maxRadius;
//                assemblyLineOut is initialized to
//                an empty ListQueue; robotArm is initialized
//                to an empty Tower
public ProductionLine(int nDisks, int maxRadius)
```

(b) Write the `unloadRobot` method of the `ProductionLine` class, as started below. The method assumes that `robotArm` holds a non-empty "inverted" pyramid. The robot "flips the pyramid over" and places it into the `assemblyLineOut` queue. The method leaves `robotArm` empty.

```
// precondition:  robotArm is not empty and holds an
//                inverted pyramid of disks
// postcondition: The pyramid in the robotArm is "flipped
//                over" and added to the assemblyLineOut
//                queue
private void unloadRobot()
```

(c) Write the `process` method of the `ProductionLine` class, as started below. The method extracts disks from the `assemblyLineIn` queue and processes them one by one. At the end, all disks are arranged into pyramids in the `assemblyLineOut` queue, `assemblyLineIn` is empty, and `robotArm` is empty.

The disks are processed in the following manner. If `robotArm` is empty or if the next disk can be placed on the top of `robotArm`, preserving its inverted pyramid order, then the disk is picked up by `robotArm`. Otherwise, `robotArm` is unloaded first. `robotArm` is also unloaded when all the disks have been processed. Assume that `unloadRobot` works as specified, regardless of what you wrote in Part (b).

```
// precondition:  assemblyLineIn holds Disk objects;
//                robotArm is empty;
//                assemblyLineOut is empty
// postcondition: all disks from assemblyLineIn have been
//                processed.  A disk is processed as
//                follows: if robotArm is not empty and
//                the next disk does not fit on top of
//                robotArm (which must be an inverted
//                pyramid) then robotArm is unloaded first;
//                the disk from assemblyLineIn is added
//                to robotArm.  When all the disks have been
//                retrieved from assemblyLineIn, robotArm
//                is unloaded
public void process()
```

3. This question refers to the code from the Marine Biology Simulation case study. We have observed that when the number of fish becomes large in an unbounded environment, each simulation step takes a long time. We want to try using a `TreeMap` rather than an `ArrayList` for holding objects in an unbounded environment and to compare the simulation speeds. For this purpose, we have introduced a class `UnboundedMapEnv`. Like the original `UnboundedEnv`, `UnboundedMapEnv` extends `SquareEnvironment`. `UnboundedMapEnv` uses the instance variable

```
private Map locationMap;
```

instead of

```
private ArrayList objectList;
```

`locationMap` associates a location (a `Location` object) with a `Locatable` object at that location. Thus a location serves as a key in `locationMap`.

`locationMap` is initialized in `UnboundedMapEnv`'s constructor as follows:

```
public UnboundedMapEnv()
{
  super();
  locationMap = new TreeMap();
}
```

(a) Implement the `add` method of the `UnboundedMapEnv` class, as started below. The method should throw an `IllegalArgumentException` if the location where the object is supposed to be placed is not empty. Debugging printout statements are not required.

```
// Adds a new object to this environment at the
// location it specifies
public void add(Locatable obj)
```

(b) Implement the `allObjects` method of the `UnboundedMapEnv` class. The method returns an array of all objects in the environment. The objects should be placed into the array in the order returned by an iterator for the set of all keys (locations) in the map. Complete `allObjects` as started below.

```
// Returns all the objects in this environment
public Locatable[] allObjects()
```

(c)   Implement the recordMove method of the UnboundedMapEnv class. The method updates the environment to record the move of a given Locatable object from its old location. If the object has not moved, the method does nothing. If the object has moved and its new location is not empty or the object at the old location is a different object, recordMove should throw an IllegalArgumentException. Complete recordMove as started below.

```
// postcondition: obj is at the appropriate location
//                obj.location() and either oldLoc is
//                equal to obj.location() (there was
//                no movement) or oldLoc is empty
public void recordMove(Locatable obj, Location oldLoc)
```

4.   This question involves reasoning about binary trees that represent arithmetic expressions. We will use `TreeNode` objects to represent nodes of a binary tree.

Consider the following abstract class that represents an "arithmetic unit" (AU):

```
public abstract class AU
{
  private int register;

  public int getRegister() { return register; }
  public void setRegister(int x) { register = x; }

  // postcondition: returns the number of inputs expected
  //                by this AU
  public abstract int numInputs();

  // postcondition: If numInputs() == 0, x and y are ignored.
  //                If numInputs() == 1, y is ignored.
  //                Sets register equal to the result
  //                of computation and returns that result
  public abstract int compute(int x, int y);
}
```

An AU can take 0, 1, or 2 inputs and compute the result of some arithmetic operation, depending on the specific type of AU. The `numInputs` method returns the number of inputs expected by this AU. The `compute` method returns the result of the operation. If `numInputs()` is 1, `compute` uses x and ignores y; if `numInputs()` is 0, `compute` ignores x and y. (If `numInputs()` is 0, the AU is a "constant" whose `compute` method always returns the same value, ignoring the parameters.)

An AU is also equipped with one "register" that can store an integer value. The `compute` method sets `register` to the result of the computation, but `register` can also be used by clients of AU for temporary storage.

Each node in an expression tree holds an AU object as that node's value. The children of a node provide inputs to the AU in that node. If AU in the node is a "constant" (takes no inputs), that node must be a leaf; if the AU takes one input, its node must have only one, left child; if AU takes two inputs, its node must have two children. The expression tree in the picture below corresponds to the following expression: `(1 + (2 * 3)) * (-(4))`. This tree has four "constant" AUs, one unary-operator type AU, and three binary-operator type AUs (two * and one +).

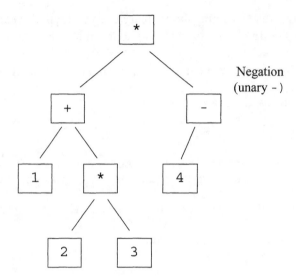

Note that in an expression tree, the subtree rooted in each node is also an expression tree.

(a)   Write a `boolean` method `isValidAUTree` as started below. The method returns `true` if and only if the tree is empty or if it is a valid expression tree: that is, the children of each node match the number of inputs for the AU stored in that node.

```
// precondition:  root is null or refers to the root
//                of a binary tree that holds AU objects
//                as values in its nodes
// postcondition: returns true if root is null or if root
//                refers to a valid AU tree; otherwise
//                returns false; in a valid AU tree the number
//                of children of each node matches the number
//                of inputs of the AU stored in that node;
//                a node with a one-input AU has only
//                a left child
public static boolean isValidAUTree(TreeNode root)
```

(b)   To evaluate an AU tree, we need to evaluate the left and right subtrees of the root, if present, then use the results as the inputs for the AU in the root. Write the method `evaluate` as started below.

```
// precondition:  root != null;
//                isValidAUTree(root) == true
// postcondition: returns the value computed from
//                the expression tree root; the register field
//                of the AU in each node is set to the result
//                of evaluating that node's subtree
//
public static int evaluate(TreeNode root)
```

(c) Write a method `findMax` that returns the largest result of evaluation of all subtrees in the tree. **Your method must work in *O(n)* time, where *n* is the number of nodes.** Assume that `findMax(root)` is called after `evaluate(root)`, so that the AU register in each node holds the result of evaluation of the subtree rooted in that node. Also assume that `evaluate` works as specified, regardless of what you wrote in Part (b).

```
// precondition:   root != null;
//                 isValidAUTree(root) == true;
//                 AU's register in each node holds the
//                 result of evaluation of that node's subtree
// postcondition: returns the maximum result of evaluation
//                 of subtrees in all nodes
public static int findMax(TreeNode root)
```

Practice Exam AB-2

COMPUTER SCIENCE AB
SECTION I

Time — 1 hour and 15 minutes
Number of questions — 40
Percent of total grade — 50

1. Given that x is *true*, y is *true*, and z is *false*, which of the following expressions will evaluate to *false*?

    (A)   (x && y) || z
    (B)   (x || y) && z
    (C)   y || (x && z)
    (D)   x || (y && z)
    (E)   x && (y || z)

2. Consider the following method:

    ```
    // precondition:  n and d are non-negative integers
    // postcondition: returns the number of times the digit d
    //                occurs in the decimal representation of n
    private int findDigit(int n, int d)
    {
      int count = 0;
      < statement1 >
      while (n > 0)
      {
        if (n % 10 == d)
          count++;
        < statement2 >
      }
      return count;
    }
    ```

    Which of the following could replace < *statement1* > and < *statement2* > to make findDigit work as specified?

	< *statement1* >	< *statement2* >
(A)	if (n == 0) return 1;	n /= 10;
(B)	if (n == 0) return 1;	d *= 10;
(C)	if (d == 0) count++;	n -= n % 10;
(D)	if (n == 0 && d != 0) return 0;	n *= 10;
(E)	if (n == 0 && d == 0) count++;	n /= 10;

3.   In OOP, programmers often arrange classes into inheritance hierarchies as opposed to implementing isolated classes. Which of the following is NOT a valid reason for doing so?

   (A)   More abstract classes at the top of the hierarchy can easily be extended in the project or reused in other projects.
   (B)   Methods from a superclass can often be reused in its subclasses without duplication of code.
   (C)   Objects from different subclasses can be passed as arguments to a method designed to accept objects of a superclass.
   (D)   Objects from different subclasses can be stored in the same array.
   (E)   All of the above are valid reasons for using inheritance hierarchies.

4.   In a regular pentagon, the ratio of the length of a diagonal to the length of a side is equal to the Golden Ratio (defined as $\frac{1+\sqrt{5}}{2} \approx 1.618$). Consider the following class `Pentagon` that represents a regular pentagon:

```
public class Pentagon
{
  public static final double goldenRatio =
                            (1 + Math.sqrt(5.0)) / 2;
  private double side;

  public Pentagon (double x)
  {
    side = x;
  }

  public double getDiagonalLength()
  {
    return side * goldenRatio;
  }
}
```

Which of the following code segments will compile with no syntax errors and display the correct length of a diagonal in a regular pentagon with side 3.0?

   I.   `System.out.print(3/2 * (1 + Math.sqrt(5.0)));`

   II.   `System.out.print(3.0 * Pentagon.goldenRatio);`

   III.   `Pentagon p = new Pentagon(3);`
           `System.out.print(p.getDiagonalLength());`

   (A)   I only
   (B)   II only
   (C)   III only
   (D)   I and II
   (E)   II and III

5. Consider the following method:

```
// precondition:  amps.length >= 2; amps is filled with random
//                 values
// postcondition: returns the largest sum of two elements in
//                 amps
public int addTopTwo(int[] amps)
{
  int k, k1 = 0, k2 = 1;

  for (k = 2; k < amps.length; k++)
  {
    if (amps[k] > amps[k1])
    {
      k2 = k1;
      k1 = k;
    }
    else if (amps[k] > amps[k2])
    {
      k2 = k;
    }
  }
  return amps[k1] + amps[k2];
}
```

For which of the following arrays will addTopTwo return an incorrect result?

(A) {1, 5, 4, 3, 2}
(B) {2, 1, 3, 4, 5}
(C) {1, 2, 3, 4, 5}
(D) {5, 4, 3, 2, 1}
(E) {5, 4}

6. One task of a compiler is to check that each pair of delimiter symbols, such as braces or parentheses, match. In writing a parsing method that checks that pairs of braces match, which of the following data structures would be most useful for temporarily saving the location of the opening brace until a matching closing brace is found?

(A) A list
(B) A stack
(C) A queue
(D) A set, implemented as a binary search tree
(E) A map, implemented as a binary search tree

7. The two versions of the `search` method shown below are both intended to return `true` if `ArrayList list` contains the target value, false otherwise.

Version 1:

```
public boolean search(ArrayList list, Object target)
{
  int k;
  for (k = 0; k < list.size(); k++)
  {
    if (target.equals(list.get(k)))
      return true;
  }
  return false;
}
```

Version 2:

```
public boolean search(ArrayList list, Object target)
{
  int k;
  boolean found = false;
  for (k = 0; k < list.size(); k++)
  {
    if (target.equals(list.get(k)))
      found = true;
  }
  return found;
}
```

Which of the following statements about the two versions of `search` is true?

(A)   Only Version 1 works as intended.
(B)   Only Version 2 works as intended.
(C)   Both versions works as intended; Version 1 is often more efficient than Version 2.
(D)   Both versions works as intended; Version 2 is often more efficient than Version 1.
(E)   Both versions works as intended; the two versions are always equally efficient.

8. Which of the following statements about interfaces and abstract classes is TRUE?

(A)   If an abstract class has no implemented constructors or methods, it is better to make it an interface.
(B)   An abstract class cannot extend another abstract class.
(C)   An abstract class cannot implement an interface.
(D)   You can declare an array of objects of an abstract class type, but not of an interface type.
(E)   A method can take a parameter of an interface type, but not of an abstract class type.

9. Consider the following method

```
public boolean isOneOfaKind(String word)
{
  int len = word.length();
  return len < 2 ||
    (word.substring(0,1).equals(word.substring(len-1)) &&
        isOneOfaKind(word.substring(1, len-1)));
}
```

For which of the following three strings will isOneOfaKind return true: "aviva", "annetta", "annabelle"?

(A) Only "aviva"
(B) Only "annetta"
(C) Both "aviva" and "annetta"
(D) All three
(E) None of the three

10. A two-dimensional array image holds brightness values for pixels (picture elements) in an image. The brightness values range from 0 to 255. Consider the following method:

```
public int findMax(int[][] image)
{
  int[] count = new int[256];
  int r, c;
  int i, iMax = 0;

  for (r = 0; r < image.length; r++)
  {
    for (c = 0; c < image[0].length; c++)
    {
      i = image[r][c];
      count[i]++;
    }
  }
  for (i = 1; i < 256; i++)
  {
    if (count[i] > count[iMax])
      iMax = i;
  }
  return iMax;
}
```

What does this method compute?

(A) The column with the highest sum of brightness values in image
(B) The maximum brightness value for all pixels in image
(C) The maximum sum of brightness values in any 256 consecutive rows in image
(D) The maximum sum of brightness values in any 256 by 256 square in image
(E) The most frequent brightness value in image

Questions 11-14 are based on the following class Table, which is used in another class, Restaurant. A Restaurant object maintains an array of Table objects and keeps track of the occupancy of tables in a restaurant.

```
public class Table
{
  private final int numChairs;
  private int numGuests;
  private List orderedItems;   // holds MenuItem objects

  public Table(int n)
  {
    numChairs = n;
    numGuests = 0;
    orderedItems = new LinkedList();
  }

  // postcondition: returns the seating capacity at this table
  public int getNumChairs() { return numChairs; }

  // postcondition: returns the number of guests at this table
  public int getNumGuests() {   return numGuests; }

  // postcondition: returns the list of ordered items
  public List getOrder() { return orderedItems; }

  // precondition:  numGuests + n <= numChairs
  // postcondition: n people added to the guests at this table
  public void addGuests(int n) { numGuests += n; }

  // precondition:  numGuests > 0
  // postcondition: order items are placed into the
  //                orderedItems list
  public void placeOrder(List items) { orderedItems = items; }

  public void clear()
  {
    numGuests = 0;
    orderedItems = new LinkedList();
  }

  // postcondition: returns the cost of all items
  // in the orderedItems list
  public double getBillAmt() {  < code not shown > }
}
```

11. Suppose a programmer decided to code and test the `Table` constructor and two other `Table` methods, temporarily leaving the other methods empty. Which of the following method pairs is the best pair of candidates for being implemented and tested first?

   (A) `getNumGuests` and `addGuests`
   (B) `getNumChairs` and `addGuests`
   (C) `addGuests` and `placeOrder`
   (D) `addGuests` and `clear`
   (E) `addGuests` and `getBillAmt`

12. Which of the following expressions would correctly refer to the first ordered item in a method of the `Table` class (assuming `orderedItems.size() > 0`)?

   I.   `(MenuItem)orderedItems.getFirst();`

   II.   `(MenuItem)orderedItems.get(0);`

   III.   `(MenuItem)orderedItems.iterator().next();`

   (A) I only
   (B) II only
   (C) I and II
   (D) II and III
   (E) I, II, and III

13. The `Restaurant` class declares and uses an array of `Table` objects:

```
public class Restaurant
{
  private Table[] tables;

  public int numTables() { return tables.length; }
  // ... etc.
}
```

The designer of `Restaurant` decided to provide the following <u>private</u> method `getTable`:

```
// postcondition: returns the k-th table in this
//                restaurant
private Table getTable(int k) { < code not shown > }
```

The programmer was instructed to use, elsewhere in `Restaurant`'s code, calls to `numTables` and `getTable` rather than direct references to the `tables` array. Which of the following best describes a valid rationale for this decision?

(A) Better run-time code efficiency
(B) Easier to replace `Table[]` with another structure (e.g., an `ArrayList`) with minimal changes in the rest of `Restaurant`'s code
(C) Easier to modify the implementation of `Restaurant` without changing its client classes
(D) The possibility to call `getTable` from subclasses of `Restaurant`
(E) The possibility to override `getTable` in subclasses of `Restaurant`

14. Which of the following are the most appropriate replacements for < *condition* > and < *missing statement* > in the following code for the `seatParty` method of the `Restaurant` class?

```
// precondition:  0 < numPeople
// postcondition: numPeople customers have been seated
//                at the first available empty table that can
//                accommodate numPeople or more people;
//                returns true if successful; false if no room
public boolean seatParty(int numPeople)
{
    for (int k = 0; k < numTables(); k++)
    {
        Table t = getTable(k);
        if ( < condition > )
        {
            < missing statement >;
            return true;
        }
    }
    return false;
}
```

	< *condition* >	< *missing statement* >
(A)	`t.numGuests == 0 &&` `Table.numChairs(t) >= numPeople`	`t.numGuests += numPeople`
(B)	`getNumGuests(t) == 0 &&` `getNumChairs(t) >= numPeople`	`addGuests(t, numPeople)`
(C)	`t.getNumGuests() == 0 &&` `t.getNumChairs() >= numPeople`	`t.addGuests(numPeople)`
(D)	`getNumGuests(t) > 0 ||` `getNumChairs(t) < numPeople`	`addGuests(t, numPeople)`
(E)	`t.getNumChairs() - t.getNumGuests()` `>= numPeople`	`t.numGuests += numPeople`

15. What is the result when the following code segment is executed?

```
String url = "http://www.usa.gov";
int pos = url.indexOf("http://");
if (pos >= 0)
    System.out.print(url.substring(0, pos));
else
    System.out.print("not found");
```

(A) Displays nothing
(B) Displays `www.usa.gov`
(C) Displays `http://www.usa.gov`
(D) Displays `not found`
(E) Displays `IndexOutOfBoundsException`

Questions 16-17 refer to the following method:

```
private int product(int n)
{
  if (n <= 1)
    return 1;
  else
    return n * product(n-2);
}
```

16. What is the output when `product(6)` is called?

    (A) 1
    (B) 8
    (C) 12
    (D) 48
    (E) 720

17. `product(25)` returns -1181211311. Which of the following accounts for this result?

    (A) Logic error that shows up for odd values of n
    (B) Stack overflow error in recursive calls
    (C) Small range of integers in the Java Virtual Machine installed on your computer
    (D) Integer arithmetic overflow
    (E) A loss of precision in calculations

18. For which of the following binary trees does preorder traversal produce APCS and postorder traversal produce CPSA?

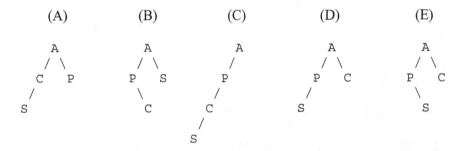

19. A master list of past contributors to a large charitable organization is maintained in alphabetical order. After each fundraising event, an unsorted relatively small list of new contributors has to be added to the master list. Which of the following sorting algorithms would be the most efficient algorithm for this task?

    (A) Quicksort
    (B) Heapsort
    (C) Mergesort
    (D) Insertion Sort
    (E) Selection Sort

20. The method below is supposed to count the number of negative values in a non-empty queue containing `Integer` objects, leaving the queue unchanged.

```
public int countNegs(Queue q)
{
  int count = 0;

  Integer first = (Integer)q.dequeue();
  if (first.intValue() < 0)
    count++;
  q.enqueue(first);

  while (q.peekFront() != first)
  {
    Integer num = (Integer)q.dequeue();
    if (num.intValue() < 0)
      count++;
    q.enqueue(num);
  }

  return count;
}
```

Assuming that `ListQueue` implements `Queue`, in which of the following code segments does `countNegs` work as specified?

```
I.        Queue q1 = new ListQueue();
          q1.enqueue(new Integer(-1));
          System.out.println(countNegs(q1));
```

```
II.       Queue q2 = new ListQueue();
          q2.enqueue(new Integer(-1));
          q2.enqueue(new Integer(1));
          q2.enqueue(new Integer(-1));
          System.out.println(countNegs(q2));
```

```
III.      Queue q3 = new ListQueue();
          Integer pos = new Integer(1);
          Integer neg = new Integer(-1);
          q3.enqueue(pos);
          q3.enqueue(neg);
          q3.enqueue(pos);
          q3.enqueue(neg);
          System.out.println(countNegs(q3));
```

(A)   None
(B)   I only
(C)   I and II
(D)   II and III
(E)   I, II, and III

21. A priority queue is implemented as a heap and contains *n* items. Which of the following describes the average running time for peekMin, removeMin, and add methods?

	peekMin	removeMin	add
(A)	$O(1)$	$O(1)$	$O(1)$
(B)	$O(1)$	$O(1)$	$O(\log n)$
(C)	$O(1)$	$O(\log n)$	$O(\log n)$
(D)	$O(\log n)$	$O(\log n)$	$O(\log n)$
(E)	$O(1)$	$O(n)$	$O(n)$

22. Consider the following method that sorts a given list of Comparable objects and returns a sorted list:

```
public static List sort(List list)
{
  if (list.size() < 2)
    return list;
  List listA = new LinkedList();
  List listB = new LinkedList();
  Iterator iter = list.iterator();
  Object x = iter.next();
  while (iter.hasNext())
  {
    Comparable y = (Comparable)iter.next();
    if (y.compareTo(x) <= 0)
      listA.add(y);
    else
      listB.add(y);
  }
  listA = sort(listA);
  listB = sort(listB);
  listA.add(x);
  iter = listB.iterator();
  while (iter.hasNext())
    listA.add(iter.next());
  return listA;
}
```

Which sorting algorithm is used in this method?

(A) Selection Sort
(B) Insertion Sort
(C) Mergesort
(D) Quicksort
(E) Heapsort

23. One of the `HashMap` constructors takes two parameters: the *initial capacity* (the number of buckets) and the *load factor* — the maximum allowed ratio of the number of items stored in the table to the current capacity. When this ratio comes to exceed the load factor, the capacity is automatically increased (usually doubled) and the entries are rehashed. If we plan to store around 3,000 items in a table, which of the following values for the initial capacity and load factor make a reasonable choice that results in not too many collisions and not too much wasted space and assures that rehashing doesn't happen?

(A) 1500 and 2.0
(B) 3000 and 0.5
(C) 4000 and 0.5
(D) 5000 and 0.75
(E) 30000 and 0.2

24. If a binary tree has 17 nodes, at most how many of them can be leaves?

(A) 1
(B) 8
(C) 9
(D) 16
(E) 17

25. Consider the following method:

```
public static int checkTree(TreeNode root)
{
  if (root == null)
    return 0;

  int x = checkTree(root.getLeft());
  if (x >= 0 && checkTree(root.getRight()) == x)
    return x + 1;
  return -1;
}
```

`checkTree(root)` returns a non-negative value if and only if the tree rooted in `root`

(A) is not empty and the root is a leaf
(B) is empty or the root is a leaf or the root has two children
(C) has no nodes with only one child
(D) is empty or the root has left and right subtrees of the same depth
(E) is a full tree

26. Suppose a method `findFirstPositive` returns the position of the first positive value in an array (or ascertains that there are none). The precondition is that the array does not have any negative values and that all zeros, if any, precede all positive values. The method works by comparing certain elements of the array to 0. If $T(n)$ is the number of comparisons that guarantees the correct result for any array of n elements, even in the worst case, what is $T(10)$ in an optimal algorithm?

   (A)   4
   (B)   5
   (C)   8
   (D)   9
   (E)   10

27. Which of the following is easier with information hiding?

   I.   Implementing IS-A relationships for classes

   II.   Making changes to the implementation of one of the classes in a project

   III.   Producing specifications for individual programmers working on the same project

   (A)   I only
   (B)   II only
   (C)   I and II
   (D)   II and III
   (E)   I, II, and III

28. A programmer is designing a database of CDs for a large music store. A CD object is described by a unique identification code, the band or performer, the date of release, a list of songs, the quantity in stock, and the retail price. A store manager must be able to obtain a list of all the CDs by a particular band, quickly check the price and availability for the CD with a given identification code, and find a CD that contains a given song. The programmer is considering some combination of the following data structures:

   S1: A `LinkedList` of all CDs, arranged in ascending order by identification code.
   S2: A `HashMap` of all CDs, keyed by identification codes.
   S3: A `HashMap` of all CDs, keyed by the band/performer name. For each band it holds a list of all CDs of that band arranged by year of release in reverse order.
   S4: A `TreeSet` of all CDs. Two CDs should be compared by the band name and, if the same, by the date of release.
   S5: A `HashMap`, keyed by song names, which associates a song name with the list of identification codes of CDs that contains that song.

   Which combination of the above structures is appropriate for this application?

   (A)   S1, S3, and S5
   (B)   S1, S4, and S5
   (C)   S2, S3, and S5
   (D)   S2, S3, and S4
   (E)   S3 and S5

Questions 29-32 refer to the abstract class House and its subclass HouseForSale:

```
public abstract class House implements Comparable
{
  private int mySize;

  public House(int size) { mySize = size; }
  public int getSize() { return mySize; }
  public void setSize(int size) { mySize = size; }

  public int compareTo(Object other)
  {
    return getSize() - ((House)other).getSize();
  }

  public abstract int getPrice();
}

public class HouseForSale extends House
{
  private int myPrice;

  public HouseForSale(int size, int price)
  {
    < missing statement >
    myPrice = price;
  }

  public int getPrice() { return myPrice; }

  public int compareTo(Object other)
  {
    return getPrice() - ((HouseForSale)other).getPrice();
  }

  < other constructors, methods, and variables not shown >
}
```

29. Which of the following is the most appropriate replacement for < *missing statement* > in HouseForSale's constructor?

    (A) mySize = size;
    (B) setSize(size);
    (C) super.setSize(size);
    (D) super(size);
    (E) super = new House(size);

30. Suppose that while coding `HouseForSale` the programmer accidentally misspelled "compareTo" in his class. What will happen when he tries to compile and run his class with the following test statements?

```
HouseForSale house1 = new HouseForSale(2000, 129000);
HouseForSale house2 = new HouseForSale(1800, 149000);
System.out.println(house1.compareTo(house2));
```

(A)   A syntax error "undefined compareTo method" in the `HouseForSale` class
(B)   A syntax error "HouseForSale should be declared abstract"
(C)   The code will compile with no errors and display `200`
(D)   The code compiles with no errors but generates a `NoSuchMethodException`
(E)   The code compiles with no errors but generates a `ClassCastException`

31. If the classes `House` and `HouseForSale` compile with no problems, which of the following declarations will result in a syntax error?

(A)   `House[] houses = new House[2];`

(B)   `HouseForSale[] houses = {new House(2000), new House(1800)};`

(C)   `House[] houses = {new HouseForSale(2000, 129000),`
      `                   new HouseForSale(1800, 149000)};`

(D)   `Comparable[] houses = {new HouseForSale(2000, 129000),`
      `                       new HouseForSale(1800, 149000)};`

(E)   `HouseForSale[] houses = {new HouseForSale(2000, 129000),`
      `                         new HouseForSale(1800, 149000)};`

32. Which of the following is the most appropriate way to define the `getSize` method in `HouseForSale`?

(A)   `public int getSize() { return mySize; }`
(B)   `public int getSize() { return super.mySize; }`
(C)   `public int getSize() { return super(mySize); }`
(D)   `public int getSize() { return super.getSize(); }`
(E)   No definition is necessary because the same code is already written in `House`.

33. Consider the following method:

```
public ListNode transform(ListNode list)
{
  if (list == null)
    return null;

  ListNode node = list.getNext();
  if (node == null)
    return list;

  list.setNext(node.getNext());
  node.setNext(transform(list));
  return node;
}
```

What is the output from the following code?

```
ListNode list = null;
for (int k = 1; k <= 5; k++)
{
    list = new ListNode(new Integer(k), list);
}

list = transform(list);

ListNode node;
for (node = list; node != null; node = node.getNext())
{
    System.out.print(node.getValue());
}
```

(A) 12345
(B) 43215
(C) 15432
(D) 45321
(E) 54321

34. The class `ListStack` implements a stack using a `LinkedList` object:

```
public class ListStack implements Stack
{
  private LinkedList items;

  public Object pop()
  {
    if (!isEmpty())
    {
      return items.removeFirst();
    }
    else
    {
      < missing statements >
    }
  }

  < Constructor and other methods not shown >
}
```

Which of the following is the most appropriate replacement for < *missing statements* > in the `pop` method?

(A)   `return null;`

(B)   `System.err.println("NoSuchElementException");`
      `System.exit(0);`

(C)   `throw("NoSuchElementException");`
      `System.exit(1);`

(D)   `System.throw(NoSuchElementException);`

(E)   `throw new NoSuchElementException();`

Questions 35-40 refer to the code from the Marine Biology Simulation case study.

35. While experimenting with the working MBS program (including breeding and dying fish) using a 5-by-5 bounded environment, Pat started with one fish (a `Fish` object) in the middle, facing north, and observed that after a certain number of timesteps, the configuration returned to exactly the same position, with one fish in the middle facing north. What is the smallest number of timesteps for which this is possible?

(A)   1
(B)   2
(C)   3
(D)   4
(E)   6

36. Trying to make the simulation results more predictable, Pat replaced the `getInstance` method in the `RandNumGenerator` class with the following code:

```
public static Random getInstance()
{
    return new Random(11843);
}
```

The modified `getInstance` method always returns a new `Random` object initialized with the same "seed" value. After some experiments, Pat discovered that with the seed 11843, the first value returned by `nextDouble()` is a small number, 0.037. The first value returned by `nextInt(n)` is 0 (for $n < 20$). Pat then incorporated the modified `RandNumGenerator` class into MBS with dynamic population and ran it on a 3-by-3 bounded environment, starting with three fish on the diagonal, all facing East:

Which of the following fish configurations did Pat see after one simulation step?

(A)   (B)   (C)   (D)   (E)

37. Suppose a fish is at the left wall of a bounded environment and is facing East (to the right). What happens when this fish's nextLocation method attempts to find and remove from its empty neighbors list the neighboring location behind the fish:

```
Location locationBehind =
        environment().getNeighbor(location(), oppositeDir);
emptyNbrs.remove(locationBehind);
```

(A)   This is not a problem because a fish can be never found in this situation.

(B)   emptyNbrs.remove(locationBehind) does nothing and the simulation continues.

(C)   The statement

```
Location locationBehind = environment().getNeighbor(
                                location(), oppositeDir);
```

throws a NoSuchElementException.

(D)   The statement

```
emptyNbrs.remove(locationBehind);
```

throws a NullPointerException.

(E)   The left "neighbor" is successfully found in the emptyNeighbors list and removed from it, even though it is not a valid location in the environment.

38. Suppose we want to introduce a new subclass of Fish, GoldFish. A GoldFish acts like a normal fish but changes color at each timestep, alternating between red and gold. Which of the following features should be added?

    I.   The act method redefined in the GoldFish class
    II. A flipColor() method defined in the GoldFish class
    III. A changeColor(Color col) method added to the Fish class

(A)   I only
(B)   II only
(C)   I and II
(D)   II and III
(E)   I, II, and III

39. Suppose f is a Fish object. Which of the following conditions correctly checks whether the environment cell immediately to the south of f is empty?

(A) `f.environment().isEmpty(f.environment().getNeighbor(`
                                    `f.location(), Direction.SOUTH))`

(B) `f.environment().isEmpty(f.getNeighbor(f.location(), Direction.SOUTH))`

(C) `f.environment().getNeighbor(f.location(), Direction.SOUTH) == null`

(D) `f.getNeighbor(f.location(), Direction.SOUTH) == null`

(E) `f.getNeighbor(f.location(), Direction.SOUTH.inDegrees()) == null`

40. Consider the following alternative MBS design:

- Simulation becomes an interface with one method:

   `void step(Locatable[] objects);`

- One or several classes implement Simulation (e.g., SimMoveBreedDie);

- An instance variable Simulation theSim is added to the environment classes and set to a Simulation type of object (e.g., a SimMoveBreedDie type of object) passed to the environment constructor;

- The method step() is added to the Environment interface and its implementations:

   `public void step() { theSim.step(allObjects()); }`

- The main MBS class calls environment's step for each simulation step.

- As before, the simulation's step method calls act for each fish.

Which of the following statements about this alternative design is true?

(A) The alternative design is more flexible but less efficient than the original design.
(B) The alternative design is less flexible and equally efficient.
(C) The alternative design is equally flexible but much more complicated.
(D) The alternative design is less flexible, more complicated, and less efficient.
(E) The alternative design is more flexible, equally efficient, and not more complicated than the original design.

Practice Exam AB-2

COMPUTER SCIENCE AB
SECTION II

Time — 1 hour and 45 minutes
Number of questions — 4
Percent of total grade — 50

1. Optical Character Recognition (OCR) software interprets images of letters or digits scanned from documents. An image may be represented by a two-dimensional array of "pixels" (picture elements). Each pixel has an intensity, represented by an integer. In this question, high intensity will represent "ink" and low intensity will represent "white space."

    A simple OCR method, suitable for one font of fixed size, is called "template matching." A template is created for each character in the font. A template is a numeric mask that has positive numbers (weights) in those places where the picture of the character is likely to have "ink," negative weights where the picture is likely to have white space, and, perhaps, zeros in the borderline areas. For example, a template for 'A' may have the size 9 rows by 11 columns and may use the weights shown in the picture below.

A digitized image of a character and a 9 by 11 template placed over it at position $row = 2$, $col = 3$.
  x — high intensity pixels
  . — low intensity pixels

Template for "A"

```
-1 -1 -1 -1 -1  0 -1 -1 -1 -1 -1

-1 -1 -1 -1  0  5  0 -1 -1 -1 -1

-1 -1 -1  0  5  0  5 -1 -1 -1 -1

-1 -1  0  5  0 -5  0  5  0 -1 -1

-1  0  5  0  0  0  0  0  5 -1 -1

-1  0  5  5  8  8  8  5  5 -1 -1

 0  5  5  0  0  0  0  0  5  5  0

 0  0 -1 -1 -1 -1 -1 -1 -1  0  0

-1 -1 -1 -1 -5 -5 -5 -1 -1 -1 -1
```

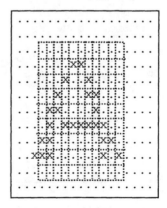

The template for each character in the font is superimposed on the digitized image at the approximate location where the picture of a letter or a digit is found and the "fit ratio" is computed for each template. The template that gives the best fit determines the recognition result.

The following class `Template` represents a template for a character:

```
public class Template
{
  private String charName;
  private double[][] weights;

  // constructors not shown

  public String getCharName() { return charName; }
  public int numRows() { return weights.length; }
  public int numCols() { return weights[0].length; }
  public double getWeight(int row, int col)
                        { return weights[row][col]; }
}
```

The `getCharName` method returns a string that represents the character name (e.g., `"A"`). The `getWeight(row, col)` method returns the value at position (*row, col*) in the `weights` matrix.

An image of a character is represented by the class `Image`, partially defined below:

```
public class Image
{
  // postcondition: returns the number of rows in this image
  public int numRows() { < code not shown > }

  // postcondition: returns the number of columns in this image
  public int numCols() { < code not shown > }

  // postcondition: returns the pixel intensity at row, col
  public int getPixel(int row, int col) { < code not shown > }

  // postcondition: returns the sum of pixel intensities in row
  public int getRowIntensity(int row) { < code not shown > }

  // pre- and postconditions are shown below, in Part (a)
  public int findVertPos(int charHeight)
  { < code not shown > }

  // postcondition: returns the left position of the
  //                template-size rectangle that contains
  //                the picture of the character in this image
  public int findHorzPos(int topRow, int charWidth)
  { < code not shown > }

  // pre- and postconditions are shown below, in Part (b)
  public double calculateFitRatio(Template t)
  { < code not shown > }

  < constructors, fields, and other methods not shown >

}
```

To find the vertical position of the character in an image, we find the contiguous block of *h* rows (where *h* is the height of the template) with the largest amount of black "ink" in it, that is the largest sum of all pixel intensities in these rows. A similar procedure is used to find the horizontal position of the character, but it works within the constraints of the found vertical position.

(a)   Write the `findVertPos` method of the `Image` class as started below. The method returns the row position `row` such that the total cumulative intensity of pixels in the rows from `row` to `row + charHeight - 1` is the largest. (If several row positions result in the same total intensity, the one with the smallest index is returned.) In writing this method, assume that `getRowIntensity` works as specified.

```
// precondition:  charHeight <= numRows()
// postcondition: returns row such that the total sum of
//                pixel intensities in rows from row to
//                row + charHeight - 1 is the largest.
//                If several row values give the same
//                maximum intensity, returns the top one
//                (the one with the smallest index).
public int findVertPos(int charHeight)
```

(b)   Write the `calculateFitRatio` method of the `Image` class. This method first finds the vertical position of the character, using the template height as `charHeight`. Then it finds the horizontal position using the template width as `charWidth` (within the constraints of the vertical position). The method then calculates the fit ratio for the template placed over the image so that the template's upper left corner is at the found position. The fit ratio is computed by multiplying the intensity of each pixel in the image covered by the template by the corresponding template weight and adding all the results. For a 9-by-11 template, for example, 99 individual products contribute to the sum. The sum is then divided by the total number of pixels covered by the template, and that number is returned as the fit ratio. Regardless of what you wrote above, assume that the other methods in the `Image` class, including `findVertPos`, work as specified.

Complete the `calculateFitRatio` method below the given header:

```
// precondition:  0 < t.numRows() <= numRows();
//                0 < t.numCols() <= numCols()
// postcondition: finds the position of the character in this
//                image for a given template and returns
//                the fit ratio for that template
//                at that position
public double calculateFitRatio(Template t)
```

(c)   Write the `ocr` method of the `OCR` class, as started below. Given an image and a list of templates that represent a font, this method returns the recognition result for the character in the image. The method returns `null` if none of the templates produces a positive fit ratio. Assume that all methods of the `Image` class work as specified, regardless of what you wrote in Parts (a) and (b).

```
// precondition:   image holds a picture of a character.
//                 The templates list contains Template objects
//                 that represent different characters in
//                 the font
// postcondition:  returns a String that corresponds to the
//                 name of the best-fitting template
//                 (or one of the best-fitting templates) from
//                 the font or null if none of the templates
//                 produces a positive fit
public String ocr(Image image, ArrayList templates)
```

2. A dictionary can be represented as a map in which each word is associated with a set of all its translations into another language. For example, in an English-Spanish dictionary, *holiday* might be associated with {*fiesta, vacaciones*}; in a Spanish-English dictionary, *fiesta* might be associated with {*holiday, party, celebration, feast*}. In a dictionary map, a word is a key and a set of its translations is a "value" associated with that key. Suppose the dictionary is implemented as a TreeMap and a set of translations for each word is implemented as a TreeSet.

    (a) Write a method that adds a word and its translation to a dictionary as started below.

```
// precondition:  dictionary != null
//                dictionary is a Map, which associates
//                a word (a String) with a set (a TreeSet) of
//                its translations (Strings)
// postcondition: if word is among the keys, translation
//                is added to its set of translations;
//                otherwise a new entry is created for word
//                and it is associated with a
//                single-element set that contains the
//                given translation
public static void add(Map dictionary, String word,
                                        String translation)
```

    (b) Write a method that takes a dictionary and generates a reverse dictionary. A reverse dictionary uses the same structure as the original dictionary, and for each pair (*word, translation*) in the original dictionary there is a reversed pair (*translation, word*) in the reverse dictionary. For example, if you can find *holiday -> fiesta* in an English-Spanish dictionary, you should be able to find *fiesta -> holiday* in its reverse, Spanish-English dictionary. Write reverse as started below. You can assume that the add method from Part (a) is in the same class and works as specified.

```
// precondition:  dictionary != null
//                dictionary associates a TreeSet of
//                translations with each word.
// postcondition: returns a reverse dictionary with
//                a similar structure and the following
//                property: word2 is in the set of
//                translations associated with word1
//                if and only if word1 is in the set of
//                translations associated with word2 in the
//                original dictionary.
public static Map reverse(Map dictionary)
```

3. This question refers to the code from the Marine Biology Simulation case study. Suppose that marine biologists want to enhance the simulation to model predator-prey dynamics in an environment. The model they have come up with is fairly simple: a fish can either be a predator or a prey. A predator fish swallows a prey fish whenever it gets a chance. Predators do not eat each other.

Assume a `boolean` method `isPredator` has been added to the `Fish` class. A regular `Fish` is not a predator, so this method always returns `false`, but it can be overridden in `Fish`'s subclasses.

(a) Write a definition for the class `Shark`, which is a subclass of `Fish`, putting only "..." in the bodies of constructors and methods. A `Shark` is a predator. Sharks act, breed, and die the same way as regular fish, with two exceptions: (1) before a shark moves, it first checks whether there is a prey immediately in front of it, and, if so it swallows the prey and takes its place. If there is no prey in front, the shark moves like a regular fish; (2) a shark keeps track of the number of "days" (timesteps) since its last meal and can breed only if the time since the last meal does not exceed 2 "days."

In writing your definition for the `Shark` class you must:

- provide the functionality specified above;

- provide a complete set of constructors consistent with the other "fish" classes;

- reuse the existing MBS code to the fullest possible degree without duplicating it;

- choose appropriate names for variables and parameters;

- make data representation consistent with the above specifications;

- make design decisions that are consistent with information-hiding principles.

Comments are not required but may be used if desired.

You DO NOT have to write the implementations of the constructors or any methods of the `Shark` class.

(b) Implement `Shark`'s `breed` and `move` methods. In writing your code, reuse `Fish`'s code, where possible, without duplication.

(c) Suppose we want to modify the behavior of fish to let prey avoid predators. Suppose we have added a `boolean` method `isDangerous(Location loc)` to the `Fish` class — `isDangerous(loc)` returns `true` if there is a predator in one of `loc`'s neighbors. The following statement has been added at the beginning of `Fish`'s `nextLocation` method:

```
protected Location nextLocation()
{
  // Get list of neighboring empty locations.
  ArrayList emptyNbrs = emptyNeighbors();

  if (!isPredator())
    removeDangerous(emptyNbrs);
```

Write the method `removeDangerous` as started below. This method should remove all the dangerous locations from a given list.

```
// precondition:  emptyNeighbors contains a list of valid
//                 locations in this fish's environment
// postcondition: all "dangerous" locations (such that
//                 isDangerous(loc) == true)
//                 are removed from locsList
protected void removeDangerous(List emptyNeighbors)
```

4. An experiment consists of tossing a coin several times until the coin falls on the same side twice in a row. A set of experiments is saved in a binary tree. A sequence of heads and tails is represented as a path from the root of the tree: heads means go left, and tails means go right. For each experiment a path is built (or retraced) and the value in the end node of the path is incremented. For example, the set of experiments below corresponds to the binary tree shown on the right.

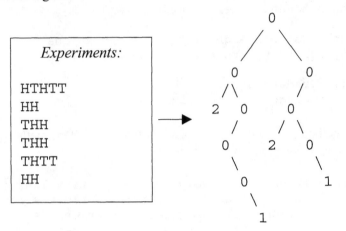

Lets call a tree that represents coin-tossing experiments an "HT tree." We will represent each node of an HT tree as a `TreeNode` object with an `Integer` value.

(a) Write a method that extracts statistics from an HT tree. The `getStats` method should return an array of four integers: the number of coin tosses in the longest experiment, the total number of experiments, the total number of heads in all experiments, and the total number of tails in all experiments. For example, for the HT tree above, `getStats` should return an array `stats` with the following values: {5, 6, 11, 7}. `getStats` can extract these statistics directly from the tree without reconstructing the set of experiments. For example, `stats[0]` is the length of the longest path in the tree; `stats[1]` is the sum of values in all the nodes in the tree, and so on. Complete `getStats` as started below.

```
// precondition:  root refers to the root of a "coin-tossing"
//                tree
// postcondition: returns an array stats of length 4.
//                stats[0] = the number of tosses in the
//                longest experiment (0 if root is null);
//                stats[1] = the total number of experiments;
//                stats[2] = the total number of heads in
//                all experiments;
//                stats[3] = the total number of tails in
//                all experiments;
public static int[] getStats(TreeNode root)
```

(b) This part is concerned with a method `isHTtree` that verifies whether a given binary tree is an HT tree. Remember that every HT tree's leaves hold positive values, its other nodes hold zeros, and any path terminates after exactly two links in the same direction.

`isHTtree` uses an overloaded recursive helper method, which takes an additional parameter that describes the path traveled so far in the last segment (after the last change of direction). The path traveled so far is represented as a string. At the beginning the path is empty. Thus the `isHTtree` method can be written as follows:

```
// postcondition: root != null;
//                returns true if root refers to
//                the root of an HT tree; false otherwise
public static boolean isHTtree(TreeNode root)
{
   return isHTtree(root, "");
}
```

In subsequent recursive calls, the path traveled so far contains one or two letters that describe the path: "L" for the left brunch and "R" for the right brunch. Complete the overloaded helper method `isHTtree`, as started below.

```
// precondition:  root is either null or refers to a
//                subtree of a binary tree;
//                path describes the path traveled to
//                root after the last direction change --
//                it can be an empty string, "L",
//                "R", "LL", or "RR"
// postcondition: returns true if root is null or if
//                this tree fits as a subtree in an HT tree,
//                as described by path.
private static boolean isHTtree(TreeNode root, String path)
```

Answers and Solutions

A-1

SECTION I: MULTIPLE CHOICE

1. A	11. E	21. E	31. C
2. D	12. A	22. B	32. A
3. B	13. C	23. B	33. A
4. A	14. E	24. D	34. B
5. A	15. B	25. E	35. D
6. C	16. E	26. D	36. C
7. A	17. D	27. B	37. E
8. C	18. A	28. C	38. D
9. C	19. D	29. B	39. E
10. B	20. D	30. E	40. B

Notes:

3. Use De Morgan's laws.
11. STARTPOS is declared final
12. After the for loop, the value of w is "banana".
23. A cast to int truncates the double value toward zero.
24. LibraryBook does not override Object's toString method.
27. list.remove(i) decrements all the subsequent subscripts, so i++ skips one value.
29. For Choice B, the compiler would report an error.
30. The code goes into an infinite loop.
33. First "Boris" is swapped with "Evan", then "Boris" is swapped with "Dan".
34. $4 + 3 + 2 + 1 = 10$
35. There is no way to get a fish at (1, 0) unless the fish at (1, 1) breeds.
38. Environment works with Locatable objects; it is not aware of Fish.
39. The choices represent boundary and exception conditions, which <u>must</u> be tested.
40. Simulation is rather specific to MBS, while Environment can be reused in many projects. The other matters are technicalities that can be taken care of.

A-1

SECTION II: FREE RESPONSE

1. (a)

```java
public boolean isFull()
{
  for (int i = 0; i < levels.length; i++)
  {
    if (levels[i].findEmptySpace() != -1)
      return false;
  }
  return true;
}
```

   (b)

```java
public boolean parkCar(Car v)
{
  if (isFull() || isCarAlreadyParked(v.getID()))
    return false;

  for (int i = 0; i < levels.length; i++)
  {
    ParkingLevel lev = levels[i];
    int spaceNum = lev.findEmptySpace();
    if (spaceNum != -1)
    {
      lev.setCar(spaceNum, v);
      totalCars++;
      return true;
    }
  }
  return false;
}
```

(c)

```
public Car removeCar(String id)
{
  for (int i = 0; i < levels.length; i++)
  {
    ParkingLevel lev = levels[i];
    for (int spaceNum = 0; spaceNum < lev.numSpaces();
                                          spaceNum++)
    {
      Car car = lev.getCar(spaceNum);
      if (car != null && id.equals(car.getID()))
      {
        lev.setCar(spaceNum, null);
        totalCars--;
        return car;
      }
    }
  }
  return null;
}
```

2.   (a)

```
public static String findFirstTag(String text)
{
  int tagStart = text.indexOf("<");
  if (tagStart != -1)
  {
    int tagEnd = text.indexOf(">");
    return text.substring(tagStart, tagEnd + 1);
  }
  else
    return null;
}
```

(b)

```
public static String remove(String text, String str)
{
  int pos = text.indexOf(str);
  if (pos != -1)
    text = text.substring(0, pos) +
                       text.substring(pos + str.length());
  return text;
}
```

(c)

```
public static String removeAllTags(String text)
{
  String tag = findFirstTag(text);
  while (tag != null)
  {
    String closingTag = "</" + tag.substring(1);
    if (text.indexOf(closingTag) < text.indexOf(tag))
      throw new IllegalArgumentException();
    text = remove(text, tag);  [1]
    text = remove(text, closingTag);

    tag = findFirstTag(text);
  }
  return text;
}
```

Notes:

1.   Not just

```
remove(text, tag);
```

— because Strings are immutable.

3.   (a)

```
public CoralReefFish(Environment env, Location loc)
{
  super(env, loc, env.randomDirection(), Color.yellow);  ¹
  placeOfBirth = loc;
}
```

Notes:

1.   Do not call `initialize` here: it is private in `Fish`. You must first call `super(...)` because `Fish` does not have a no-args constructor.

(b)

```
protected double distanceFromHome(Location loc)
{
  int x = loc.col() - placeOfBirth.col();
  int y = loc.row() - placeOfBirth.row();
  return Math.sqrt(x * x + y * y);
}
```

(c)

```
protected Location nextLocation()
{
  ArrayList emptyNbrs = emptyNeighbors();
  int index = 0;
  while (index < emptyNbrs.size())
  {
    if (distanceFromHome((Location) emptyNbrs.get(index)) > 4)
      emptyNbrs.remove(index);
    else ¹
      index++;
  }

  if (emptyNbrs.size() == 0)
    return location();
  Random randNumGen = RandNumGenerator.getInstance();
  int randNum = randNumGen.nextInt(emptyNbrs.size());
  return (Location) emptyNbrs.get(randNum);
}
```

Notes:

1.   `index` is incremented only if the location is not removed. That's why a `while` loop is used instead of a `for` loop.

4. (a)

```
public class APStudent
{
  private String studentName;
  private ArrayList exams;

  public APStudent(String name) { ... }
  public String getName() {...}
  public ArrayList getExams() { ... }
  public void add(APExam exam) { ... }
  public double getAverageGrade { ... }
}
```

(b)

```
public int getAwardLevel(APStudent student)
{
  ArrayList exams = student.getExams();
  int len = exams.size();
  double years = 0.0;
  int award = 0;

  for (int k = 0; k < len; k++)
  {
    APExam exam = (APExam)exams.get(k);
    if (exam.getGrade() >= 3)
      years += 0.5 * exam.getLevel();
              // adds 1 for a full-year and .5 for a
              //   half-year course
  }

  if (years >= 4.0 && student.getAverageGrade() >= 3.25)
    award = 2;
  else if (years >= 3.0)
    award = 1;

  return award;
}
```

(c)
```
public double[] getStats(ArrayList list)
{
  int[] counts = new int[3];
  int award;

  for (int i = 0; i < list.size(); i++)
  {
    award = getAwardLevel((APStudent)list.get(i));
    counts[award]++;
  }

  double[] percents = new double[3];
  for (award = 0; award < 3; award++)
    percents[award] = 100.0 * (double)counts[award] [1]
                                         / list.size();

  return percents;
}
```

Notes:

1. The cast to `double` is optional here.

Answers and Solutions

A-2

SECTION I: MULTIPLE CHOICE

1. B	11. D	21. B	31. D
2. C	12. C	22. B	32. C
3. A	13. C	23. D	33. E
4. B	14. A	24. D	34. E
5. E	15. D	25. B	35. A
6. E	16. E	26. A	36. C
7. D	17. B	27. E	37. B
8. C	18. A	28. B	38. C
9. A	19. C	29. D	39. D
10. E	20. A	30. D	40. C

Notes:

4. $(-1 + 2) + (- 3 + 4) + (- 5 + 6) + (- 7 + 8) + (- 9 + 10) = 5$
5. `count++` is missing.
10. 4 / 3 yields 1
12. `filter` makes a new string from `str` with all the occurrences of `pattern` in `str` removed.
24. `s` is not an array (A); `amps` is private in `Sample` (B, C); and `Sample` has no public field `length` (E).
26. `numbers` holds two elements: two copies of an `Integer` with value 1. The element at index 1 is deleted twice from `names`.
31. References to objects are passed "by value" (i.e., `swap` receives copies of addresses of `a` and `b`).
32. "Dynamic method binding" is a technique that implements polymorphism. The MBS narrative prefers this term.
33. `msg` is `null`; you can't call its methods.
35. To get 3, start with two fish next to each other; the first breeds and dies and the second dies. To get 7, again start with two fish next to each other; both breed and die.
40. The whole idea of the `Locatable` interface is to isolate `Environment` from `Fish`.

A-2

SECTION II: FREE RESPONSE

1. (a)

```
    private int printWord(String nextWord, int cursorPos,
                                        int lineWidth)
    {
      int len = word.length();

      if (cursorPos > 0 && cursorPos + len + 1 > lineWidth) 1
      {
        System.out.println();
        cursorPos = 0;
      }

      if (cursorPos > 0)
      {
        System.out.print(" ");
        cursorPos++;
      }

      if (cursorPos + len <= lineWidth)
      {
        System.out.print(word);
        cursorPos += len;
      }
      else
      {
        System.out.print(
                word.substring(0, lineWidth - cursorPos)); 2
        cursorPos = lineWidth;
      }
      return cursorPos;
    }
```

Notes:

1. `cursorPos + len + 1` counts one space character before the word.
2. At this stage `cursorPos` must be 0, so you can write simply `word.substring(0, lineWidth)`

(b)

```
public void print(int lineWidth)
{
  int cursorPos = 0;
  for (int i = 0; i < storyWords.length; i++)
  {
    cursorPos = printWord(storyWords[i],
                      cursorPos, lineWidth);
  }
  System.out.println();
}
```

2.　(a)

```java
public static String toZodiacString(int year)
{
  return animals[(year - startYear) % 12] + ", " +
                    elements[(year - startYear) % 10];
}
```

(b)

```java
public String shortZodiac(int year)
{
  String z = ChineseZodiac.toZodiacString(year);
  String animal = z.substring(0, z.indexOf(","));
  String element = z.substring(z.indexOf("(") + 1,
                                    z.indexOf(")") );
  return animal + "/" + element;
}
```

(c)

```java
public int getYear(int year, String animal, String element)
{
  for (int y = year; y < year + 60; y++)
  {
    String z = ChineseZodiac.toZodiacString(y);
    if (z.indexOf(animal) != -1 && z.indexOf(element) != -1)
      return y;
  }
  throw new IllegalArgumentException();
}
```

3. (a)

```
public class AgingFish extends Fish
{
  private double probOfDying;
  private int myAge;

  public AgingFish(Environment env, Location loc) { ... }

  public AgingFish(Environment env, Location loc,
                                    Direction dir) { ... }

  public AgingFish(Environment env, Location loc,
                          Direction dir, Color col) { ... }

  public void act() { ... }
  public String toString() { ... }
  protected void generateChild(Location loc) { ... }
}
```

(b)

```
public AgingFish(Environment env, Location loc)
{
  super(env, loc, env.randomDirection(), Color.blue);
  probOfDying = 1.0/7.0;
  myAge = 0;
}
```

(c)

```
public void act()
{
  if (!isInEnv())
    return;

  if (myAge < 3 || myAge > 10 || !breed())
    move();

  if (myAge >= 3)
    probOfDying += 0.1;

  Random randNumGen = RandNumGenerator.getInstance();
  if (randNumGen.nextDouble() < probOfDying)
    die();
  else
    myAge++;
}
```

4.   (a)

```
public DataPacket getBestPacket(double minIntelFactor)
{
  DataPacket packet, bestPacket = null;
  double intelFactor, bestIntelFactor = minIntelFactor;

  for (int i = 0; i < dataPackets.size(); i++)
  {
    packet = (DataPacket)dataPackets.get(i);
    intelFactor = packet.getIntelFactor();
    if (intelFactor >= bestIntelFactor)
    {
      bestIntelFactor = intelFactor;
      bestPacket = packet;
    }
  }
  return bestPacket;
}
```

(b)

```
public int filterList(int minStrength, int minDuration)
{
  int i = 0, count = 0;

  while (i < dataPackets.size())
  {
    DataPacket packet = (DataPacket)dataPackets.get(i);
    if (packet.getStrength() < minStrength ||
                        packet.getDuration() < minDuration)
    {
      dataPackets.remove(i);
      count++;
    }
    else
    {
      i++;
    }
  }
  return count;
}
```

(c)

```java
public ArrayList alienMessage(double minIntelFactor,
                      int minStrength, int minDuration)
{
  filterList(minStrength, minDuration);
  DataPacket bestPacket = getBestPacket(minIntelFactor);
  if (bestPacket == null)
    return null;

  ArrayList msg = new ArrayList();

  for (int i = 0; i < dataPackets.size(); i++)
  {
    DataPacket packet = (DataPacket)dataPackets.get(i);
    if (packet.getSource().equals(bestPacket.getSource()) &&
          packet.getQuadrant() == bestPacket.getQuadrant())
      msg.add(packet);
  }
  return msg;
}
```

Answers and Solutions

AB-1

1. A	11. E	21. E	31. E
2. B	12. C	22. A	32. E
3. A	13. D	23. A	33. D
4. D	14. B	24. A	34. B
5. C	15. D	25. B	35. C
6. C	16. A	26. C	36. D
7. A	17. C	27. E	37. A
8. C	18. C	28. E	38. E
9. B	19. B	29. E	39. E
10. C	20. D	30. D	40. B

Notes:

3. Choices D and E are not invariants because the conditions do not hold before and after the loop.

4. `remove` decrements subsequent indices and list size.

10. `public int hashCode() { return upc.hashCode(); }`
    `public boolean equals(other) { return upc.equals(other.upc); }`

11. `mince` repeatedly unlinks the first node and links it to the head of the new list `p`.

12. Can't assign a `Party` to a `BDayParty`.

13. III only works because `Party` has a no-args constructor.

14. `public String getOccasion() { return "Birthday " + getName(); }`

16. The presence of `compareTo` in itself does not mean the class implements `Comparable`.

21. `list` is modified even as it sits on the stack.

28. None of them is a complete tree.

32. Should be:

    ```
    it.previous();
    it.add(x);
    ```

    However, `previous` is not in the AP subset.

33. The subtree of each node with one child should become symmetrical.

35. It would be possible in an unbounded environment if the fish on the right acted first and died, then the fish on the left bred and died.

38. `Fish`'s constructor has already added this fish to the environment; the second attempt to add it causes an exception.

AB-1

SECTION II: FREE RESPONSE

1. (a)
```
public boolean hasStuckSensor()
{
  int row, col;
  boolean stuck;

  for (row = 0; row < SCAN_HEIGHT; row++)
  {
    stuck = true;
    for (col = 1; col < SCAN_WIDTH; col++)
    {
      if (scan[row][col] != scan[row][0])
        stuck = false;
    }
    if (stuck)
      return true;
  }
  return false;
}
```

(b)
```
public int getScanValue(int col)
{
  int count = 0;

  for (int row = 0; row < SCAN_HEIGHT; row++)
  {
    if (scan[row][col] == 1)
      count++;
  }

  if (count > SCAN_HEIGHT / 2)
    return 1;
  else
    return 0;
}
```

(c)
```java
public int[] getBarCode()
{
  if (hasStuckSensor())
    return null;

  int parity = 0;
  int barcode[] = new int[SCAN_WIDTH - 1];

  for (int col = 0; col < SCAN_WIDTH - 1; col++)
  {
    barcode[col] = getScanValue(col);
    parity += barcode[col];
  }

  parity += getScanValue(SCAN_WIDTH - 1);

  if (parity % 2 != 1)
    return null;

  return barcode;
}
```

2.   (a)

```
public ProductionLine(int nDisks, int maxRadius)
{
  assemblyLineIn = new ListQueue();
  Random gen = RandNumGenerator.getInstance();

  for (int i = 1; i <= nDisks; i++)
    assemblyLineIn.enqueue(
                   new Disk(gen.nextInt(maxRadius) + 1));

  robotArm = new Tower();
  assemblyLineOut = new ListQueue();
}
```

(b)

```
private void unloadRobot()
{
  Tower pyramid = new Tower();

  while (!robotArm.isEmpty())
    pyramid.push(robotArm.pop());

  assemblyLineOut.enqueue(pyramid);
}
```

(c)

```
public void process()
{
  while(!assemblyLineIn.isEmpty())
  {
    Disk disk = (Disk)assemblyLineIn.dequeue();

    if (!robotArm.isEmpty() &&
                (disk.compareTo(robotArm.peekTop()) <= 0))
      unloadRobot();

    robotArm.push(disk);
  }

  unloadRobot();
}
```

3. (a)

```
public void add(Locatable obj)
{
  Location loc = obj.location();
  if (!isEmpty(loc))
    throw new IllegalArgumentException("Location " + loc +
                  " is not a valid empty location");
  locationMap.put(loc, obj);
}
```

(b)

```
public Locatable[] allObjects()
{
  Locatable[] objectArray = new Locatable[numObjects()];

  Iterator iter = locationMap.keySet().iterator();
  int index = 0;

  while(iter.hasNext())
  {
    objectArray[index] =
                  (Locatable)locationMap.get(iter.next());
    index++;
  }
  return objectArray;
}
```

(c)

```
public void recordMove(Locatable obj, Location oldLoc)
{
  Location newLoc = obj.location();
  if (newLoc.equals(oldLoc))
    return;

  if (objectAt(oldLoc) != obj || !isEmpty(newLoc))
    throw new IllegalArgumentException();

  locationMap.remove(oldLoc);
  locationMap.put(newLoc, obj);
}
```

4. (a)

```
public static boolean isValidAUTree(TreeNode root)
{
  if (root == null)
    return true;

  int numChildren;
  TreeNode left = root.getLeft();
  TreeNode right = root.getRight();

  if (left == null && right != null)
    return false;

  if (left != null && right != null)
    numChildren = 2;
  else if (left != null && right == null)
    numChildren = 1;
  else
    numChildren = 0;

  return numChildren == ((AU)root.getValue()).numInputs() &&
            isValidAUTree(left) &&
            isValidAUTree(right);
}
```

(b)

```
public static int evaluate(TreeNode root)
{
  TreeNode left = root.getLeft();
  TreeNode right = root.getRight();

  int x = 0, y = 0;
  if (left != null)
    x = evaluate(left);

  if (right != null)
    y = evaluate(right);

  return ((AU)root.getValue()).compute(x, y);
}
```

(c)
```
public static int findMax(TreeNode root)
{
  int max = ((AU)root.getValue()).getRegister();

  TreeNode left = root.getLeft();
  if (left != null)
  {
    int leftMax = findMax(left);
    if (leftMax > max)
      max = leftMax;
  }

  TreeNode right = root.getRight();
  if (right != null)
  {
    int rightMax = findMax(right);
    if (rightMax > max)
      max = rightMax;
  }

  return max;
}
```

Answers and Solutions

AB-2

SECTION I: MULTIPLE CHOICE

1. B	11. A	21. C	31. B
2. E	12. D	22. D	32. E
3. E	13. B	23. D	33. B
4. E	14. C	24. C	34. E
5. A	15. A	25. E	35. B
6. B	16. D	26. A	36. C
7. C	17. D	27. D	37. B
8. A	18. B	28. C	38. E
9. A	19. D	29. D	39. A
10. E	20. C	30. C	40. E

Notes:

5. 5 is eliminated at the beginning.
8. Then a class that implements that interface can extend something else.
9. Checks if word is a palindrome.
12. Option I doesn't work because orderedItems is declared as a List, not as a LinkedList.
13. Note that getTable is private, so its use only affects this class.
15. pos is 0.
20. In Option III, the list holds copies of the same object, so the loop quits earlier than intended.
21. removeMin and add need to repair the heap.
24. *number of leaves <= (number of nodes + 1) / 2*
25. As long as the left and right subtrees have the same depth, checkTree returns the depth of the tree.
26. Binary Search applies.
31. Can't assign a House to a HouseForSale.
33. transform moves the first node to the end of the list.
35. (1) the fish breeds and dies; (2) the fish to the south moves north, the rest die.
36. The first call to nextDouble or nextInt after RandNumGenerator.getInstance always returns a small double or a 0. Therefore, each fish always breeds and dies (and a child fish always faces north).
40. In the alternative design, a simulation is attached to the environment as a "strategy." This design is more flexible, because we can easily switch between different simulation strategies. For example, in an extended MBS application, the user may be able to choose a simulation strategy from a menu at run time.

AB-2

SECTION II: FREE RESPONSE

1.   (a)

```
public int findVertPos(int charHeight)
{
  int maxSum = 0, sum;
  int maxRow = 0, row;

  for (row = 0; row <= numRows() - charHeight; row++)
  {
    sum = 0;
    for (int r = row; r < row + charHeight; r++)
      sum += getRowIntensity(r);
    if (sum > maxSum)
    {
      maxSum = sum;
      maxRow = row;
    }
  }
  return maxRow;
}
```

  (b)

```
public double calculateFitRatio(Template t)
{
  int topRow = findVertPos(t.numRows());
  int leftCol = findHorzPos(topRow, t.numCols());
  int tRow, tCol;
  double fit = 0;

  for (tRow = 0; tRow < t.numRows(); tRow++)
    for (tCol = 0; tCol < t.numCols(); tCol++)
      fit += t.getWeight(tRow, tCol) *
                getPixel(topRow + tRow, leftCol + tCol);

  return fit / (t.numRows() * t.numCols());
}
```

(c)

```
public String ocr(Image image, ArrayList templates)
{
  double bestFit = 0;
  String result = null;

  for (int k = 0; k < templates.size(); k++)
  {
    Template t = (Template)templates.get(k);
    double fit = image.calculateFitRatio(t);
    if (fit > bestFit)
    {
      bestFit = fit;
      result = t.getCharName();
    }
  }
  return result;
}
```

2. (a)

```
public static void add(Map dictionary, String word,
                                        String translation)
{
  if (dictionary.containsKey(word))
  {
    ((Set)dictionary.get(word)).add(translation);
  }
  else
  {
    Set translations = new TreeSet();
    translations.add(translation);
    dictionary.put(word, translations);
  }
}
```

(b)

```
public static Map reverse(Map dictionary)
{
  Map reverseDictionary = new TreeMap();

  Iterator wordsIter = dictionary.keySet().iterator();

  while (wordsIter.hasNext())
  {
    String word = (String)wordsIter.next();
    Set translations = (Set)dictionary.get(word);

    Iterator translationsIter = translations.iterator();
    while (translationsIter.hasNext())
    {
      String translation = (String)translationsIter.next();
      add(reverseDictionary, translation, word);
    }
  }

  return reverseDictionary;
}
```

3. (a)
```
public class Shark extends Fish
{
  private int daysSinceLastMeal;

  public Shark(Environment env, Location loc) {...}
  public Shark(Environment env, Location loc,
                                 Direction dir) {...}
  public Shark(Environment env, Location loc,
                       Direction dir, Color col) {...}

  public String toString() {...}
  protected boolean breed() {...}
  protected void generateChild(Location loc) {...}
  protected void move() {...}
  protected boolean isPredator() {...}
}
```

(b)
```
protected boolean breed()
{
  return daysSinceLastMeal <= 2 && super.breed();
}

protected void move()
{
  Environment env = environment();
  Location inFront = env.getNeighbor(location(), direction());
  if (env.isValid(inFront) && !env.isEmpty(inFront))
  {
    Fish fish = (Fish)env.objectAt(inFront);
    if (!fish.isPredator())
    {
      env.remove(fish);
      changeLocation(inFront);
      daysSinceLastMeal = 0;
      return;
    }
  }
  super.move();
  daysSinceLastMeal++;
}
```

(c)
```
protected void removeDangerous(List emptyNeighbors)
{
  Iterator it = emptyNeighbors.iterator();
  while (it.hasNext())
  {
    if (isDangerous((Location)it.next()))
      it.remove();
  }
}
```

4.   (a)

```
public static int[] getStats(TreeNode root)
{
  int[] stats = {0, 0, 0, 0}; ¹
  if (root == null)
    return stats;

  int[] leftStats = getStats(root.getLeft());
  int[] rightStats = getStats(root.getRight());
  stats[0] = Math.max(leftStats[0], rightStats[0]) + 1;
  stats[1] = ((Integer)root.getValue()).intValue() +
                          (leftStats[1] + rightStats[1]);
  stats[2] = leftStats[2] + rightStats[2] + leftStats[1]; ²
  stats[3] = leftStats[3] + rightStats[3] + rightStats[1];
  return stats;
}
```

Notes:

1.   Or `int[] stats = new int[4];` — initialized to zeros by default.
2.   `leftStats[1]` is the number of experiments that start with an "H."

(b)

```
private static boolean isHTtree(TreeNode root, String path)
{
  if (root == null)
    return true;

  if (path.length() < 2)
  {
    String leftPath = "L", rightPath = "R";
    if (path.equals("L"))
      leftPath += "L";
    if (path.equals("R"))
      rightPath += "R";

    return ((Integer)root.getValue()).intValue() == 0 &&
                 isHTtree(root.getLeft(), leftPath) &&
                 isHTtree(root.getRight(), rightPath);
  }
  else // if (path.length() == 2) ¹
  {
    return ((Integer)root.getValue()).intValue() > 0 &&
        root.getLeft() == null && root.getRight() == null;
  }
}
```

Notes:

1.   Must be a leaf

Index